Advance Praise For
The Attitude Equation

"Understanding the power of your attitude allows you to truly serve, contribute, engage and inspire. Our attitudes are instrumental in driving the attitudes of others.... The AxB=C formula simply breaks down the process of how we convert attitude into measurable outcomes. Awareness of your attitude can be challenging and elusive, but self-awareness is imperative to manifest outcomes that not only serve you but those that are in your work and life space."

—TIFFANI BOVA, global growth evangelist, business strategist, keynote, bestselling author, and top sales podcaster

"Sometimes the greatest obstacle in the path to living our happiest, most productive life is merely our personal attitude toward what life throws at us. Mark Schulman and Dr. Jim Samuels have curated the wisdom of some of the world's greatest 'Attitude Adjusters' who share their stories of strength and courage in making the shifts necessary to achieve success—I'm honored to be among them! This book is essential to surviving life in the twenty-first century."

—BONNIE ST. JOHN, Paralympic medalist, Rhodes Scholar, and CEO of Blue Circle Leadership

"Attitude is one of the most powerful forces affecting human behavior and outcomes. By defining such a simple formula—Attitude x Behavior = Consequence, Dr Jim Samuels and Mark Schulman have created a simple blueprint to allow you to drive desirable outcomes in your life. And if you reverse engineer the formula by deciding on the consequences you want to achieve, then you can more clearly see the behavior that would create those consequences and the attitude(s) you would need to generate the appropriate behavior. You get thirty-nine interviews with some of the great thinkers on the planet giving examples of their experiences supporting this formula. This book is a declaration of the absolute power of attitude!"

—Josh Linkner, tech entrepreneur, *New York Times* bestselling author, venture capital investor, and jazz musician

"Just as he lays down the drumbeats that are the foundation of every live show, here Mark Schulman lays down an extraordinary foundation for living life right. He and Dr. Jim share an extraordinary tapestry of insights that will help you understand how to optimize your own potential as well as spotting and defusing any pitfalls that may be in your path, whether they are internal or external. Sit back and be prepared to take notes as the wisdom unfolds."

—Andrew Macpherson, author, artist, and photographer

"When Mark takes stage, he's in 'the zone' and (similarly) we all need more of this in our personal and professional lives. *The Attitude Equation* is a practical guide for getting us closer to peak performance with each passing day."

—Jared Kleinert, TED speaker, award-winning author, and *USA Today*'s "Most Connected Millennial"

"People think they got to see Mark Schulman on stage because of what a great drummer he is. And they do—Mark is one of the best rock drummers in the world. But what's so incredible is how Mark takes his energy, his talent, his excitement, and his attitude and pours it into everything he does. You just have to see—and hear—it to believe it! Rock on Mark!!!"

—Bruce Turkel, author, consultant, and keynote speaker

"I met Mark when I was a young, teenage girl, aspiring to land a 'big gig' similar to what he had with P!nk. What stood out to me was not just his incredible playing or charisma on the stage, but his positive attitude and inclusive nature off of it. What he and Dr. Jim have put together as *The Attitude Equation* is sure to inspire, equip, and prepare anyone, not just musicians, with the tools necessary to accomplish their dreams and change lives in the process. If you are looking for something to spark a flame of motivation and intentionalism in your life, you cannot NOT read this book."

—HANNAH WELTON, musician, vocalist, drummer, and
 Christian minister

"In *The Attitude Equation*, Mark Schulman and Dr. Jim Samuels unlock the secrets of the Rock Star Attitude. Dr. Jim and Mark provide the formula that allows you to shift your attitude in almost any situation, empowering you to change your behaviors and thereby positively influence the outcomes and consequences of your business and personal lives. But they go far beyond that. Mark has interviewed 'rock stars' from entertainment, sports, and business—people like Howie Mandel, Michael Franti, Martina Navratilova, and Jeffrey Hayzlett who share how one attitude shift impacted their lives. The stories are entertaining...but be careful... you might also learn something that changes your life!

"Mark is a creative catalyst. His positive energy is contagious. I have enjoyed working with Mark's radiant creativity both on and off the stage. He is a bona fide rockstar and he is a bona fide student on the creative process. If you are an artist, you are gonna love this book. If you are an executive looking to implement creative strategies for your team, you are gonna love this book. If you are an artistic executive this book is gonna blow you away. Enjoy."

—ERIK WAHL, artist and author

The ATTITUDE EQUATION

ROCKSTARS IN ALL FIELDS SHARE THEIR SECRET ATTITUDES

BY MARK SCHULMAN & JIM SAMUELS, PhD

PERMUTED
PRESS

A PERMUTED PRESS BOOK
ISBN: 979-8-88845-384-1
ISBN (eBook): 979-8-88845-385-8

The Attitude Equation:
Rockstars in All Fields Share Their Secret Attitudes
© 2024 by Jetty Jewels, INC
All Rights Reserved

Cover art by Michael Murphy
Cover photo by David Phillips

PERMUTED
PRESS

Permuted Press, LLC
New York • Nashville
permutedpress.com

Published in the United States of America
1 2 3 4 5 6 7 8 9 10

TABLE OF CONTENTS

Foreword..11
Preface...15
Introduction: Attitude Defined 17

SECTION 1 - BESTSELLING AUTHORS
Chapter 1: Possibility *featuring Alex Banayan* 27
Chapter 2: Self-Awareness *featuring Tiffani Bova*.........................32
Chapter 3: Action *featuring Grant Cardone* 38
Chapter 4: Appreciation *featuring Chester Elton* 42
Chapter 5: Aspiration *featuring Shep Hyken*..................................50
Chapter 6: Preparation *featuring Jared Kleinert*............................54
Chapter 7: Reflection and Renewal *featuring Josh Linkner*.........60

SECTION 2 - BUSINESS LEADERS
Chapter 8: Leadership *featuring Jeff Clarke* 67
Chapter 9: Positivity *featuring Lee Cockerell*.................................74
Chapter 10: Inspiration *featuring Ken Freirich* 81
Chapter 11: Adaptation *featuring Tony Hsieh* 88
Chapter 12: Confidence *featuring Julie Masters*.............................94
Chapter 13: Gratitude *featuring Bob Pritchard* 101
Chapter 14: Performance *featuring Dr. Gary F. Russell*..................109
Chapter 15: Identity *featuring Bruce Turkel*...................................115

SECTION 3 - ATHLETES AND COACHES
Chapter 16: Repetition *featuring Jim Abbott*..................................123
Chapter 17: Ambition *featuring Julia Landauer*.............................130
Chapter 18: Soul *featuring Keith Mitchell* 136
Chapter 19: Focus *featuring James Samuel Morris Jr.* 140
Chapter 20: Experience and Emotion *featuring Martina Navratilova* 148
Chapter 21: Hard Work *featuring Bonnie St. John* 154

Chapter 22: Magic *featuring Shelli Varela* 161
Chapter 23: Focus *featuring Dr. Jen Welter* 168
Chapter 24: Resilience *featuring "Bronco" Billy Wright* 174

SECTION 4 - DRUMMERS
Chapter 25: Knowledge *featuring Kenny Aronoff* 181
Chapter 26: Joy *featuring Gregg Bissonette* 189
Chapter 27: Service *featuring Dom Famularo* 193
Chapter 28: Intention *featuring Hannah Ford-Welton* 201
Chapter 29: Logic *featuring Thomas Lang* 209
Chapter 30: Improvisation *featuring Stanton Moore* 214
Chapter 31: Adventure *featuring Nate Morton* 220
Chapter 32: Enthusiasm *featuring Rich Redmond* 225
Chapter 33: Differentiation *featuring Antonio Sánchez* 232
Chapter 34: Inspiration *featuring Matt Sorum* 240

SECTION 5 - CREATIVES
Chapter 35: Freedom *featuring Judd Apatow* 247
Chapter 36: Truth *featuring Michael Franti* 257
Chapter 37: Empathy *featuring Andrew Macpherson* 266
Chapter 38: Confidence *featuring Chef Andre Rush* 275
Chapter 39: Service *featuring Jade Simmons* 279
Chapter 40: Abundance *featuring Erik Wahl* 287

SECTION 6 - ACTORS AND HOSTS
Chapter 41: Control *featuring Jeffrey Hayzlett* 295
Chapter 42: Fulfillment *featuring Howie Mandel* 301
Chapter 43: Direction *featuring Suzanne Sena* 310
Chapter 44: Dreams *featuring Tom Todoroff* 319

Addendum: The Attitude Scale 327
Acknowledgments 332
About The Authors 334

FOREWORD

I HAVE KNOWN Mark Schulman since we were introduced by a mutual friend, Aussie mover and shaker Julie Masters, in June 2021. I later interviewed Mark for my *Remarkable People* podcast during which we talked about anxiety, confidence and world-class performance. I am intrigued by the science behind success and how individuals can control the outcomes of their lives, and I was thrilled when Mark asked me to write the foreword for this book, co-authored with his longtime friend and mentor, Dr. Jim Samuels.

Throughout my career, I have been a judicious analyzer of behavior and outcomes, starting with my degree in psychology from Stanford in 1976. As a marketing executive at Apple in the 1980s, it was imperative that we keenly understand the transformative change we shepherded, the positive impact technology has on users and the science that creates brand loyalists.

For many years, I studied these phenomena—both in qualitative field research and in the quantitative information, we began to collect at the cutting edge of the data revolution. What strikes me most about the methodology herein—that attitude begets behavior which begets consequences, both positive and negative—is its simplicity and immediate application. Anyone can change their personal and professional outcomes by modifying their perspective and approach. And this scenario plays out in interview after interview of incredibly successful individuals in a variety of fields.

When I was younger and dumber, I thought I knew it all. Among my delusions was that an interview-style book (or podcast) was easy. You turn on a recording device, ask a few questions and the wisdom flows. Nothing could be further from the truth. You must identify ideal interviewees (and gain their buy in), explain the concept, ask penetratingly intelligent questions, catalyze insightful responses, and edit those responses into a succinct and valuable format.

Given this degree of difficulty, why not simply write the book yourself, or—in my case—feature only yourself on a podcast? The answer is that proof of concept comes from the preponderance of stories that play out in similar fashion. And Mark has done a remarkable job of selecting individuals who graciously share their stories and wisdom in the pages to come.

I admire Mark's capacity and ability to embolden and empower people with his unique exploration of human behavior through speech and song. He's taken the wisdom gained from his decades-long career as a world-class drummer for the likes of P!nk and Cher and transformed it into practices and tactics that move people and spark positive change.

His inspiration for this comes from longtime mentor and philosopher, Jim Samuels, PhD, who has spent a half century motivating thousands of people with ideas and tools that lead to successful outcomes. He is a distiller of ideas, breaking down complicated formulas and concepts and making them easy to learn and apply. You will find that the driving methodology herein follows this course.

(A)ttitude × (B)ehavior = (C)onsequence

Thinking back upon my time as a technology executive, serial entrepreneur, and critical industry leader, and now as a keynote, consultant, and podcaster, I can pinpoint myriad times when my attitude led to successful outcomes.

Enjoy herein the wisdom, practices, and ideas from successful business leaders, athletes, artists, and creators who share why and how their attitudes led them to positive outcomes. And then consider how your outcomes can change, grow, and excel when you take a more focused approach to how you perceive the world.

Mark and Dr. Jim have thus done a great service for readers. The interviews will inspire, inform, and incite you. Then, the onus shifts from the authors to you.

What you need to know to "dent the universe" is in the pages that follow. It's up to you to invest the attitudes and behaviors that lead to your own desired consequences.

GUY KAWASAKI
Business leader, author and venture capitalist

PREFACE

I AM GRATEFUL for so many people and moments in my life, and I take special note now of all the knowledge I gained. As a young drummer in the '80s with a myopic definition of success, I was surprised when my bandmates wanted to leave Los Angeles for Portland, Oregon. I dug my rock 'n' roll boot heels into the ground, resisting even the thought of leaving. My friends were adamant about making a change, drawn by the lure of playing original music and paid gigs. So, we packed the van and cars and drove one thousand miles north to live with a real estate agent/music manager and chase a new dream. The band broke up six months later, but I met Dr. Jim Samuels, the co-author of this book.

Under his guidance, I stayed in Portland another four years, formed a new band, refined my attitude and skills and expanded my awareness of what was and is possible. Dr. Samuels flipped the script for me, informing a new world of self-exploration, emotional growth, and mind-blowing knowledge that would be the foundation of my life and success moving forward. Nothing proved more profound or powerful than the ABC Formula (as he called it back then).

Dr. Samuels taught classes three times a week. As time went on, I became increasingly committed to his philosophy. I had (and have) a voracious appetite to learn. I did the work, and the deep realizations and personal evolution inspired me to function with more clarity and joy and be of greater service to others. My drum, production, leadership skills, and career continued to expand.

Dr. Samuels has thousands of pages of brilliant ideas full of robust acronyms that are each worthy of their own book, but the ABC Formula (Attitude × Behavior = Consequences) has enough potency to power a lifetime. I have been sharing it with hundreds of corporate audiences of all roles and industries from interns to CEOs over the past several years, and now I'm sharing it with you.

My keynotes showcase the power of attitude, but they are just a taste of how my friends and I have used this power to achieve success. This book goes into greater depth, demonstrating all the components necessary to enable you to control your life's consequences by using the power of attitude. We mold the technical aspects of the power of attitude around the stories of people who have used it to achieve great success.

The world's top business people, athletes, influencers, actors, movie producers, writers, photographers, coaches, speakers, and—of course—musicians have extraordinary stories that can empower all of us with their unique perspectives on the power of attitude.

We are so honored and grateful to present this body of work that will entertain, engage, challenge, and intrigue you while enabling you to take greater control of your attitude and life.

–Mark Schulman

INTRODUCTION

ATTITUDE DEFINED

ATTITUDE SITS AT the heart of human behavior and interaction. It has significant bearing on positive outcomes, including the achievement of individual and business goals. It is fundamental to perception and your responses to the world. Attitudinal improvement is the single best investment you can make in life because of its direct impact on your future outcomes and your impact on others. Consider this formula:

$$A \times B = C$$

Attitude (A)
multiplied by Behavior (B)
equals Consequence (C)

It may be easier to notice the attitudes of others than your own. Whether you encounter a neighbor, coworker, executive, or government leader, a hostile and aggressive attitude establishes specific outcomes, as does a cooperative and encouraging attitude. Consider your life journey and the influence that the attitudes of others have played and continue to play in your personal and professional success. Conversely, your attitudes can have profound effects on others.

This book introduces you to a simple yet profound equation that will assist you in moving toward desired outcomes in all areas of your life including relationships, business, health and creativity. Your attitude first modifies your perception and feelings, then your behaviors, and, finally, the consequences you create, which can be negative or positive depending on the variables *you* control.

Consider the above formula in reverse: $C = B \times A$. The consequences you produce are the result of your behavior (or actions), which are significantly influenced by your attitude as attitude underpins every aspect of human interaction.

It's been my privilege to work with people on improving their lives for more than fifty years. I've learned a lot from their willingness to share their experiences and thoughts, giving me invaluable insights into the relationships among how people think, feel, and act.

In this book, Mark Schulman and I have collected valuable insights and actionable knowledge from people who have leveraged the power of attitude to produce powerful results for themselves, their communities, and their businesses.

Mark is not only an accomplished, world-class drummer, he is a student and life-long learner, always seeking to understand how and why people behave and the role that plays in their personal and professional outcomes.

Together, along with a host of business leaders, athletes, and entertainers, we're going to show you how shifts in attitude can change the consequences of your professional and personal lives and lead to greater success for you, your business, and your career.

–Dr. Jim Samuels

Focus on Attitude

Why concentrate on attitude in the search for positive outcomes? Leverage.

People immediately respond to attitude and for good reason. We intuitively understand its importance. Take a moment to recall a coworker, client, or even family member who exhibited a bad attitude. Was it periodic or consistent? Now, recall someone who presented a good attitude or even someone with a great attitude. How did your experiences with these individuals differ?

Using the formula $A \times B = C$, consider every goal that you or your business has set as a desired consequence. This consequence can change depending upon your behaviors—behaviors colored, modified, and controlled by your underlying attitude. Plans are the sequence of behaviors that are designed to produce desired outcomes (consequences).

Hence, your attitude determines the quality of your feelings and behaviors, and these behaviors determine the quality of your consequences. Your *attitude* fundamentally controls your chance of success, and control of your attitude can give you enormous leverage when it comes to ensuring the outcomes you want.

Ultimately, success is dependent on the quality and execution of a plan, defined as a sequence of behaviors tailored to bring about a desired outcome. The success of these behaviors is ultimately determined by the attitudes of everyone involved, and this is true regardless of a project's size—from individual life goals to the KPIs of Fortune 500 companies.

If attitude is such a critical component of successful outcomes, what exactly is it, how is it defined, and in what ways can it be controlled?

Attitude is a settled way of feeling and/or thinking
about something or someone, evidenced by behavior.

Desired outcomes can be achieved by applying more attention to your attitude and approach.

Attitude determines the quality of your behaviors and those behaviors lead to observable consequences.

Thus, even a small investment in attitude can produce life-altering consequences, and this is true for individuals, families, communities, organizations, institutions, corporations, and governments.

The leaders of these entities, and their attitudes, make or break organizational reputations, which often encapsulate the attitude of the brand itself. This is defined by an organization's approach to customer experience, product quality and longevity, service, and level of commitment. What is more important to the business, maximizing profits or customer loyalty?

I recently bought a toaster from a brand I have known and trusted for decades. Within a few weeks, the edges of my bread began to burn while the center was barely toasted. My investigation into the cause revealed that poor-quality material had compromised the heating coils. Someone sold the organization on short-term profit. That decision may have led to increased profits in the short-term, but I will never buy from that brand again. The attitude of their decision-makers was to focus on today's profit at the expense of quality and user experience. Building back a good reputation is significantly more expensive than maintaining an already established one.

The same is true in personal relationships. Attitude multiplied by behavior equals consequence, regardless of the situation. Your true attitude toward a friend is evidenced by your behavior and, over time, will produce predictable consequences. In all settings and circumstances, A × B = C.

Here is an abridged version of the Attitude Scale:

Attitude	Behavior	Consequence
+4 Successful	Follows through	Completion
+3 Focused	Takes correct action	Correct results
+2 Careless	Distracts	Mistakes
+1 Determined	Struggles toward	Progress
0 Critical Choice	**Conflict**	**Complaint/Correction**
−1 Rebellious	Struggles against	Regress
−2 Undermining	Disintegrates	Mistakes
−3 Failing	Takes wrong action	Wrong results
−4 Failed	Gives up	Incompletion

ATTITUDE AND PLANNING

Before beginning any planning process, from strategic to tactical, conduct an attitude check. Plans made with a less-than-optimal attitude tend to be less-than-optimal plans. Mitigate against negative mindsets individually or as a team and address negative feelings that would adversely impact the creation of plans that lead to positive change.

If you establish universally positive attitudes, you are far more likely to create functional plans that produce desired consequences. A well-built plan lays out the step-by-step behaviors that clearly produce desired consequences or achievements. This is intuitive (and obvious), but often overlooked.

Ask yourself (and your team) what attitude best supports or drives efforts to create a plan that is likely to produce the desired goal. This attention to attitude will dramatically improve the development and execution of a winning plan. It will positively change your organization's motivation. Different attitudes generate different perceptions. And, these perceptions generate different feelings and awareness of possibilities that play a huge role in personal and organizational productivity and creativity. Different attitudes produce different possibilities and results. For a deeper exploration into predictable outcomes as a result of specific attitudes, we have included the complete *Attitude Scale* in the addendum at the end of the book.

Your attitude can be considered your literal point of view or from where you are looking, and that changes how you see things. Consider a chicken egg. If you are hungry, it's food. If you are a farmer, it's product. If you are a chicken, it's family. The egg is the same, but it is perceived differently and, therefore, responded to and handled differently. Your attitude modifies your perceptions, and your perceptions guide your behavior and the consequences you produce.

Have you engaged with a salesperson with a careless attitude? Was that person successful in converting you into a customer? Compare that to speaking with a salesperson demonstrating a successful attitude, who is inspired and passionate about their product or service. Who was more successful? A salesperson who acts as an enthusiastic partner, joining with you to learn about your challenges and goals and contributing to your overall success makes a world of difference to your motivation, efforts, and results—often with life- or business-altering consequences.

It goes far deeper than a business transaction. The same equation is true for a friend, mate, colleague, investor, bank, or government because attitudes create mindsets and define possibilities. These perceived possibilities are the foundation for goal-setting and problem-solving.

Planning should not start before you have achieved positive attitudes among all involved. Start with the desired outcome, and then backstep into the behaviors (or tactics) necessary to achieve that outcome.

Ask yourself or your team the following:

- ➢ What is the optimal final consequence (C) we are trying to produce?
- ➢ What behaviors (B) are likely to produce that optimal final consequence?
- ➢ What attitude (A) will best support or drive our efforts to fulfill this plan and produce the desired goal?

We decided that a potent and entertaining way to exemplify the power of attitude would be to tap into the insights of some of the world's top performers. Mark enthusiastically interviewed these amazing people, guiding them to express stories, successes, failures, and wisdom into how the Attitude Equation molded their life experiences. Many of these folks became aware of the attitudes they chose through these interviews. Jessie, our editor, came up with the idea of identifying the unique learning keys of each interview and stating them upfront, so you have greater insights into what to look for in each interview. Enjoy this journey into $A \times B = C$.

SECTION 1

● ● ●

BESTSELLING AUTHORS

CHAPTER 1

POSSIBILITY

*Featuring **Alex Banayan**, bestselling
author, consultant, and commentator*

ALEX BANAYAN IS the youngest bestselling business author in US history. His book, *The Third Door*, chronicles his seven-year quest to uncover the definitive mindset of exponential growth and success. It has been acclaimed by *The New York Post* as "a joy to read." Over the course of his journey, Banayan's research led him to interview the most innovative leaders of the past half-century, including Bill Gates, Lady Gaga, Larry King, Maya Angelou, Steve Wozniak, Jane Goodall, Jessica Alba, Quincy Jones, and more. Named to *Forbes'* 30 Under 30 and *Business Insider*'s "Most Powerful People Under 30," Banayan is his generation's leading expert in high-performance and personal development, having been featured by *Fortune*, CNBC, Businessweek, *The Washington Post*, MSNBC, Fox News, and NBC News.

WHAT TO ◉◉ FOR

➤ Develop an attitude of possibility, and nurture that attitude in others.

➤ Turn disappointing moments into opportunities for future successes. If you get turned down for a job, ask if there is a future role you can play.

Alex Banayan: After spending ten years researching how the world's most successful people reach unimaginable heights, I realized that no matter where they came from and no matter what they do, they all treated life, business, and success the exact same way.

It's like getting into a nightclub. There are three ways in. There's the main entrance, where the line curves around the block and where 99 percent of people wait hoping to get in. Then, there's the second door, the VIP entrance, where the billionaires and celebrities enter. You either wait your turn, or you're born into it. But there's always a third door. You jump out of line, run down the alley and bang on the door a hundred times. Or you crack open a window. Or you go through the kitchen. There's always another way in. It doesn't matter if that's how Bill Gates sold his first piece of software or how Steven Spielberg became the youngest director in Hollywood; they all took the third door.

Mark Schulman: I'm that guy. I auditioned for Foreigner, got the gig, and found out they were recording without me. The producer didn't know me and hired someone else. So, I called the producer and left a message: "I know the drummer you normally use, and I love him. If he's ever not available, give me a call." Three months later he wasn't. They were in a bind, gave me a call, and asked me to play on a track for *Beverly Hills Cop III*. I nailed it on the first take. From that point on, I was his guy, too. Very few people would have gone through the third door. Essentially, that third door is really based on attitude.

Banayan: There are a lot of subcategories of attitudes. Some people have attitudes of gratitude or tenaciousness or perseverance. But the one overarching attitude that every single person I interviewed and researched has in common is possibility. You can give someone the best tools, wisdom, and knowledge in the world, and they can still feel stuck. But if you change what someone believes is possible, they'll never be the same. You can have someone who's the most talented person you've ever met. But if they have an attitude of "it's not possible," then they're right, it's not possible.

Schulman: Henry Ford said, "Whether you think you can, or you think you can't—you're right."

Banayan: When you change what you believe is possible, you change what becomes possible.

It's Steven Spielberg's story. It's Maya Angelou's story. It's Warren Buffett's story. On the surface, all the stories look different. Buffett is in finance. Maya Angelou is in poetry. Spielberg is in film. They all took different paths. They came from different backgrounds. But if you look beneath the surface, it's that attitude of possibility that they all have in common.

There are so many implicit messages that tell you why you're not enough and you are not capable, that only special people are capable of doing special things. The only thing you can control is how much you turn up the volume in your own life.

Schulman: When I first met business leader, consultant, and author Tim Sanders, he told me, "Feed your mind good stuff." I'll never forget that. I want to help people develop such an extraordinary attitude that it supersedes their talent, ability, and even intelligence. We're not all celebrities. We are not all at the top of our game. We don't all have bestsellers. Do you think that the attitude of possibility would be able to carry somebody above and beyond their talent and ability?

Banayan: I don't know if anyone goes beyond or above their talent and ability. The whole purpose of attitude is to unlock and reach that potential and capability.

I was once talking to Naomi Levy, the author of one of my favorite books, *Einstein and the Rabbi*. She told me that there's a theory among rabbis that human beings are born with potential within them, like a flickering flame. It's our job while we're alive to fan the flames and cultivate that talent. At the end of the day, it's up to you as an individual. Not everyone has parents or support figures who see into their souls and help them on their paths. You really have to choose yourself.

The challenge many times is that circumstances can be difficult. I think about this a lot. If you're born in a developing nation or you are a refugee, it might be really hard for you to become the lead drummer for P!nk. Even if you have that innate talent in you. But at the end of the day, no matter how hard your circumstances are, if you don't have an attitude of possibility and perseverance, it's not that the game is over—you didn't even enter the game. You didn't start.

Schulman: What did computer scientist Qi Lu say about luck?

Banayan: "Luck is like a bus." He says that if you miss the bus, another one's going to come around the corner. But if you're not prepared, you'll never be able to get on. It's attitude and behavior. Michael Jordan was not born shooting three pointers. He was born with an aptitude, with potential. He worked harder than everybody else. He wanted it that much and that badly. That's what Qi Lu did with sleep packing, creating more hours in a day.

Schulman: He discovered he had two extra months a year because he was sleeping less. So, he had those extra hours to work. He knew at some point the bus would come around. It's like my chance with Foreigner. After I did it in the first take, I went into the control room and the producer gave me a big hug. He also worked with Simple Minds and Billy Idol. If you look at my résumé, you'll see I worked with Simple Minds and Billy Idol, all because of one call.

When I committed to pursuing a speaking career, I was relentless. I cold called every speaker's bureau. I knew there were twenty other people doing the same. So, I had a pretty good opening line. "My name is Mark Schulman. I'm the drummer for P!nk. I do a unique top-performance, high-energy keynote. Can I have thirty seconds of your time?" Not one person said no. But when it was time to actually deliver the keynote, I needed to come through with quality. I studied with two speaking coaches, an acting coach, a storyteller, and a director to amplify my chances and my abilities.

Banayan: You've been living it for a while.

Schulman: I'm a constant student, and I love the journey.

FOOD FOR THOUGHT

1. How can you benefit from a positive attitude about what is possible?
2. How can others benefit from a positive attitude about what is possible?
3. How can you search for lessons in disappointment or failure?
4. How can you use disappointment to improve your knowledge and skills?
5. How can asking the right question open opportunities for your future?
6. How can a longer time frame reveal new opportunities to you?

CHAPTER 2

SELF-AWARENESS

*Featuring **Tiffani Bova**, global growth evangelist,*
business strategist, keynote, and author

TIFFANI BOVA IS the global growth evangelist at Salesforce and the author of the *Wall Street Journal*–bestselling book *GROWTH IQ: Get Smarter About the Choices that Will Make or Break Your Business*. Bova has been named to the Thinkers50 list of top management thinkers and is a welcomed guest on Bloomberg, BNN, Cheddar, MSNBC, and Yahoo Finance, among others. As host of *What's Next! with Tiffani Bova*, an iTunes' all-time business and management bestseller and a top sales podcast according to *Top Sales Magazine*, Bova has interviewed a growing number of leaders including Arianna Huffington, Chester Elton, Dan Pink, Ginger Hardage, Bonin Bough, Mark Victor Hansen, Seth Godin, and Tom Peters. Bova is a top Twitter influencer in business growth, customer experience, digital transformation, the future of work, and sales.

WHAT TO 👀 FOR

➤ Be ambitious. Learn, grow, accept new opportunities and responsibilities. Seek out new ones if they don't manifest in your current circumstances.

➢ Think beyond who you are as an individual contributor. Think about how you can have outsized impacts leading teams and people.

➢ Consider how unfortunate circumstances could lead to unexpected positive outcomes.

➢ Surround yourself with an orchestra of people whose strengths complement yours and who bring different perspectives that you may have missed.

➢ Be aware and cognizant of your attitude and how it impacts others. You can only change and improve what you are aware of.

➢ Take a beat when you need one. Go outside, change your environment, reflect, and adjust.

Tiffani Bova: Sellers can control one thing. They can't pick their quota, territory, technology, or brand message, but they can control how they show up. How you show up gives customers the feeling you care. I was one of very few women selling technology back in the '90s. I might not have been technical, but I showed up prepared every time. And I'm a student of my profession. I consumed information about the industry I was selling. I might not have known the answer, but at least I knew what they were asking. And that set me up for tremendous success.

In my thirties, I changed jobs every eighteen months and created my destiny, saying, "If you're not going to give me more responsibility and things to do, I'm going to go find where I can get more responsibility and more things to do." That was the attitude—the more I know, the more I can do. The more I can do, the more I want the opportunity to do it. And if I can't make that happen where I'm at, I'm going to go. It wasn't just about money, it was attitude. If I don't invest in myself, nobody else will. If I don't create my opportunities, nobody else will. And not in a negative way, in a very thoughtful way of trying to align my career.

Mark Schulman: How has your attitude shifted over the years?

Bova: In my twenties, I didn't know what I wanted to do. I was born and raised in Hawaii and my mom was just happy I didn't end up staying there and surfing the rest of my life. In my thirties, I wanted more—money, influence, responsibility. In my forties, I changed jobs and started working for Gartner, the world's largest analyst and consulting firm. I started as a senior director, and I left as a research fellow, which was the highest rank you can get in sales transformation, go-to-market, and growth, learning from really smart people who were forward-looking.

My superpower was taking disparate points of data and telling stories that were compelling to an audience. My ability was to aggregate signals in the market and get leaders to think differently, figuring out where I could have the greatest impact. In my thirties, I was an individual contributor. In my forties, I was advising some of the largest tech companies in the world how to grow. My attitude was "How do I help? How do I serve? How do I contribute and be part of a team?" It was having influence and understanding its power and privilege. That's when my attitude changed, when I understood the power of that platform. When I stood on stage and said something, it had implications.

Now, my attitude has shifted to contribution. How do I give back to an industry that's been so good to me? How do I use my voice for women and girls in 2030, work with the United Nations, speak on equality and diverse teams? That is a different level of attitude and impact. I went from consumption to contribution, which was an attitude adjustment.

Schulman: It was a natural evolution for you to shift your attitude. It's interesting to view yourself from a position of service. People who lead with service respond differently and produce different behaviors and consequences.

Bova: Over the course of fifteen years of keynoting, I've flown millions of miles and given hundreds of keynotes in front of hundreds of thousands of people. People ask, "Are you nervous when you do that?" I am not nervous about my content. I'm not nervous about knowing what I'm talking about. I'm not nervous that someone's going to ask me something that's going to catch me. What I'm nervous about is can we all make more money? Because we cannot make more time. Is it engaging? Is it inspiring? Is it getting them to think differently? Is it challenging? Is it motivating? Is it insightful?

Schulman: Can you think of any specific time where you feel like your attitude failed you?

Bova: When the pandemic hit, it was really disruptive to me. Virtual speaking was a medium I was not used to. Onstage, I'm being filmed, but it's very different from virtual-only. Initially, I needed an attitude adjustment because I was wallowing in what I had lost versus seeing what opportunity I had in front of me. It really challenged me to think of new ways to be interesting and deliver content in new ways, to stretch myself, to put it up on IGTV, which is something I would not normally do. My "think time" was during flights. My research time was conversations on the road, backstage, and meeting really interesting people. It's just not the same at scale. I'm fried at the end of eight video calls. Eight conversations at an event don't frighten me the way Zoom calls do.

I am not an academic, I play one at work. I don't have an MBA. I was a horrible student. It is all about who you surround yourself with. I call it my orchestra. My friends play very different instruments. And when I need someone to really kick my butt, I go to my drummer. And when I need someone to softly walk me off the edge, I go to my violinist.

Schulman: Do you have any stories about consciously shifting your attitude to produce a different behavior and consequence?

Bova: Being aware of your attitude is the hardest thing to do. People may not innately understand what their attitude is in a moment. There is a lack of self-awareness between what you think your attitude is internally on your own talk track versus what you're actually giving externally. If you're self-aware, you realize when you just don't have a good attitude. So now, if I feel like I'm in one of those not-great attitude moods, I'll say, "Please take the tone or how I say something with the fact that I'm just having one of those days. It has nothing to do with anybody I'm talking to." Self-awareness and attitude are where you start, otherwise you don't know you need to adjust or work on it.

Schulman: With that self-awareness, can you consciously shift your attitude?

Bova: Sometimes, if I'm in the thick of it, I need a beat. If I feel like I need it, I shut down. I go for a ten-minute walk around the neighborhood. I change the environment. I clear my mind, and I get the attitude adjustment.

FOOD FOR THOUGHT

1. What new opportunity can you explore or engage in?
2. What leadership position could you accept and explore?
3. How can you turn a negative experience to your advantage or the advantage of others?
4. How can including others improve your own understanding and capabilities?

5. What attitude are you approaching these questions with and how can that expand or limit your awareness?
6. How often would it benefit you to "take a beat?"

CHAPTER 3

ACTION

*Featuring **Grant Cardone**, entrepreneur,
author, and master salesperson*

GRANT CARDONE IS an American entrepreneur, *New York Times* best-selling author, and motivational speaker. His books, audio packages, and seminars provide people of all professional backgrounds with the practical tools necessary to build their own economies. Cardone is the author of four sales and business books, including *New York Times* bestseller *If You're Not First, You're Last* and Axiom award winner *Sell or Be Sold*. He has created customized sales training programs for Fortune 500 companies, small businesses, success-minded individuals, and entrepreneurs. Cardone regularly appears on CNBC, Fox Business, Fox News, and MSNBC, and contributes to Entrepreneur.com and *Huffington Post*.

WHAT TO ◉◉ FOR

➤ Find what attitude drives you beyond complacency and into action.
➤ Seek harmony between your personal and professional lives, as opposed to balance, which can be a harder metric to achieve.

Grant Cardone: What drives me is seeing other people do phenomenal, extraordinary things. It inspires me, and it fuels me. Why am I not doing that? There's some honesty in me that I know I can do more. It's not arrogance. It's this demand on self. I'm very unhappy that I haven't done more. That's the attitude.

People see me and say, "Look what you've done." But I see myself and say, "Why haven't I done more?" I know the decisions I've made. I know the things that I've not taken risks on. I know where I play it safe. I know the secrets of Grant Cardone.

Mark Schulman: You've said that you use fear to combat complacency. You always know that there's more to do. That is a powerful attitude because that's what drives you to be diverse in who you are and what you do. You're audacious and authentic; that's why you've been able to affect people.

Cardone: Hate is also a massive driver for me. People count me out. You shouldn't do that. The haters fuel me. I grew up a little guy. I got bullied and pushed around. That chip on my shoulder has been a driver. It's the people who have settled for two cars, the gate and fence, the puppy, and the welcome mat, and they're unhappy. It's the dash between the time you're born and the time you die. Am I living or not? It's not about money or fame. It's about people saying, "I can't."

People asked what I was doing selling an event on Super Bowl weekend. I'm a genius. Number One: No one else will be. I could've picked any weekend. I picked Super Bowl weekend to sell out thirty-four thousand seats. That was the biggest event we've ever done by ten times. I said, "If we do this, people will talk about us at every event going forward. It will be free promotion forever."

Schulman: What is that underlying attitude that's driving your behavior and your consequences?

Cardone: Sick of failing, of being satisfied, of making sense, of being scared, of being worried about money, of being stuck with the same people in my life. Why am I not friends with Warren and Jay Z and Kevin and Kanye? Why can't I have access to these people? Because I haven't gone for it. I'm just being honest with myself. It's not like I'm greedy. I don't have a yacht. I've got a great life. It's phenomenal, but I don't need anybody pushing me. I'm being pulled towards something. It's not my wife, it's not the kids, it's not God. I wasn't predestined. I don't believe in any of that stuff. I'm being pulled by me towards something that I know is true, that I can do more. And until I do more, I'm going to be perpetually unsatisfied with myself.

Schulman: Was there a time when your attitude was a critical factor in failure?

Cardone: I knew I didn't have enough things going on when the 2008 recession happened. I knew I was too dependent on one vertical. Legends are made in crisis. They're not made in good times. So, some people will contract out of crisis, and some people will expand. But no one will be the same.

Schulman: Fear and excitement are basically identical—our perception of that chemistry creates an experience. You invite fear because it becomes a big motivator for you.

Cardone: Fear is like the bully. I can avoid him on Monday and again on Tuesday and again on Wednesday, but sooner or later I'm going to get my butt kicked. And when you get your butt kicked once, you realize it wasn't that bad. Or maybe he doesn't kick my butt, and I take care of myself. Either way, I'm going to feel better because I confronted the boogeyman.

Schulman: Are there any other times when attitude shifts drove different behaviors or consequences?

Cardone: When I recovered from drug addiction, I came back from the treatment center, and I knew my biggest enemy was no longer drugs—it was time. Free time was the devil because if I had any free time, I misused it. So, I try to cram everything I can into every day.

Schulman: What about family? What about balance?

Cardone: I don't really do the balance thing. I've created a life where we punch into it together. I look for harmony more than balance—harmony through expansion rather than contraction.

FOOD FOR THOUGHT

1. Take one fear and think about how you can reframe it into something exciting.
2. Recall a time when you could have done more. Take one action that provides a sense of closure.
3. Recall a time when you were angry and rebellious and reframe that rebellion into determination.
4. What can you do today that pushes you outside your comfort zone to either accomplish something that serves you or helps someone else?

CHAPTER 4

APPRECIATION

*Featuring **Chester Elton**, Apostle of
Appreciation, author, and keynote*

CHESTER ELTON HAS spent two decades helping clients engage their employees to execute on strategy, vision, and values. In his provocative, inspiring, and entertaining speeches, the No. 1 bestselling leadership author provides real solutions to leaders looking to manage change, drive innovation, and lead a multi-generational workforce. Elton's work is supported by research of more than one million working adults, revealing the proven secrets behind high-performance cultures and teams. Elton has been called the "apostle of appreciation" by Canada's *Globe and Mail*, "creative and refreshing" by the *New York Times*, and a "must read for modern managers" by CNN.

WHAT TO 👀 FOR

➤ Assume positive intent. Too often, we judge situations negatively by seeing them through the lens of negative intentions. Assume people are cheering you on.
➤ Be kind, and treat others how you want to be treated. This attitude is contagious, and often leads to better outcomes for everyone.

➤ Focus on how you make other people feel and how you can make them feel even better.

Chester Elton: Attitude is everything. Great talent with poor attitude equals not-great talent. I asked executive coach Marshall Goldsmith if he would endorse one of my books. I didn't know him well, I met him at a conference through a mutual friend. He asked, "Would you like me to write the foreword?" He was so magnanimous and generous. I said, "Marshall, you're so giving! I really appreciate it." He gave me this bit of advice. "I look at the work we're in from two standpoints. One is that everybody's your competitor. The other is that we're all in this together, and the tide raises all ships. I prefer the latter."

I grew up in a very competitive family, and I brought that to my work. And while my work was all about appreciation and giving, there was this part of me that was competitive. And that was a moment when I thought, he's right. Instead of charging people another thousand dollars to videotape our session, I'll say, "Look, our goal is to make a difference, and if videotaping my presentation to show your employees is going to help, let's do that." You need a couple more books, they're on me. You want me to meet with sponsors before the conference, absolutely. That has made all the difference in how I approach my work and how I approach people.

My friend, Prudential Center CEO Scott O'Neil, said, "Many times in business, or even in relationships, we assume the worst. If somebody doesn't respond, they don't care. But the reality in most cases is, they're just busy. Their day got away, they got a call from school, their kid was throwing up, and they didn't get back to you." He has this philosophy of assuming positive intent. Assume people are cheering for you.

This happened to me the other day. For the first time in my life, I missed an appointment. It was a pro-bono meeting with the CEO of a bank in New Jersey, and Adrian Gostick and I were launching our book in Manhattan. There was no way I was getting from Manhattan to the middle of New Jersey. So, I called him, left a message, and apologized. He didn't get back to me for a week. I stewed about it. So, I called and I said, "We haven't been able to connect. I really want to make this good." He called me back and said, "I really appreciate your message. I'm not really that upset. Life is too short. I've been meaning to get back to you, I just haven't. Seriously, don't worry about it."

Assume that people have the best intentions at heart instead of assuming the worst. It just comes right back to attitude. How do I look at this situation? My dad would say, "Ches, don't tell me not to worry about stuff because 99 percent of the stuff I worry about never happens."

Mark Schulman: Your attitude is your launching point and your viewpoint. It determines what you see. Depending on your assumption, your jumping-off point is going to be very, very different. A positive assumption is going to drive different behaviors.

Elton: I'll share with you my keynote introduction. "I'm delighted to be with you here today. I get to speak in a lot of different places all over the world to a lot of different associations, industries, and companies. I like to hear the other speakers speak, too, so I've sat in your seat. I've come to the conclusion that the quality of any presentation is directly proportionate to the volume of applause that welcomes the speaker to the stage. So, if you really want this to be world class, you have to do better." It's a cheap trick, but I really like it. It makes me feel good, and it makes them feel good, too.

Schulman: You rile them up. We are there to move energy. These are attitude shifts. You are asking them to step out of their comfort zones and drive you with more appreciation, with more applause. You're changing their chemistry. You're opening them up for a greater experience. It is an attitude shift that is producing different behavior and driving different consequences. You want them to have the greatest experience possible.

Can you think of a time when you shifted your attitude to produce a better result?

Elton: My Marshall Goldsmith moment. Why are we doing this? We want to make a difference. How do we make a difference? We want people to be happier at work. What creates a great culture at work and an engaging and a high producing team? A lot of that is attitudinal, and it comes from the boss. If we're going to make a difference, people have to access our knowledge. And if we're so obsessed with charging for every little thing we do, it makes it prohibitive. So that's the attitudinal shift. It changed a lot of things that we did in our business.

We have an online assessment. It's a hundred questions, it takes you about twenty-five minutes, and it spits out this amazing report on your top motivators. We used it for our book *The Best Team Wins*. There are common motivators, and then there's diversity. Where do you have a disconnect? If I value family and you don't, and we don't address that, it could cause friction. You want me to work every weekend, but I coach my kid's soccer team. I'm not coming in.

Schulman: Can you think of any specific times when you failed based on an attitude?

Elton: That happens more often than we realize, in subtle ways. As humans, we're wired to be negative. That's our defense mechanism. We assume negative intent. My college-age son says, "The man's always trying to get you, Dad." And then we laugh. Who is the man? "Anybody who's trying to get you, Dad!"

We organized a bunch of kids from our church to go to the Community FoodBank of New Jersey and work for half a day. I remember thinking that the kids weren't going to enjoy it. I went in with a negative attitude. It was goofy work. People send products that are broken, open, and spilled. You have to clean things up and deal with it. The founder, Kathleen DiChiara, came out and said, "I've run the numbers, and you've literally put together food-stuff and supplies for more than 350 families today. You did that. Here's their situation." She shared what a difference we'd made in four hours. Everybody's crying and, and I'm thinking my attitude coming into this thing was not great and could have easily taken us off the rails. And yet at the end, it was so worth it.

My dad would say, "Ches, happiness is a choice. Choose to be happy." You can wake up in the morning, look at all the things you have to do and be overwhelmed. Or you can say, "It's gonna be great!" Why not? A completely different outcome! Ninety-nine percent of people who show up to work today want to do a good job.

Schulman: Regardless of the attitude we choose at any moment, we can be miserable or we can be joyful. By driving your attitude, you're creating a different behavior, which is controlling the outcome of your experience. But there are still some things we can't control.

It's the concept of being in traffic. I can be in traffic and get myself riled up, anxious, and angry or I can just turn on music, listen, and enjoy the ride. I'm not having much of an effect on the traffic either way. But if I'm tense, it could make me more dangerous—which could promote a more challenging outcome for myself and others. Who and how do I want to be?

Elton: I was trying to get to Columbus, Ohio. I flew out of Newark to Detroit. There was bad weather, and I wasn't able to get to Columbus. I called my client and apologized. I went to the airport lounge, and there's a man in front of me—older, dressed up, and clearly aggravated. He is just ripping the woman behind the counter, saying, "I gotta get back to Newark! There's a flight leaving. I don't think you understand who I am." He's got a negative attitude, and he's giving her a really hard time. She said, "Sir, there's only so much I can do. Getting angry with me isn't helping. Here's your pass, please go sit down. If I can figure something out, I'll call you back, and we'll tell you what your options are. Right now, we've got you on the first flight out tomorrow morning."

I watched this whole thing, waited for him to leave, and said, "Rough day?" She said, "Little bit. What can I do to help you?" I said, "I listened to the whole conversation. I was trying to get to Columbus, Ohio, and I would love to be on that Newark flight, but overheard it's full." She said, "It's not full. There's a seat available. Give me your boarding pass. If you leave right now, you'll make it." That guy could've been in that seat! If his attitude had been: "I hope you can help me. I understand this isn't your problem. Is there any way we can get back to Newark?" She would have moved heaven and earth. People want to do business with people who make them feel better about themselves.

My dad, John Dalton Elton, was the program director for CJCA, a rock station in Edmonton, Alberta. Dad would talk to parking attendants the same way he would talk to captains of industry. Here is a story he told me. A couple goes to a big gala, they get separated, and they're talking to various people. The wife comes back to her husband, and her husband asks, "Did you meet so-and-so?" And she says, "Yes, I did. After talking to him, I am convinced he is the most interesting person on the planet." Her husband asks, "Did you meet so-and-so?" She says, "Yes, I did. After talking to him, he convinced me that I am the most interesting person on the planet." My dad said, "Be the latter." That was his outlook. Be nice to everybody. Everybody's having a tough day. Being kind costs you nothing. It can change attitudes. It can change somebody's whole day by just being kind.

Schulman: What a fantastic reminder—the value of individual relationships. My boss P!nk spends five minutes of her show having banter with individual people because she knows the value of nurturing every single relationship. Even if you are a huge company or a popular entertainer or you have a client base of millions or billions, every single person needs to feel that individual attention.

Elton: I'm a big fan of random acts of kindness. What did I do today to be encouraging? What was my random act of kindness? What did I do to make somebody else's day just a little nicer and smoother?

Schulman: What shift did I create? Look at the butterfly effect—what seems to be a nuanced and subtle thing can shift consciousness and evolution over time. All the small moments eventually make a big difference. You don't know how your day could have been different had you approached one early instance with a positive attitude.

Elton: What did your parents teach you when you were five years old? It's better to give than to receive. By giving, you always receive.

Schulman: I don't want people to walk away from my keynotes thinking, "Mark is a rock star." I want them to walk away saying, "I am a rock star!"

FOOD FOR THOUGHT

1. How can you measure your attitude for positivity?
2. How can you manifest a positive attitude in those around you?
3. In what ways can you interpret someone's attitude as positive, whether it is or not?
4. How can you be more kind to yourself and others?
5. How can kindness improve all of your relationships?

CHAPTER 5

ASPIRATION

*Featuring **Shep Hyken**, Chief Amazement Officer and customer service expert*

SHEP HYKEN IS a customer service and experience expert and the Chief Amazement Officer of Shepard Presentations. He is a *New York Times* and *Wall Street Journal* bestselling author and has been inducted into the National Speakers Association Hall of Fame for lifetime achievement in the speaking profession.

Some of his clients include American Airlines, AAA, Anheuser-Busch, AT&T, AETNA, Abbott Laboratories, American Express—and that's just a few of the As!

WHAT TO 👀 FOR

➢ Life's outcomes are determined by how you react to both positive and negative situations.
➢ Create lifetime aspirations and decide what steps you can take daily, weekly, and monthly to achieve them.
➢ Write down your wins, and focus on how you will create more positive outcomes in the future.
➢ Have fun.

Shep Hyken: I was an optimistic child. I played music. I did magic shows. I practiced card tricks for hours. I still have a childlike enthusiasm for things that give me joy. I still like to have fun. I call my music buddies, go to Los Angeles, and jam on a soundstage. I call my magic buddies, and we stay up all night doing card tricks.

I was at an event doing an exercise where we're supposed to find somebody we know in the group and share something about them. One gentleman shared something about me. He said, "What I like about Shep, he's like a child. He's got this wonder, enthusiasm, and excitement that you don't often see in people our age."

Life should be fun. It should be interesting. Sure, there's a lot of seriousness and sometimes tough things happen, but I love the philosophy that at the end of a bad day, it's time to move on. It's not what happens to you. It's what you do about it. I'm a resilient person, and part of that might be my optimism. I'm able to see good, even in bad situations. There's always some way out.

I was coming home from a speaking engagement, and my driver owned his own transportation service. I was one of his regular clients. He said, "I have a little something for you for Christmas. Do you use a day planner?" And he pulled out one of those small planners that fit in your jacket breast pocket. You open them up, and you can see a week at a time, little squares for each day. I said, "I don't really use a day planner. You shouldn't waste it on me, but that's very nice. Thank you." Then, I thought about it. And I said, "You know what, I'd like to take that day planner, and instead of planning my days, I'm going to reflect on my days. This is a day reflector." For one year every single day, I wrote down something good that happened to me professionally and personally. Within a short period of time, I was finding the good in almost everything.

Mark Schulman: I do the same thing using Dr. Jim Samuels's WINS Formula. The "W" stands for yesterday's wins. I write down my wins, so I'm primed and excited about everything I accomplished—big or small. The "I" represents improvements and the "N" stands for next wins. I forecast the most important wins for today. "S" is the state you want to create. I do this every morning.

Hyken: It is a ritual, a practice, a habit. I have five lifetime aspirations. And if you ask me without even looking at the list, I can tell you what they are. I want quality of life. I want to play golf when I'm one hundred years old. I'm healthy. I have a personal mantra to have fun and make my kids (and eventually grandkids) smile, and a business mantra to be amazing for my clients and teach my clients to be amazing. I want to be charitable. I want to leave a mark and help others. I want fulfillment. I want to spend time with my wife and kids.

Schulman: It begins with perspective, your vantage point or your disadvantage point, depending on the attitude you choose. Have there ever been times when you weren't feeling optimistic, when you were running into trouble because you needed to shift your attitude or make a change?

Hyken: I get over things pretty quick—that's part of resilience. At age twelve, my parents got divorced and that freaked me out. I came home from hockey practice. My brother, sister, and I sat next to each other on the couch, and my mom and dad said, "We're getting divorced." We all nodded our heads. I took it pretty hard. I remember going into my mom's room and crying. "What's life going to be without him?" She said, "You're still going to see your dad. It's not like he's out of your life. It's just that he's out of *my* life." She didn't say that, but I know that's what she was thinking. It took me a while to figure that out.

I'm a conscientious person. I've only missed one speaking engagement. My airport was closed because of the weather. We were on the tarmac getting ready to take off, and they shut the airport down. The pain I felt by not being able to meet my obligation was so extreme that here we are close to thirty years later, and I'm still thinking about it. I thought, how can I keep that from ever happening again? I remember a speaking engagement that I couldn't get to because of weather, and I called a private plane an hour away. "What's the weather like?" "It's fine here." I got into a cab and chartered a jet that cost almost as much as what I was getting paid to speak. It wasn't about making money. It was about meeting the obligation.

Throughout my life, as things were thrown at me, I asked, "What do I need to do to get out of this?" I exhaust all possibilities until there's nothing left. Nobody's going to ever question my lack of effort and, perhaps, even a little ingenuity on making things happen.

FOOD FOR THOUGHT

1. What attitude can you create daily to ensure you take action on lifetime aspirations?
2. What action will you take today to manifest those aspirations?
3. What attitude could make you more childlike?
4. What actions can you take to be more ingenious and find new, alternative, or adjunct paths to your desired outcomes?

CHAPTER 6

PREPARATION

*Featuring **Jared Kleinert**, business owner,*
consultant, author, and speaker

JARED KLEINERT IS the founder of invite-only mastermind community Meeting of the Minds, as well as a TED speaker, a two-time award-winning author, and *USA Today*'s "Most Connected Millennial." Kleinert started his first company at fifteen years old. At sixteen, he served as the first intern (and later one of the first ten employees) for enterprise SaaS company 15Five, which has raised more than US $40 million. He was a delegate to US President Barack Obama's 2013 Global Entrepreneurship Summit in Malaysia. Kleinert has written multiple books including *2 Billion Under 20: How Millennials are Breaking Down Age Barriers and Changing the World*. His insights on entrepreneurship and networking have been featured in major media such as *Forbes*, *TIME*, *Harvard Business Review*, *Fortune*, NPR, *Entrepreneur*, *Mashable*, Fox Business, and more.

WHAT TO ◉◉ FOR

➤ It's never too early to start being conscious and cognizant of your attitudes and how they impact behavior and consequences.

> ➤ Own your mistakes and failures, apologize to those who were impacted, and learn how to do better next time.
> ➤ Prepare. Prepare more. Be more than ready for every experience, project, or opportunity.

Mark Schulman: How important do you believe attitude has been in the development of your career?

Jared Kleinert: I'm twenty-three, and I've had the fortune of starting at a very young age. And I've become more and more mindful that I have the ability to shape my attitude. Initially, I had a certain way of doing things that represented youthfulness and optimism. I was really just trying to get my foot in the door, but as I've matured and as I've grown conscious of the fact that I am still so young and have so much more to go, I've taken a more reflective and constructive view toward my attitude. Today, I employ an executive coach every other week. I do meditation and journaling to bring my best self to the table.

I know I have a long way to go, and these are things I'm not perfect at, but it's something that can be molded and shaped. You can do this at any age, but there is advantage to building these at a young age because there might be bad habits you don't want that you have to deconstruct before constructing good ones. Like any part of the business world, if you start at a younger age, you get more time to build relationships. You get more time to experience things.

Then, you get to bring all that experience and wisdom to the table. I'm actively working to do more of that. It's showing as I speak, as I facilitate sessions with diverse CEOs, entrepreneurs, and business owners, many twice or three times my age—people who I admire or who I consider mentors. It's beginning to feel more and more like I belong, and I do belong, but I'm garnering a different type of respect and interest in my work and a different type of feedback than I did when I was first starting out, and that's due to attitude and how I am getting myself ready to show up.

Schulman: Have you found that changing your attitude was necessary or helpful in developing your career?

Kleinert: A lot of my work started by studying hundreds of top performing millennials, people from my generation in business, athletics, and entertainment. Now, I'm seeing how I can take these top performers—regardless of their age or industry—and bring them together for mastermind groups and CEO roundtable experiences.

When I first got started as an entrepreneur, there was an urgency to it. There still is some urgency to growing my business, but there is more balance now than there was at the beginning. I've sensed more mindfulness around how I relate with people. I'm more focused on building deep and meaningful relationships that will sustain ten or twenty years and multiple companies, as opposed to trying to just build one company as quickly as possible and sell it or be successful by any means. In the beginning, there was a lack of consciousness not only with my day-to-day performance, but also the short- versus long-term sense of it. Over time, as I've matured, there is more mindfulness around how each day can impact long-term outlook.

The stakes are rising, and I need to bring a better and better self. I need to be on my game every single time I talk to someone. Whereas, when I was younger, I didn't have assets to protect as far as my brand or my network were concerned.

Schulman: You have more to gain and you have more to lose, and you're cultivating relationships that are more meaningful, and, therefore, have more longevity and can create a bigger benefit for both you and other people on a long-term basis.

Kleinert: With that comes more confidence, but also more humility. I see how easy it could be to ruin that reputation. I see how easy it could be to get an important meeting and have it go absolutely nowhere.

Schulman: It's not just you, and it's not just about your age. You have a lot of integrity, and integrity is a critical part of your attitude. Integrity creates sustainable relationships. But was attitude ever a critical factor in a failure?

Kleinert: A few years ago, I tried to get into the online course space, which was not something I had any expertise in. I hadn't built an online course. I was looking to pre-sell a product. It was called "Yourself with Wealth." I lined up all these successful businesspeople and high-level experts and told them that I would pay for their time to do an interview and then forecast the potential revenue from a joint partnership.

I hadn't tested this sort of launch before bringing in partners. I hadn't even developed a product or service yet. I hadn't done market research to determine if the product that I was looking to sell was needed or not. Maybe there was an over-confidence as opposed to a healthy slowness or preparation.

Here I am, thinking that I can come in with a catchy sounding online course and have a successful launch. Sure enough, I went to launch the thing and not a single sale registered.

Thankfully, I had tried to pre-sell it, so I wasn't down in the hole too much. But I put myself in a position where I had jeopardized a half dozen relationships with very important people in that space. I ended up acknowledging my failures. I did whatever I could to correct those mistakes and wrote a blog post or two about it for *Forbes*. I don't think I've torched any relationships or burned any bridges, but I put myself in a position where I could have.

That taught me to be more careful about asking for other people's time and energy and the weight behind my asks or requests. It taught me that when something does go wrong, all you can control is how you respond.

If you make a mistake, how do you fix it? You can't control if someone is going to forgive you or not. That didn't stop me from trying to right the wrong. The *Forbes* piece was probably the article that I got the most individual emails and comments from because I was vulnerable and shared.

Schulman: People like it when you're vulnerable. They like it when you tell the truth. We learn so much from each other's mistakes. You had a conscious idea about the attitude you chose. You couldn't affect everybody else's attitude, but you could control your own attitude to best fix the harm. Has your attitude ever been a critical factor in success?

Kleinert: One of the things I've been doing to promote Meeting of the Minds—our invite-only, high-end mastermind group—is running private, free-to-attend CEO roundtables. We did one Saturday.

Because of the coaching that I've been doing and because of my awareness of the power of attitude, I woke up early and went for a short run, even though it was cold out in New York. I meditated on the ride over to the venue. I showed up with plenty of time to spare—the opposite of everything I did with the online course. I was very prepared.

[My guests included] a current NFL player, multiple seven-figure business owners, people who had recently sold companies for eight figures and Emmy nominees, directors, and show producers.

I had a table of twenty-five very diverse and successful entrepreneurs, and I brought my best self. I not only held my own, I facilitated the interactions among all these people for four hours and did not lose any energy. In fact, I was energized by it. That is the feeling I want to have every single time I'm hosting one of these or every time I'm leading a Meeting of the Minds, which is a three-day experience. I need to be on my game the whole time.

Schulman: That's what you have created consciously with your attitude shift—your approach.

FOOD FOR THOUGHT

1. How can you increase your attitudinal awareness and the impact it has on behavior and consequences?
2. How can you take more responsibility for your mistakes?
3. What is the best way to apologize to people affected by your mistakes?
4. What is the best way to learn from your mistakes?
5. How do you know when you are ready to fulfill responsibilities?

CHAPTER 7

REFLECTION AND RENEWAL

*Featuring **Josh Linkner**, entrepreneur,*
author, and keynote speaker

JOSH LINKNER DELIVERS inspiring and actionable keynotes to drive meaningful outcomes worldwide. He is the perfect balance of energizing and practical, entertaining and result-focused, fun and impactful. As an innovation keynote speaker, *New York Times* best-selling author, successful five-time entrepreneur, venture capitalist, national columnist, and well-respected jazz musician, Linkner blends deep, real-world experience with a magnetic stage presence to help people and organizations thrive. Every keynote is customized to drive the biggest possible impact, combining engaging stories, gorgeous visuals, and practical techniques that push audiences to jumpstart their creative energy and solve challenges in fresh, innovative ways.

WHAT TO 👀 FOR

➤ Positive attitude doesn't just help you succeed, it helps you recover from failure.

➤ Do what others won't do, not what they can't, to differentiate yourself from them.

➤ Take time to reflect on your successes and where you want to go next. Use this moment to cleanse any negative thoughts from the week and refocus on your goals.

Josh Linkner: The energy you bring can create opportunities that determine outcomes. If you have two people, and everything else is the same, but one has a bad attitude and the other one does not—then that becomes the difference maker. There's so much negativity out there, but when you take the stage, you have to have a great attitude. You have to pour your heart and soul into it. That's the mark of a professional. When you do that, you elevate others around you. It's an intentional approach because that type of attitude can be contagious. Likewise, if you're a big whiny complainer, that's going to rub off on people, as well.

Mark Schulman: I am there to perform, to be of service to the audience, my boss, and the other band members. For me, it's a conscious attitude shift. I'm going to put everything I have into being present. My mind becomes senior to my body with the necessity of top performance because that's what I'm hired to do.

Linkner: I play something on guitar, and you hear the rhythm and you play it on the drums. Then, the bass player picks it up, and you create something collectively. Attitude has that same factor. If I'm with people in a meeting or business setting, I will try to be the elevator. How do I bring others up? In business, you have achievements, and it's not only what you say, it's how you say it. There's so much communication that is nonverbal. If you communicate with a dumpy, grumpy attitude, no one is going to get behind you.

Schulman: You've had enormous success in a variety of areas with a variety of businesses. We tend to revel in our successes, but we learn a lot from our failures. Can you think of a specific time when attitude was a critical factor in a failure for you?

Linkner: You choose to respond. If you wallow in self-pity and pout, you get knocked down and stay down. If you have tenacity and proper attitude, even in the face of defeat, you'll rise from it.

I had a situation with a partner who was a very successful guy, but it became toxic. It didn't work out. I could have blamed myself and become miserable, but I said, "Time to reinvent the next chapter." I gave myself permission to feel bummed about it, but I didn't waste time and energy on it. I didn't become angry about it.

Schulman: We get wounded, but we get back up. Can you think of any other specific examples when you definitively shifted attitude and it made an absolute difference?

Linkner: Public speaking is a good example of that because so much of it is the energy you give on the stage. You have to have good content, obviously. It has to be original and compelling. But, if you're just reading a transcript, that's not what people are paying for. You open your heart on stage and give energy to people. I like to say, "I do what others won't, not what others can't." A lot of people won't do what I do. They wouldn't do a morning speech in New Orleans, fly to New Jersey, and the next day go to Boston. Then, it's Hawai'i at 1 a.m., taking a helicopter to my gig, and then immediately flying on a red eye so I can get to Austin for another one. Part of it is attitude, having streetfighter grit.

Schulman: I'm thinking about that schedule, and I'm drooling. I love that, too. Are you making conscious shifts to create the attitude you need to have? Because you could be physically exhausted, as well. What are you doing to change your state?

Linkner: I don't have a particular ritual. I keep super high energy all the time. For me, it's about staying connected to a bigger purpose, which is my kids, my family, and this desire to make an impact on people's lives. If I allow myself to mope or be less than fully energized, it hurts my impact.

Schulman: Your energy is just infectious. I feel like going back to the gym I just left.

Linkner: Getting work done, that's transactional. I take time to reflect at least once a week for forty-five minutes to an hour. We spend our professional lives "heads down," getting the to-do list done. I use this time to be "heads up," when I put the transactional work aside. I think about the long term, about my goals or the impact I'm making or the broader trajectory of the work that I'm doing. This is a high-level, fifty-thousand-foot reconnect. It is grounding because you're always bombarded with so much negativity throughout the week. For me, that's my reset button.

Schulman: It connects you with your "why" with a fundamental purpose.

FOOD FOR THOUGHT

1. How can a positive attitude help you spot opportunities to succeed? How can it help you deal with failure?

2. What is the difference between what people won't do and what they can't do?

3. How can doing what others won't do bring you exceptional results?

4. How can recounting your successes help you determine what to succeed at next?

5. How can long-term goals bring more integrity to your short-term goals?

SECTION 2

● ● ●

BUSINESS LEADERS

CHAPTER 8

LEADERSHIP

*Featuring **Jeff Clarke**, author,*
consultant, and keynote speaker

JEFFREY J. CLARKE is co-CEO of E.Merge Technology Acquisition Corporation and chairman of the board for FTD. He served as CEO of Kodak for five years. Prior to joining Kodak, Clarke was a managing partner of Augusta Columbia Capital (ACC), a private investment firm he co-founded in 2012. From 2012 to 2014, he was the chairman of the board at Travelport Inc., a private, travel technology firm, where he also served as CEO, after leading its sale from Cendant Corporation to the Blackstone Group for $4.3 billion. Clarke earned an MBA from Northeastern University and holds a bachelor's degree in economics from SUNY Geneseo.

WHAT TO ◉◉ FOR

➢ Good leaders are optimistic. No one wants to follow someone who looks at the world with frustration.

➢ Be true to yourself and seek out other leaders who match and elevate your attitude and approach.

➢ Be transparent about present conditions, the attitudes, and behaviors you seek out of others and your honest expectations about the future. Dishonest optimism leads to unrealistic expectations that can't be delivered on and costs your credibility.

➤ Help people see the big picture and how what they do daily contributes to something important.

➤ Attitude is emotional. If you want to change people's behavior and create more positive outcomes, touch people's emotions.

Mark Schulman: I am inspired by your philanthropy, your passion for film, and your celebration of art. How important do you believe attitude has been in developing your career?

Jeff Clarke: Attitude is critical to leadership. As you work in corporations, which has been my business career, you quickly see the people who are optimists and leaders and who get things done. People watch behaviors that are successful and try to mimic them.

I define culture as how you get things done. Sometimes you can have a culture that's nefarious, like organized crime. They get things done by breaking rules and exploiting lives. In corporations, we get things done by processing, building positive reinforcement, changing markets, and, ultimately, satisfying customer needs. Attitude is critical because no one wants to follow someone who's either a pessimist or looks at the world with frustration. If you're going to lead and grow an organization, you have to have an attitude that excites people. There are really two motivational tools in the world. One is excitement and showing people rewards and culture. The other one is fear. Some people manage by fear. By doing that, you're threatening and you have a negative attitude. You're always talking about the downside, saying that people will be fired if they don't do this or that. That is not a sustainable culture. It's not anything that anyone really wants to work for. People want to work for people who are inspiring, who show them the way, who paint an exciting picture, and who talk about what that means for employees, the market, and the company.

From an attitude perspective, you can't be successful in life or business unless you are optimistic about the future. It must be real and specific. If we do this, we're going to win this way, and here's what it means for you. That's attitude.

Schulman: The big misconception is that positive consequence begins with behavior manipulation. It begins with attitude shifting.

Clarke: Why would people change their behavior if their leader doesn't show an attitude or intent they want to follow? Wednesday, I flew to Houston to meet with twenty of Kodak's biggest Texas customers. We took them to a Houston Astros baseball game. If I wasn't smiling and happy and excited about the company and spending the evening with them, how would I change their behavior to buy a product? Attitude is critical.

When I took over Kodak, the decision had been made to shut down the last film factory in the world. I went to Hollywood and met with the six major studios and high-profile directors. I told them that I was willing to change that decision in partnership with them. What succeeded was me going in with excitement and saying, "You all know we have a lot of competition from digital, video, and advanced high-definition television. But film is still really important. Look what's happened with vinyl. People care about it. People want differentiative experience." If I couldn't paint excitement with my attitude, I wouldn't have gotten their support. I painted them a future that I fundamentally believed in. That attitude and my personal excitement about the product helped them say, "Yes, we'll double down. We're willing to sign contracts with you. We didn't believe in it because you guys didn't believe in it. Now, we think you believe in it."

Today, *Wonder Woman, James Bond, Star Trek, Mission Impossible,* everything Quentin Tarantino does, everything Steven Spielberg does—it's all shot on Kodak film. All of those were at risk of going digital. We invested in the product, even though it was a product that many people thought was dead. We believed in it and showed the attitude with real actions that allowed them to change their behaviors. Their attitude was, "Why are we going to invest in a product that even the manufacturer doesn't care about?"

Schulman: Look at the consequence it produced. It's magnificent. It affected art; it affected experiences. Your attitude is joyful and incredibly motivating. But can you share a story when your attitude was a critical factor in a failure?

Clarke: I was recruiting a star executive to be the chief financial officer for our company, Computer Associates, a large software company. The company had gone through a difficult financial scandal. I was brought in by the board after the chief financial officer, the chief executive officer, the general counsel, and the chief of talent all went to prison. We needed to change about a hundred top managers who were deeply complicit in the crime. Not all of them went to jail, but half of them needed to. So, when I was hiring a new CFO, I gave candidates a sober but positive view. My attitude was positive, but realistic. In other words, you're going to find more problems that we haven't found yet, but the underlying strength of the company is good. In fact, it ended up being a strong turnaround in retrospect. But despite having an honest and positive attitude, I failed in recruiting that candidate. He would have been a great CFO. His attitude was that we needed to tear everything down.

My experience had been that you can't tear everything down. My view was that while this had been a horrific example of corporate malfeasance, there were real strengths in the company. I think he viewed my attitude as being Pollyannish. I was too optimistic. I was too positive. Some of the people we kept are still there today. They're extraordinarily good people. They were misled by their executive management. But my attitude was viewed as unrealistic by someone who was more somber. He just had a different prescription and a different style. Looking back, I would have had to modify my optimism to recruit him, and I couldn't do that. Fundamentally, I believed in the direction I was going, and as such, I failed in not getting a strong executive into the company. Everything worked out fine, but my goal was to hire this person and persuade him to my viewpoint, and I couldn't do that.

Schulman: Would you have done it differently if you were to do it again?

Clarke: No, I wouldn't. I learn from my mistakes. I am pragmatic and adjusted, but on this one, I needed to build a culture that was aligned to my view of the crisis. And my view of the crisis was not to just burn everything down. My view was to make surgical changes where needed and keep the good things alive.

Schulman: It was a difference in attitude and approach, and it was authentic to you.

Clarke: Success and failure are blunt end spectrums. Usually something's in the middle. Circumstances can always be a little bit better or a little bit worse.

Schulman: What is your day-to-day approach to maintaining this attitude? Is there anything you do or communicate to others specifically to influence their attitudes?

Clarke: Your attitude has to be rooted in reality. We've all seen cases where people have a positive or negative attitude, yet neither works towards changing behavior. In fairness, both should

MARK SCHULMAN AND JIM SAMUELS, PHD

work, but achieve different outcomes. I try to create transparent communications that support my attitude. I show a positive, let's-get-it-done, optimistic attitude. I need to back that up with real specifics and transparency. Equally, when I'm trying to get the troops to climb the next hill, I have to be realistic with them about what's on the other side. If I paint a too-positive picture, I lose the credibility of having an optimistic or positive attitude. So, I'm constantly reinforcing the transparency underneath the actions I'm asking people to do and the behaviors that I'm trying to influence with my attitude.

Schulman: My co-author, Dr. Jim Samuels, says, "Reality is the one possibility that destroys all others."

Clarke: You have to paint a broad picture, or you can't see the forest for the trees. You spend so much time in business in the trees, and you have to see the forest. At Kodak, the whole mission was serving the artists. We're here as a company to serve our customers who are the creative class, whether they're photographers, filmmakers, graphics arts printers, or people who design packaging.

We have to paint for our employees and management a realization that they're doing more than making ink that goes on paper or cellulose. They're doing something that will allow Christopher Nolan to make a movie like *Dunkirk*. They are part of that picture. They may be a small cog in it, but they're part of it. That makes everyone excited. If I can reinforce that, it drives attitude and behavior. Everyone wants to go home at the end of the week and say, "I contributed to something." You're giving them the reason why. It's not just what we do or how we do it. It's why we do it. If we're in touch with that reason, then you're creating purpose.

We had people who worked in the film factory for more than forty years. They literally work in the dark every day manufacturing a product. After Christopher Nolan did *Interstellar*, he did a special interview about the film just for Kodak and he thanked Kodak for manufacturing. We had two thousand seats in our film auditorium in Rochester, New York, and we invited all seven hundred members of the factory and [their spouses] and children to a special screening. They came and watched a product made by Kodak film that they had actually made. In the opening he said, "I'm a filmmaker, but you make films." It was incredibly empowering to the people who are working for an hourly wage in the dark, doing hard work with chemicals. For them to actually be able to share with their families that they are part of it was really important. Nolan showed understanding that changed behavior for my staff and my employees for a long time.

Attitude is emotional. If you want to change behavior, touch people's emotions.

FOOD FOR THOUGHT

1. How can you increase your optimism?
2. Why do you think optimists are attractive to others?
3. How can you be more (honestly) optimistic and true to yourself?
4. What tactics can you take to deliver on your optimism?
5. How can you remind yourself and those around you how work contributes to the bigger picture?
6. How can you include emotional content in your communications?

CHAPTER 9

POSITIVITY

Featuring **Lee Cockerell**,
former Walt Disney World Resort Executive,
keynote speaker, author, and consultant

LEE COCKERELL IS the former executive vice president of operations for the Walt Disney World Resort, where he led a team of 40,000 cast members and was responsible for the operations of twenty hotels, four theme parks, two water parks, a shopping and entertainment village, and the ESPN sports and recreation complex, in addition to the ancillary operations that supported the No. 1 vacation destination in the world. One of Cockerell's major legacies was the creation of Disney Great Leader Strategies, which was used to train and develop 7,000 leaders at Walt Disney World. He held various executive positions in the hospitality and entertainment business with Hilton Hotels for eight years and the Marriott Corporation for seventeen years before joining Disney in 1990 to open the Disneyland Paris project.

WHAT TO 👀 FOR

> ➤ If your attitude is negative, people won't want to work with you, and they may consciously or unconsciously help you fail.

➤ If you respect and care for your colleagues, you should always be truthful with them, even if it includes a difficult conversation. Otherwise, you will be complicit in their failures.

➤ When you receive positive or negative feedback, it's up to you to use it to improve.

➤ Decide what you want to be best at, and take the time and effort to become the best.

Mark Schulman: We often can't control what happens to us, but we do have the power to change, control, and choose our attitudes. How important do you believe attitude has been in developing your career?

Lee Cockerell: I didn't graduate from college. I went for two years and didn't go to class, so I flunked out and joined the Army. There are two reasons I had success with no college degree, growing up on a farm in Oklahoma to running Disney World for ten years. Attitude. When you don't have a college degree, you better have a good attitude. And even if you do have a degree, a bad attitude is probably the number one reason people lose their jobs or their careers don't work out well. Because it really doesn't matter how smart you are, it's how you get along with people, your flexibility, and your ability to make hard decisions and have hard conversations.

My attitude has taken me the furthest. Even when I'm having a hard time or I'm in a tough situation, I keep a positive attitude. I don't share any negative issues with anybody. I don't bring anybody down. I just bite my lip and get through it. The second thing? I'm organized. Keep your promises, get it done, and be reliable and credible. If you don't have a good attitude, nobody wants to work with you, and they help you fail.

Schulman: Organization unto itself is an attitude. It is a choice that drives different behavior and produces positive consequences. Have you ever made a conscious effort to shift your attitude to produce a different behavior?

Cockerell: I'm always professional. I'm pretty loose with most people and tough on results and desired behavior. I had a vice president working for me who was resisting me because he thought he should've had my job. He didn't do what I wanted him to do. It wasn't outright, but I could tell his attitude was poor. He didn't care for me. He wasn't going to do what I told him to do. I sat down with him and had a conversation for a couple of hours. I told him, "I feel bad about having to have this conversation. You've been here a long time. I just got here. But if you don't improve over the next ninety days, I'm going to terminate you." He and I became best friends. He was very successful after that and had a great career.

If we get into a situation, and you're not hearing me, I'm going to step it up. But I'm not going to demean you or make you feel bad about yourself or hurt your self-confidence or -esteem. In difficult situations, I tell the truth. Whether you're doing a good job or a bad job, it's dishonest and unethical not to tell people the truth. If you don't, they will end up failing, and it'll be partially your fault. It's like kids. We always tell our kids when we want them to behave, or when they make a mistake, because we love them so much. If you respect your people at work, you should tell them the truth. And that's an attitude. Everybody in my organization knew that if they wanted the truth, they could just ask me. When you get the truth, you can either get worse or better. It's up to you.

Schulman: I never graduated college either, and I teach and consult executive leaders. Sometimes I see my father, who earned his doctorate degree in grammar and composition looking down on me with a smile (he passed away). "You didn't get a college education, but you sure learned a lot anyway."

Cockerell: Everybody learns in a different way, and we need to accept that. I learn by doing. I didn't learn well in school by studying and reading. I didn't have discipline when I was young. I could do it now, but I've found another way. Show me, let me do it and I will learn.

Schulman: As a leader, do you employ different techniques to help people learn or relate to what you're saying?

Cockerell: I don't use PowerPoint or slides. I'm high energy. I don't use podiums or notes. I'm open to adjusting my speech as I read the audience. Maybe I learned something during the coffee break from someone, and I can work it in when we come back. I don't give speeches. I tell stories. Kids don't want to hear about theory anymore. They want reality. They want to know how and not just what. One of the big problems we have is kids not working when they're teenagers. They're not getting exposure to work, to being on time, to getting along with other people.

Schulman: Millennials are experiential. They value experience, and experience is doing. It is action.

Cockerell: You can become an expert in anything if you focus on it long enough. I say to people, "I'm an expert in leadership, customer service, and time management." They ask, "How can you say that?" I reply, "I read about it, study it, talk about it, think about it every day, and observe it." Figure out something you want to be the best at, better than everybody else. And do it.

Schulman: Just deciding is a powerful attitude because you cut off all other possibilities. And when you tell somebody else about it, they become your notary or witness. Then, you have culpability.

Can you share a time where your attitude was a critical factor in a failure?

Cockerell: I've had a lot of failures. When I started working, everybody was pretty autocratic. I worked that way for ten or fifteen years until it became clear to me that that was not the way to lead. Some of my direct reports suffered from great anxiety when they heard I was coming to visit them. One guy had to go to the hospital because he got so upset. I had dinner with him. We talked. And I started to change. I was insecure. I had low self-confidence. Anybody who raises their voice at you or tries to intimidate you is a person with low self-confidence. I worked on that for him. I had to start trusting him. The more success I had, the more trust I had in people. And then, I got better at hiring people. So, I had the right people around me I could depend on.

Schulman: That's a big attitude shift. Congratulations on recognizing that.

Cockerell: My career would not have turned out the way it did if I had stayed on that track. I would not have had the success I had. People would not have promoted me. I was defensive. I didn't want any feedback. I had to go through tough times because when you grow up in an insecure environment, which I did with an insecure family, it becomes your own environment and your own culture. I had to work my way out of it. And it was not easy. I try to understand people when I'm working with them. "What's going on? What happened in their past? Why is this person behaving this way?" Instead of getting negative about a situation, I try to get it out of them.

Schulman: You've done a lot of wonderful things for a lot of wonderful people by understanding essentially the importance of shifting your attitude.

Cockerell: I was at Disney World, and I wanted to develop a newsletter for the fifty thousand cast members and five thousand managers. Human resources didn't want me to do that; it wasn't my job. But I'm persistent, so I did it anyway. They were really mad at me, but it turned out to be one of the best things I did and became the foundation for my book, *Creating Magic.*

I have a problem with people saying "no" to me. And that's not always good because you can make mistakes. I learned to surround myself with great people who will say "no" to me, and I trusted them. But with people who I didn't have a lot of regard for, I just did it anyway. Sometimes you have to do your thing. People are going to try to hold you back, stop you, and tell you it's a bad idea—nothing would ever get done. I'm glad we don't have a world full of those people, or we'd still be plowing the fields with a horse instead of a tractor.

Schulman: A lot has to do with authenticity and just knowing it is going to work. By that point, you've had enough experience and accumulated enough hours to know.

Do you do anything on a day-to-day basis to shift your attitude?

Cockerell: I'm into routine. I don't care for uncertainty. It gives me anxiety. So, I get up every morning at 5:30, and I go to Starbucks from 6:30 to 7:30. I meet with people who want to meet with me every day. I work out every day. I have strength training twice a week to avoid breaking a hip someday.

I schedule all the events in my life. I plan ahead months and months, blocking time to be off, as well. I get enough sleep. I don't really drink alcohol anymore, so I have more energy. And I've learned these things as I go along, what helps me feel better and have more energy and a better attitude. I love wine, but the wine doesn't love me if I drink too much of it.

I'm clear with myself about what I should be doing and what I shouldn't be doing. I could do whatever I wanted, but I know that's not the way to go. Because I have done that in my life. I've done anything I wanted and got in trouble because of it. It's usually you who are the problem, not other people. It's like that song from *Frozen*, learn to let it go. That's what I've done, and I'm happier. I feel better. I'm healthy. I have better relationships. You must change it on purpose and know that attitude makes you better or makes you worse.

FOOD FOR THOUGHT

1. How can a negative attitude infect the attitudes of those around you?
2. How can the negative attitudes of others lead you to failure?
3. Why is truthfulness a requirement in relationships?
4. How can you use positive feedback to improve your performance? What about negative behavior?
5. What are you willing to invest to become the best you?

CHAPTER 10

INSPIRATION

*Featuring **Ken Freirich**, CEO, business
leader, and healthcare executive*

KEN FREIRICH HAS successfully launched, built, operated, and grown a variety of world-class organizations. For fifteen years, he helped transform Health Monitor Network into the leading patient-engagement company in the US. The company grew tenfold during his tenure and the employee base quadrupled during his last four years. Prior to joining Health Monitor Network, Freirich was CEO of TransLocal Health Corporation, a leading multimedia health information provider to the pharmaceutical and healthcare industries. He has served as president of InteliHealth, an executive with Thomson/Medical Economics, and the founder and publisher of *The Collegian Magazine*. He plays drums in the rock band MedROCK and is an active international philanthropist.

WHAT TO ◑◐ FOR

➢ Follow your dreams (or pursue your goals), and do everything you possibly can to make them happen. Don't let anything stand in your way.

➢ Practice so that you are prepared when opportunity comes along. Don't wait for the opportunity to be ready.

➤ Life is not a dress rehearsal. Whatever it is you want to do in life, professionally or personally, just do it.

➤ As a business leader, you can instill attitudes in others. Ensure they are positive positions and that you encourage employees and peers to believe in themselves. Think big and take risks.

Mark Schulman: I met you at a Teen Cancer America benefit featuring Kenny Loggins, P!nk, the Foo Fighters, and The Who. You bid on and won a chance to jam with The Who on drums, and you killed it. Talk about someone creating an attitude shift.

Ken Freirich: There were a lot of elements that ultimately contributed to that moment. It was obviously an incredible experience for me, a childhood dream. My philosophy in life is to find ways to make things happen.

The Monday night before that benefit, I practiced for an hour. I hadn't played in three months. I got home at eleven that night, and the headline of the evening news was about the forest fires in California, right in Pacific Palisades where the benefit was going to take place. My first thought was, "Well, this thing isn't going to happen." The next morning, I emailed the host, "First and foremost, I hope you and your family are OK. By the way, do you think that the forest fires are going to pose any issues for the benefit?" He said, "Nope, we're in a different part of the area. It's okay." I got out there Wednesday night, and I spoke to the host on Thursday. I really wanted to check out the venue, house, and facilities. When I got there, the guys from The Band and The Who said, "Hey, did you know you're going to be playing on electronic drums?" I said, "No." They said, "Did they call you?" I said, "No!"

I don't like electronic drums. It made me a little bit uncomfortable, truthfully. They said, "We'll come back tomorrow during sound check so you can play them." I thought, "Oh man, this is a monkey wrench." All this buildup to hopefully what could have been one of the greatest nights of my life, and now I was on electronic drums. I was prepared for everything; I wasn't prepared for that. Then, I started smelling a little bit of the forest fires, and I get asthma from smoke. I thought, "Is there going to be smoke tomorrow night? Am I going to have to stay inside the house for the whole concert and just take a cameo?"

The next day came, and I played the drums. I was impressed. I don't know what I expected, but they were pretty good electronic drums. It was still very different. Everything felt different. The hi-hat was on the right side. I usually like it on the left. The cymbals were different. I played for a while, became comfortable—even though I didn't love it. The evening of, I'm hanging out backstage, chilling out. I had every reason to be nervous. The biggest stage of my life, real rock stars surrounding me, all of Hollywood, playing with one of the greatest rock and roll bands of all time. I played that same song "Pinball Wizard" when I was eight years old in my first band. I said, "Boy, I'd love to one day play with The Who." Here was that moment.

My mind was just in the zone. I was prepared, and I was ready. I should have been nervous. I had all these people coming up to me—Howie Mandel: "Oh, Ken, great leather pants." Adam Sandler: "Oh, Ken's playing with The Who." I had all these distractions that should have made me nervous. But I just stayed focused. And everything just happened naturally. Playing with them brought out my best. I just felt the music. It was an incredible experience. And when you circle back to attitude, that attitude was one of appreciation and fulfillment, but it was also pure focus and not letting anything get in the way. There was also an element of preparation meeting the moment of opportunity. When I practiced in the studio, I did some solos at the end just to have some fun. A few days later, Pete Townshend [was] doing windmills, egging me on to do a solo. And I was prepared. I went with it, and it was a blast. I was humbled after—a standing ovation from the crowd, people chanting my name.

I was humbled to have that experience and positively affect a charity that was near and dear to my heart. My mom is a cancer survivor. But what I didn't realize was the unintended consequences of impacting so many other people—from friends to celebrities who shared and posted about the experience. That circles back to attitude, staying in the zone with peak performance, and how your performance can move other people. I didn't expect that to happen. I did it for me, for my dream. I'm still hearing from people about how it impacted them, and that is a really cool thing.

Schulman: Attitude is contagious, both positively and negatively. You helped others relive their childhood dreams. I would love to sit in with The Who. And I've played with some of the greatest artists on the planet. Your attitude made all the difference.

You were the CEO of Health Monitor Network. You're a philanthropist, and you constantly give back to others. At Skidmore College, you offer an entrepreneurship competition for students. Have there been pivotal moments in your life when you've noticed that a situation could turn out well or poorly based on your attitude?

Freirich: When I went to college, I was very fortunate. I was a financial aid student at Skidmore. I've always been grateful for the opportunity to study there, and I always believed in myself. I wanted to start businesses and companies, but didn't know the first thing about how. I was passionate, focused, and driven. And I was willing to do whatever it took to make it happen.

I started my first company when I was nineteen at Skidmore. I went to see a mentor, Nick Platt, who was an executive for the American Stock Exchange—a financial aid student going to meet a guy on Wall Street. He told me my hair was too long, to take my earring out, and to come back next time with pinstripes on my suit that were closer together, and he'd see me. Or don't come back. I cleaned up my act and came back. He said, "You're too focused on business. You need to do something well-rounded—bartend. If you do, I'll find you a job after you graduate. And if you don't, don't come back." So, I tried to find a bartending job and couldn't. I ultimately started a business. Late one night, I was watching a program and saw Wally Amos of Famous Amos Cookies. He said that people talk about starting businesses their whole lives with their friends and family, and you just have to do it.

Two days later, I drove up to Saratoga Springs, New York, and started a magazine without having any background in publishing. It started at Skidmore, and ended up in thirty-five colleges in three states. The first week, I remember calling my dad after I had a rough day. He said, "Son, you can do anything if you put your mind to it." A switch went off. In eight business days, I raised enough revenue for the first magazine. My dad couldn't give me business mentorship—he didn't have a lot of financial resources—but he gave me the confidence and that has lasted a lifetime.

During college, I also spent my junior year living in London. I started a few businesses while we were there, too. I was supposed to be on Pan Am Flight 103 that went down over Lockerbie, Scotland. I came back three days earlier to see a girlfriend. I knew people on that flight, and I'll never forget that day. I can still visualize right now the moment when I heard about it.

Life is not a dress rehearsal. Whatever it is you want to do in life, professionally or personally, just do it. Call that an attitude shift. It changed everything for me. Every day I say a mantra: I want to make the world a better place. And I'm actually committed to doing that. That's what has gotten me involved in philanthropy all over the world. I do global projects, and I do little stuff every day. After we finish today, I have a yoga instructor in Mexico who I'm going to help because she's stuck. She's a single mom. Rather than just give her money, I'm going to buy virtual yoga sessions from her. If I give them to people who may then become customers, how great is that? The gift could keep giving. I do a lot of those things, and I live by that every single day.

Attitude is everything. But it's the positive not the negative aspects of attitude. The glass can be half empty or it can be half full. I'm always looking at it half full. I'm practical about it, but I'm looking at angles to make things happen. Because that's what you need.

What you can do as leaders in any kind of organization, whether it's two people or twenty thousand, is inspire others to believe in themselves and to have a positive attitude, to push themselves beyond their comfort levels. So, when they succeed, they realize they can leap even higher. As you lead an organization, you're only as good as your people. You need to lead them, encourage them, have them take risks.

In business, you have to be practical because sometimes you think you have the right people and you don't. You must adjust situations accordingly. Alongside attitude is the burning desire to succeed and never, ever give up, no matter how hard it gets. Because no matter what—business, industry, music, athletics—

everyone struggles. And you're always at that turning point. You just have to continue to keep that positive attitude and succeed.

Schulman: Part of what you've done is build wins. I calculate my wins every day, even the small ones. Stacking up success becomes fuel for future successes.

FOOD FOR THOUGHT

1. What have you been thinking about doing that you will commit to accomplish this week?
2. What positive action or communication can you activate that pushes you beyond your comfort zone?
3. What immediate action can you take to make the world or at least one person's life better?
4. What extra work can you do to prepare yourself for unexpected opportunities that may arise?
5. Are there areas in your life about which you have doubts that a conscious attitude shift could change?
6. Once you shift your attitude to see new possibilities, are you willing to take immediate action?

CHAPTER 11

ADAPTION

*Featuring **Tony Hsieh**, former Zappos
CEO and bestselling author*

TONY HSIEH WAS the author of No. 1 *New York Times* bestseller
Delivering Happiness and CEO of Zappos. At the age of twenty-four,
Hsieh sold his company, LinkExchange, to Microsoft for $265 mil-
lion. He joined Zappos.com as an advisor and investor, and eventually became CEO. He helped Zappos grow from almost no sales
to more than $1 billion annually, while simultaneously making
Fortune magazine's annual "Best Companies to Work For" list. In
November 2009, Amazon acquired Zappos in a deal valued at $1.2
billion. Hsieh's first book, *Delivering Happiness*, outlines his path
from starting a worm farm to leading Zappos. In it, he shows
how a distinct model of corporate culture can help organizations
achieve success.

*Note from Mark Schulman: I became friends with Tony Hsieh in
2014 and am honored to have gotten to know him and interview him
for both of my books. Sadly, he passed away in 2020. This interview also
features co-author Dr. Jim Samuels.*

WHAT TO ◑◑ FOR

> Instead of trying to change other people's behaviors, reset your expectations of them and create interactions that will be successful for everyone.

> Understand your core values as an individual, department and organization. Write them down and review them regularly with your team (or family).

Mark Schulman: Attitude is your point of view. Where you look from determines what you see, and if you see no opportunity, then there won't be any. Do you recall consciously creating an attitude shift because you knew you wanted to produce a different result?

Tony Hsieh: Have you been to a county fair where they have a ride called the Zipper? In elementary and middle school, I used to go to our county fair every Fourth of July week with my best friend. He wanted me to go on the Zipper and the other roller coasters. I said I didn't really like roller coasters because I got a tingly sensation. And he said, "Don't you like that feeling?" I went on the Zipper and reinterpreted that feeling as a positive thing, and now I love roller coasters.

Schulman: That *is* an attitude shift. So, interview over! Do you have any specific stories where you noticed your negative attitude created a failure?

Hsieh: One of my pet peeves is when people are late. You made a commitment, and one of my values is honoring commitments, and it reflects not valuing other people's time as much as your own. I used to get upset if people were late, especially if they were consistently late. But if you harp too much, then you ruin the rest of the night versus just missing the first half hour of a movie or show.

I have something I refer to as my "Cat Philosophy," which is all about managing expectations. A cat is generally pretty selfish. You feed it, take care of it, provide it with shelter, and it never says thank you. But nobody gets upset at a cat, even though it is an unfair relationship, because you know it is a cat and that is what cats do. There is no sense in getting mad at a cat or expecting your cat to act towards you in the way you might act towards a cat. I started taking that same philosophy and applying it to people. Rather than get upset at someone who is consistently late, realize that's just who they are.

If I know some people who are consistently late, I just stop putting myself in situations where being late has an impact on my experience. If there is a friend who is consistently late, I will stop inviting them to movies or shows. But I will invite them to a party, where there are other people and it doesn't matter if they are late. Or if they are consistently late the same amount of time, then I will just tell them the movie starts half an hour earlier than it does and that works. For me, it became about realizing that my role in making this situation worse was partly due to my expectations of them; if I just changed my expectations, then everyone would be happy.

Schulman: Is there anything you do daily to drive specific behaviors that are critical to specific outcomes?

Hsieh: Seth Godin wrote a blog post, "On Being Irritated."

> *Irritation is a privilege.*
>
> *It's the least useful emotion, one that we never seek out.*
>
> *People in true distress are never irritated. Someone who is hungry or drowning or fleeing doesn't become irritated.*
>
> *And of course, irritation rarely helps us get what we need.*

Irritation clouds our judgment, frustrates our relation-
ships and gets our priorities all wrong.

Irritation tries to persuade us that it's justified, but it
merely pushes us away from what we actually need.

In order to be irritated, we need to believe we're not
getting something we deserve. But of course, that expec-
tation is the cause of the irritation. We can choose to
lose the expectation, embracing the fact that we're lucky
enough to feel it, and then get back to work doing some-
thing generous instead.

It turns out that irritation is a privilege and irritation
is a choice.

Every Friday, we do a GT weekly review, which is from the book *Getting Things Done: The Art of Stress-Free Productivity*. Once a week you review your goals. One of my goals is to reframe annoyance or irritation as the delta between expectations and events, and then decide whether to change expectations or disengage in the future.

I also try not to be judgmental. I used to judge people if they were late or flaky. So, just like I don't judge cats, I try not to judge people. Instead, I just don't take them out on walks or invite them to movies.

Schulman: Can you think of any other ways that attitude relates to how you run your business or the company culture?

Hsieh: We have ten core values, and you could think of each one as an attitude statement.

1. Deliver WOW through service
2. Embrace and drive change

3. Create fun and a little weirdness
4. Be adventurous, creative, and open-minded
5. Pursue growth and learning
6. Build open and honest relationships with communication
7. Build a positive team and family spirit
8. Do more with less
9. Be passionate and determined
10. Be humble

If you frame them as attitudes, it sounds more temporary than if you call them values. You can always change your attitude but changing values doesn't happen as often.

Schulman: You can immediately drive different behaviors with attitude shifts, and a core attitude is going to drive behaviors that produce consequences. A core value would do the same thing.

Dr. Jim Samuels: The value is the why. It is why you make an attitude shift. We refer to an attitude scale of human temperament and emotions and how you can raise yourself to a more successful attitude. For example, to escape rebelliousness, which can be destructive, we need to move up the scale to being determined, which is also an anger-based emotion, but drives constructive behaviors and creates different, more valuable consequences than rebellion.

You can call it managing expectations by identifying peoples' attitudes and then modifying your expectations accordingly. This allows you to expect (predict) different behaviors. You are affected differently, get along better, and can identify potential shared successes.

Hsieh: I have read a few articles about raising kids and changing their behavior. If "Smiths" throws a tantrum, you can say, "Don't throw tantrums or there will be these consequences." But what they found most effective was, "Smiths don't do that." It anchors their identity for certain behavior and has more sustainable results.

Samuels: I would add, "Smiths do this instead." Do you think your expectations consciously drive some of the culture at Zappos? Do you do that intentionally?

Hsieh: Core values are expectations. We interview for them. It is much easier to catch on the front end because if we only hire people whose values match our corporate values, then we don't have to drive unnatural behavior; we just tell people to be themselves.

Schulman: You are consciously picking people based on continuity, their belief systems, their attitudes, and their core values. P!nk does the same thing because if someone on tour doesn't have a foundational value that she subscribes to, they are not going to produce the behavior and the consequences she is looking for. You need to have continuity and establishing your core values up front helps that.

FOOD FOR THOUGHT

1. What are some of the core values at your organization?
2. How can you regularly discuss them with your peers?
3. How can you ensure that enjoyment is part of your organization's culture?
4. How can you better reward creativity?
5. How can you use humility to increase productivity?

CHAPTER 12

CONFIDENCE

*Featuring **Julie Masters**, co-founder, and CEO of Influence Nation, podcast host, consultant, and keynote speaker*

JULIE MASTERS HAS spent a career decoding influence. As a leading authority in the speaking world, she has earned a reputation for launching and advising some of the world's most respected thought leaders. Co-founder of ODE Management, the world's largest dedicated speaker management agency across the US and Australia, she is now the Founder and CEO of Influence Nation, working with business leaders and organizations to become the voice of authority in their spaces. Clients include industry-leading CEOs, entrepreneurs, speakers, bestselling authors, and media personalities—voices that have reached millions of people globally through speaking, publishing, and digital channels. Masters also hosts the iTunes Top 100 podcast *Inside Influence*. Having won numerous communications industry awards across the US, Australia, and Europe, Masters now regularly advises CEOs, entrepreneurs, and executive teams on how to stand out in their marketplaces by turning expertise into influence.

WHAT TO ◉◐ FOR

> Rely on and project confidence that your experiences, failures, successes, and learned lessons are valuable to others, be they individuals, organizations, or sectors.

> Say "yes" to new opportunities to grow in positive ways and into new spaces and places, even if they make you uncomfortable or scared.

> Encourage your stories to change when you do. What you say may reflect an old version of who you are, but you can change your stories to be an authentic reflection of who you are today.

> Stop running from the question "who do you think you are?" Answer it in such a compelling way that it reminds you of your competence and worth.

Mark Schulman: You're the master decoder, the CEO of Influence Nation, and a brilliant thinker. How important has attitude been in the development of your career on the cutting-edge of what you do?

Julie Masters: It has been interesting spending twenty years around influential people at the forefront of ideas, political parties, and industry in the privileged position to witness that and decode it so we could replicate it. When you take a powerful idea and a powerful human, put them together, and it flies, what does that look like? It takes getting it wrong, trying different things, and watching things play out in action. There's a myth that one day, the sky opens, angels start singing, and there's a sunbeam on you. "We have chosen you. You have permission to go forth and be brilliant and share your ideas." It doesn't work that way.

People who stand out in their careers decide to take a mindset of certainty, to step out and look. I don't feel any more confident than I felt yesterday. I don't feel any more chosen or have any more permission, but this is what I know with certainty. I know what is useful. I know what is important. I know I have insights that are helpful and valuable. Shift your positioning from waiting for confidence to developing a mindset of certainty. I give you the best I have today, where all my experiences, failures, and successes have led me. Tomorrow, if I get new information or if somebody challenges me and it's interesting or if something new arises, I'll change my mind. I'll pivot. But today, I'm not going to let the fact that I might learn something new tomorrow stop me from contributing. That's the biggest attitude shift.

Schulman: Do you remember a specific event or thought process—an aha moment for you—on your road to success?

Masters: I spent ten years of my career behind the scenes, supporting other influencers on the stage, taking an idea and a person and building a movement. I was happy. I could work on multiple ideas at the same time. Then, I started another business. I went to a client one day and pitched it. It was one of the biggest clients I had gone for. They said, "We'll think about it." And I said I could come back in a week. When I came back, they brought me into a room with a woman I'd never met before. She said, "I'm head of events. Everything you've been talking about when it comes to decoding influence in a new age when all the rules have changed—would you talk about it at our event in six months?"

I remember looking at her stunned for a second. She didn't know I was absolutely petrified of speaking in front of other people. All the speakers I met knew you never asked Julie to introduce you. My knees would shake. My voice would break. My whole body would shut down. What she asked me—that's my worst nightmare. But I really wanted this client, so I said, "Sure. Yeah."

I said to my husband, "This is either going to be the dumbest thing I've ever said 'yes' to or I'm going to address this mindset of I'm not meant to be there." I'd worked with some of the greatest speakers on the planet—the Top 1 percent. I knew what good looked like. Either I was going to rise to it or I was going to use that knowledge as a battering ram to keep myself really small. I set about doing it. I got coaches. It took a massive mindset shift for me, from "I'm not meant to be here." It was good. It wasn't world-class, but it was good. Good enough to be asked to come back and do it again, and then again and again.

I had this moment, "Oh, my goodness, I'm doing it. This is part of who I am now. It's not a question of if I'm meant to be here. Different places bring out different parts of me and they have different advantages and I can inhabit both spaces. I get to choose which space I inhabit." That was a massive mindset shift.

Schulman: My first book deals with conquering life's stage fright based on three Cs—clarity, capability, and confidence. If you have a clear goal and develop your capability, it leads to indisputable confidence—real, not false confidence. Even if you have deleterious stage fright, you can calm down enough because you've done the work. You had six months, and you knew exactly what you wanted to do. You studied with the right people. You created the content. By the time you hit the stage, you knew you could do it.

Masters: You have to do the work. You make a decision, do the work, and show up. Those are really the only three things within your control. And the attitude: "I get to do this," not "I have to do this." I chose to give this a go. And I may or may not be world-class at this. It's OK if it doesn't work out. It's OK to see if this is something I want to do and that if I show up hard enough for it, the universe is going to show up back." Sometimes it does, and sometimes it doesn't. Sometimes you show up hard, and the universe doesn't show up back. But a door opens up somewhere just for the very fact you showed up.

"Having the courage" and "taking a moment to reset" are my attitudes. I'm going to examine it and reset it. Sometimes, I require an attitude adjustment. I can hear it. When you hear a story come out of your mouth and it suddenly strikes you that you don't know if it's true anymore, that it doesn't feel helpful anymore. Recognize old stories and then reset them.

Schulman: When I'm trying to get to the root of an issue I have, I ask where it is coming from. Who is talking? Is it my mother, father, or brother? Where did that get seated in my brain? I want to catch it before it develops into a prejudice or prejudgment, a belief system and then an attitude, when it could consume me.

Masters: "Who do you think you are?" That one question has kept more brilliant ideas and people on the sidelines than any other set of words. Because that's our biggest fear, that somebody will ask us that question. Who do you think you are to get up and say that? Who do you think you are to claim to be an expert?

What's worse than anybody else asking this is when we ask ourselves that question. Who do I think I am to try that? Who do I think I am to say no, to raise my hand, to use my voice to step out? The cure is in the poison. The cure is to stop running from the question and answer it. Give yourself a compelling answer to that question.

Ask yourself every time you hit on the edges of your competence. Answer the question, and come up with such a compelling answer that every time it gets asked, you answer it and it's a reminder. The answer is a reminder to step back into the journey.

Schulman: The inflection has such implications because it can be "Who do you think *you* are?" or "*Who* do you think you are?" It can be something you are proud to be, rather than having a negative association—the audacity of "Who do you think *you* are?" It becomes possibility.

Masters: It's the shift from judgment to curiosity. Take the exclamation point away, and add a question mark at the end. Who do you think you are? Compare that to who you want to be. When I approach high-intensity situations, I think of someone who embodies who I want to be right then. How would they be? How would they hold their body? How would they breathe? Where would they come from? How would they listen? It gives you a frame of reference to start becoming. You can't be what you can't see. It gives you a visualization of who you're trying to be.

Schulman: That's how children form their personalities; they pretend to be somebody else, somebody they admire, like a superhero, scientist, or musician. It gives them the wherewithal to have the confidence, or at least the confidence to pretend.

Masters: We are not static creatures; we are forever evolving, forever shifting. We have hardware and software. The hardware is the wiring we install when we are young, and the software includes new ideas and tools we learn along the way. We have the ability to rewire, to see someone and say, "That's what I want to be." It's not easy, and it involves repetition, effort, discipline, and focus. It's shifting your mindset from fixed to experimental.

Schulman: Is there anything you do on a daily basis to shift your attitudes?

Masters: I go for a walk every morning, and I think about who I want to become. I envisage the life I want to create, the places I want to go, the people I want to meet, and I adjust how I walk. I do this every morning. "How would someone who does that walk? How would they hold themselves? How would they vibrate? Would they be fuzzy and yum?" I adjust as I walk.

FOOD FOR THOUGHT

1. Who do you think you are and who do you think you could be?
2. Think of someone you want to emulate and answer the following questions:
   a. Where would they come from?
   b. How would they breathe?
   c. How would they listen?
   d. How would they hold themselves?
   e. How would they vibrate?

CHAPTER 13

GRATITUDE

*Featuring **Bob Pritchard**, marketing leader and business consultant*

BOB PRITCHARD HAS more than thirty years of experience as a business and marketing consultant for many of the world's leading companies, including The Coca-Cola Company, Citibank, Anheuser Busch, Mercedes Benz, Frito Lay, and dozens more. In sports, he directed marketing programs and corporate relationships for Formula 1, the Los Angeles Raiders, former World Heavyweight Champion Evander Holyfield, Legends Tennis, Skins Golf, Indy Racing teams, and the "100 Years of Hollywood" global celebration. Pritchard's newsletter reaches 1.8 million people each day.

WHAT TO ◉◉ FOR

➢ A positive attitude and gratitude for the successes you have had are paramount to future success. Keep your mind in a positive headspace, and be thankful for what you have accomplished and done.

➢ Bite off more than you can chew. With a strong mind and a lot of hard work, you can reach your career goals—and more.

> Allow your attitude to shift in positive ways according to your current mindset and environment. Individualism can get you many places, but teamwork can create real change for you and your business.

> Don't give up. Determine the worst possible outcome, and decide whether or not to accept the risk.

Bob Pritchard: I'm not about banking money, I'm about banking experiences. Money will follow. The day you're on your deathbed you won't sit there and think, "Wow. I've got $2,135 in the bank." You'll remember when you saw Lady Gaga in Las Vegas. That's what you remember.

Mark Schulman: How important do you believe attitude has been in the development of your career and bringing you to where you are now?

Pritchard: Attitude is absolutely fundamental to my career. I grew up very poor. There were eight of us in a one-bedroom apartment in a really crappy inner-city neighborhood. There seemed to be no way out. But I knew we were young. If I was going to survive and become successful, it was up to me to create the change to get out of there.

My work ethic was born from that attitude. I was driven; I started working very young doing odd jobs. I remember delivering papers and milk and packaging things for people, and I did that to make extra money because I wanted to get out of my environment. I was focused and driven to achieve at school and go to university. I did what I needed to do to get where I wanted to go. There are so many people who don't like where they are, but they're not doing anything to change it. They post lots of really philosophical Facebook posts, but they don't activate any change. I realized when

I was really little that *if it's to be, it's up to me.* Nobody is going to do it for me. I have to do it.

Bite off more than you can chew; chew like hell and hope it works. You might not get 100 percent of what you're trying to achieve, but you might get 90. If you don't bite off more than you can chew, all you're going to get is whatever you settle for.

Schulman: You are quite the overachiever. I've never seen anybody post more articles than you. You post an article a day?

Pritchard: Every day. I use it as a funnel. I use the radio show and the newsletter. The newsletter goes out to 1.8 million people, and 30 percent of them read it. Every day six hundred thousand people read the newsletter, and people think of me when they want someone to speak or they want someone to consult with. It pays dividends.

Schulman: It's hard work.

Pritchard: It's paid off.

Schulman: I read most of your articles, and they are incredibly informative, diverse, and relevant. And sometimes shocking.

Pritchard: Sometimes shocking.

Schulman: I like that because it stimulates really necessary thought processes—and that has a lot to do with your attitude. Did you make conscious attitude shifts or changes when you were younger, or was it just in your blood because you so desired to get out of the negative situation you were in?

Pritchard: There were obviously shifts, but changing attitude is always important. I was headhunted by Australian media tycoon Kerry Packer, and he had interests in dozens of industries. I had developed this attitude where I was going to do what I wanted to do and not put up with anybody who treated me in a condescending way or who didn't show me respect. He promoted an environ-

ment where performance was rewarded, and it provided phenomenal experiences all over the world because of all these interests.

During that period, my attitude softened, and I realized that I
needed to weigh the pros and the cons of situations. If it was just
me against the world, I never would have had those experiences,
and I got to be marketing director for Formula 1 and World Series
Cricket, which is the second biggest sport in the world. There are
all sorts of things that I never would have had the opportunity to
do, if I hadn't mellowed a bit in that environment and realized that
I was part of an extremely talented team.

If it hadn't been for my drive and my belief that whatever I
wanted to do was about living my life, then I wouldn't have had
all those opportunities and met all the incredible people that I did,
which has put me in pretty good stead these days. I know people
everywhere in the world that I can call on when I need something.

Schulman: You needed to evolve your attitude to become successful in a different situation and evolve your career, essentially.
Do you remember any specific time where your attitude brought
you to the point of failure?

Pritchard: I was the first member of my family to graduate
from a university. I finished my science degree. I was on television
six nights a week and did the science degree because…everybody
did it, I suppose. My family wanted me to get a "proper" job and
felt that seeing me on television probably wasn't a "real" job. I felt
pressured to conform to my family's wishes, and I was guided by
the fact that I needed to be "responsible." So, I started my job as
a chemist, and I hated it from the minute I walked in the door. It
lasted five days, and my family was absolutely horrified. In one
sense, that's a failure. But if I hadn't done that, I'd still probably be
working as a chemist somewhere, bored. I wouldn't have traveled

the world; I wouldn't have done what you do and give speeches all over the planet.

So, while that could have been judged as a failure, I shifted my attitude and realized that my life was mine to live, and it was not to be lived the way other people wanted me to live it. I really can't think of a time in my life when I haven't really been where I wanted to be. Sure, there have been ups and downs, and things didn't go the way I wanted them to, but overall, it's been an upward trajectory ever since I could ever remember.

Schulman: That's truly amazing. You're a very unique and fortunate individual as a result of this circumstance. I asked you about failure, but this situation was truly a success for you because you made a decision that created an attitude shift, changed your behavior, and drove different consequences quickly and profoundly.

Pritchard: It was five very long days. Trust me.

Schulman: Have you had challenging moments?

Pritchard: Around 1980, a group of Japanese business people visited me and wanted my assistance introducing karaoke to North America. From the start, I had a pretty negative attitude. I was influenced by the fact that I'd been a singer. I thought it would be really embarrassing for people who can't sing to get up in front of other people with a microphone and sing to an image with a bouncing ball. I said, "Look, nobody is going to do that. People are not going to get up in front of a television screen and sing words to songs they don't know and make themselves look stupid." My mind was closed to looking at the proposal.

Schulman: Your attitude is your point of view. I've done a few fun karaoke nights myself.

Pritchard: The guy who invented Pet Rock pitched it to me, and I said, "You are crazy." So, I knocked him back, too. A couple of years later he came and picked me up in his Rolls Royce and took me to lunch.

Schulman: You started out with a sense of complete determination and made attitude adjustments as you went along to become more of a team player. And you realized that experience is the most important thing to you—more than money. If you're authentic with that experience, then you're going to drive money and drive cash flow.

Pritchard: You have to be really dedicated and committed to what you're doing as well.

Schulman: How does your attitude affect your behavior on a day-to-day basis?

Pritchard: I was working on a project in Canada around sports teams. Australia didn't have any privately owned sports teams at that time. So, I decided to see if I could buy a professional football team in Australia. When I got back to Sydney, everybody said it was impossible. "We've never had privately owned sports teams, and it cannot be done." I thought, "This is really achievable if I work hard and smart, and I really want to do it." After six months of struggle and negotiation, I finally got the league to agree to sell me a team—the first privately owned team in Australia.

But I only had seven days to come up with the equivalent of US$50 million dollars in today's money. So, I sat on the phone eighteen hours a day and contacted every person I've ever met. After every knock back, I got straight on and dialed the next number. Six days in, a really wealthy Australian said, "I'll do it." He flew to Sydney the next day; we did a deal, and we brought the Sydney football team.

I could have given up after the fifty-seven thousandth knock back, but I was determined to do it. Too many people give in easily.

My attitude that I would succeed stayed strong, and I didn't let the negativity of dream-takers steal my patience. One of the reasons that I don't like some lawyers and accountants is because they'll tell you twenty thousand reasons why you can't do something. Anybody can achieve anything they want to if they want it badly enough, if they're paid to work for it, and if they stay positive. Don't worry about the people who criticize you on the way.

Schulman: That's an unyielding tenacity.

Pritchard: If you believe in yourself, and you've got a "what's the worst thing that can happen to me" attitude, then you can constantly push the envelope and get away with it. Sometimes, we worry too much about our financial future and forget about living a dream. If you work hard, money will come. It won't be as much as you want, but keep working at it; projects will come, money will come, speeches will come.

Schulman: Your brand is your reflection, your attitude is a reflection of your brand, and that is part of who you are. Attitude can be viewed as your point of view—where you are looking from.

Pritchard: One of my driving forces now is to give back to people, give back to society that has been so good to me. So, that's a change in attitude. There are so many great people in this world; it gives me faith in humanity. There are too many negative people. That's just a lack of respect and self-confidence. It's a reflection of you, not of the people around you.

Schulman: It's easy to be selfish. You're exercising gratitude based on what you've gotten. The power of gratitude is incredibly strong because you're focusing on your abundance, successes, and wins and helping others shift their minds toward a focus on what they have.

Pritchard: I don't do things half-cocked. And more success gives you more confidence. One of the great things about this daily newsletter is I learn from all the research I do, which means I can hold a conversation with most people, and they think that I know what I'm talking about. Usually. When you're selling something, you don't actually sell the product. You sell your energy. People buy your energy. And you can't manufacture positive energy. You're either a positive person, and that's part of your DNA or you're not.

Schulman: It's critical, my friend. Thank you for that.

FOOD FOR THOUGHT

1. How can you be more positive?
2. How can you assist others in being more positive?
3. How can you develop a more positive team attitude?
4. How can you raise your ambition?
5. How can you choose better priorities?
6. How can you compare choices in more productive ways?

CHAPTER 14

PERFORMANCE

*Featuring **Dr. Gary F. Russell**, CEO of*
Winning Profile and performance consultant

DR. GARY F. Russell has been studying human behavior his entire life, alongside raising four children and creating programs for millions with the National Football League, Major League Soccer, The Football Association, Jack Nicklaus (Golden Bear), and Boys Scouts of America. After years of research, trial and error, and working with world-class athletes and executives from billion-dollar corporations, Russell's original work in activation, teaching, and coaching has led him to create Winning Profile, a way to accurately measure talent, discover its origins, and determine how to replicate it. In other words, a way to see the best in people and put them in positions to be their best. Helping others reach beyond their vision of capability is Russell's definition of winning. As he says, "I might not be able to pick who is going to win, but I can tell you who wants to."

WHAT TO 👀 FOR

➢ Skill is the foundation of performance, but behavior is the foundation of skill.

> ➢ Everyone has talent. Identify yours and the critical actions you can take to turn that talent into success.
> ➢ The ways you think, feel, and act all must sync with each other for optimal performance, regardless of what you are trying to accomplish.

Dr. Gary F. Russell: I've always had this burning interest in understanding people. I knew people were different. I knew I was different, but I didn't know why. I got involved in education. I loved teaching and working with kids. And I ended up getting the kids nobody else wanted. I could handle them. I could tell you what I did, but at that point I couldn't tell you why it worked. I can now.

I've studied what causes the differences in people. I've looked at psychometric instruments to figure out if there is a way to help discover people. I found that these were limited in scope. They were linear, and they didn't give us the complexity or the contextuality of a person. So, I thought, "I'll make one."

I studied medicine, not to become a doctor but to find out how the medical model was put together. I studied psychology, and I was disappointed because it was all based on qualitative information, what everybody thought or felt. I wanted to study neurology, and then, I really began to find my way.

Look at the [NFL Scouting] Combine. We invite athletes. They run, jump, and lift, and each team is allowed fifteen minutes to talk to them. We get it backwards. In the 2000 NFL draft, the greatest quarterback ever was picked 199th in the sixth round.

When they invited him to play at the University of Michigan, he said, "I'll come but I just want to warn you I can't run." They said, "That's alright. Come anyhow." So, he went, and they wrote him up and said, "Beware. This guy can't run." And he will tell you he still can't run. His name is Tom Brady. A multibillion industry can't figure it out.

Skill is the foundation of performance. If you don't have skill, you can't perform. Behavior is the foundation of skill. And talent is the pre-wired condition we have at birth.

There is a progression in how attitudes form. It's an imbuing of thinking, feeling, and acting that comes together and forms a picture. That picture turns into perception, perception leads to attitudes, attitudes lead to values, and then we act or we behave.

So, 7.5 billion people have a profile; they have talent. It's my job to figure out what it is and give people the opportunity to feel really good about themselves.

If we're going to help people develop attitudes, the best thing we can do is give them information, and that's the winning profile. When I profile you, I go in and find out your psychological DNA. I figure out the patterns of how you're mentally, emotionally, and physically put together—like a fingerprint.

The profile doesn't care who you are—Black, white, female, tall, rich, or poor. It's like a doctor says, "You have appendicitis." "But I'm from Italy." "I don't care. We're going to take your appendix out."

The beauty is we all have talent.

Mark Schulman: It makes sense. What is within our control are the decisions we make relative to our attitudes, and attitudes are pliable. We can't control what happens to us, but we can control how we view the world. We can create attitude shifts that drive behaviors that determine the consequences or outcomes of our lives.

Dr. Russell: There are many people—whether it's cooking, singing, instruments, science—who know "their calling" very early on. My son's a film director in Los Angeles. We gave him an old Kodak camera when he was seven. We thought, "He can't do anything with that. He won't break it." He came back that night and showed us what he had done. We looked at each other, and said "There's something here." So, we kept buying him cheap cameras.

You're absolutely correct that attitude leads to behavior. It goes back further than attitudes in the wiring we have. When you ask someone to change their attitude, or you suggest they should, we go back in with the profile and begin to teach the person those connecting points in the wiring.

The wiring creates a picture, and it isn't just visual. Smell is a picture, touch, our senses. All this energy from outside comes in and turns on the wiring. And once the wiring goes on, a picture begins to form. When we teach athletes who have a good attitude to change their behaviors, we start with the picture. We present a new picture for them to learn through their talent themes.

We had a client who wanted to become a professional golfer. We profiled her to see if she had the talent themes that elite athletes have. If we were going to pick a drummer for P!nk, not only would we watch what you did with the drums, but we would pick the mental, emotional, and actionable things inside you to see if you're the same type of person that P!nk would like to play the drums.

We measure that. One of our client's talent themes was competition, which you would expect. It was in the seventh position out of thirty-four, and we had never seen anybody who didn't have it in the top five. So, we created this idea that competition was a talent. We coached talent, and after six months, by creating new pictures of what competition was, she began to change her picture to a perception.

We took two-hour practices, and we built them into fifteen-minute segments and put a score next to them so that competition would resonate, resonate, resonate. As that score began to change externally, that began to change the picture in her head to a perception. That settling is the absorption of a new perception that comes from the picture that she's being introduced to. That settling leads to the next step, which is an attitude—a sense, a thinking, or feeling that goes back to the wiring. Once I have a new attitude about it, I begin to value that attitude and that valuing pushes me to do—to behavior.

You build the picture, you begin to believe it, and then you act.

With athletes, we don't say, "Practice makes perfect." We say, "Good practice makes perfect." And a good practice is following the procedures of the brain and the body that will lead you in the right direction.

I have a performance program that teaches people how to do it, so that they can take these ideas and implement them together in everyday life and practice. That's when it really is a home run. That's when I take Olympians from bronze to gold.

That's the process I would add to your attitude/behavior formula. It comes back to the wiring of how we're put together. Thinking, feeling, acting. If you get those themes going in the right direction that creates a new picture. That picture solidifies into a perception, and the next step is attitude.

FOOD FOR THOUGHT

1. What skills do you want to enhance, and how can you accurately measure them?
2. What behaviors impact the talent underlying those skills?

3. How can you improve your attitude about those skills? How can you practice them?
4. Do you have thoughts, behaviors, and actions that can be more harmonious?

CHAPTER 15

IDENTITY

*Featuring **Bruce Turkel**, author,*
consultant, and keynote speaker

BRUCE TURKEL HELPS leaders and companies thrive in the new world of increased consumer expectations and choice. He helps clients and audiences uncover creative solutions and messaging strategies that future-proof their brands in a world of disruptive upheaval. Turkels's clients include Fortune 500 companies and industry associations around the world. Bruce founded Turkel Brands, a global brand consultancy that has worked with clients including Discovery Networks, Bacardi Limited, Miami Jewish Health Systems, and more. His fifth book, the bestselling *All about Them*, was chosen as one of Forbes's top ten business books of the year. He is a frequent guest on Fox Business, CNN International, and CCTV (Chinese State Television).

WHAT TO 👀 FOR

➤ Don't talk yourself out of your dreams. Maintain a positive attitude.
➤ Customers don't choose you based on what you do. They chose you based on who you are. It's all about attitude.

Bruce Turkel: Operational function is cost of entry. You have to be able to do your job. If you're not a good jeweler or surgeon or drummer, you're not getting the work. But just because you are good, doesn't mean you're getting the work either.

Consumers have many choices. The Internet means they can work with people around the world. Schools are cranking out professionals all the time. We're working later in life. Companies are offloading people. You have all these professionals in the workplace looking for opportunities. Companies and freelancers have unbundled what they do; customers can buy from you, or they can buy from lots of other people.

Are other people as good as you? I'll give you the benefit of the doubt and say they're not. But that's irrelevant because if you don't get the work, it doesn't really matter how good you are; nobody will know. Ability, function, operational superiority are the costs of entry.

So, there has to be something else. They don't choose what you do. They choose who you are. And what is who you are other than attitude? It's what you bring to the table, the stage, the operating suite, the sales center, the restaurant, the office. You tell me I'm a good dentist or I'm a good accountant? I'm sorry, but that isn't enough. It's all about attitude.

Remember that one kid on the diving board, "Hey, look what I can do. Look what I can do. Hey, look what I can do. Hey, look what I can do." You don't want to be that person. You want to be able to sing the song, crochet, make the flambé, but also be a pleasure to be around.

Mark Schulman: Have you found that changing your attitude was necessary or helpful in developing your career?

Turkel: As an art director, I had to open the portfolio and show my work. And you never know what turns someone on or what turns someone off. I might design something using a type style you hate, and instantly, you're turned off. I was selling something that was very judgeable. I'd open my portfolio, and you'd look at it. You either dug it or you didn't.

You may or may not have liked what I did, but I'm never going to do those things again. You're hiring me for creativity. So, I better do something new that I've never done before.

Some clients would say, "We want to do something new, unique, different, and special." And the next thing out of their mouths was, "Do you have something like that in your portfolio?" That's like saying "We want to hear how well you improvise. Here's the sheet music."

The first thing I do when I land at an airport for a speaking engagement, I take a picture of myself in front of a sign that reads Minneapolis or Memphis or Albuquerque. I take a selfie, I send it to the meeting planner and I say, "I'm here. Go worry about something else." At the hotel, I take a picture of me in front of the sign that says Memphis Hilton or Minneapolis Marriott, and I say, "I'm at the hotel. My stuff is here. Go worry about something else."

Why do I do that? Because I know my customer, the meeting planner, is nervous. They're trying to wrangle three different speakers. They're trying to make sure the CEO gets what they want. They're dealing with the person who doesn't like their room. And all I want them to know is they don't have to worry about me.

I can't tell you how many meeting planners come up to me afterwards, and they may or may not say, "You are awesome. That presentation was great. I learned so much." But they *always* say, "When I got your photo, it made me smile."

My attitude is, "I'm happy to be here, and I'm gonna kick some butt and make them feel that way, too."

Schulman: Can you just give me an example when you felt that you had a failure as a result of an attitudinal misjudgment?

Turkel: One of the dream clients that I always wanted for my agency was a cruise line—the opportunity to do great work, to go to great places, and to build your career. I worked so hard to get inside cruise companies. But we weren't big enough to win cruise business. Eventually, I got lucky. We got into a review, we did the work, and we won the business. We got a cruise line.

I'm meeting with the CEO, the CFO, the COO, the CMO—all the Cs. I have my team there: my account executive, my art director, my copywriter, my media person, my strategy person. I'm talking about how the business is going to move forward, what we're going to do.

I'm introducing each person. And, from my attitude and point of view, I'm being supportive of my people, and I'm really making them feel good. I want the client to understand I've put the best people on this piece of business and that we are a team.

At some point, the CEO said to me (in a condescending voice), "And what do you do?" I said, "I'm the glue that keeps this all together. But truth be told, with people like this," and here was my fatal flaw, "I'm always willing to do less." I was trying to be funny and not presumptuous.

She canceled the contract. She didn't do it at that moment, but she did it soon afterward. When I did the debriefing to find out why, they said, "She thought you were obnoxious and lazy." That was not my intention at all. My intention was to say, "I'm Vince Lombardi, I have the greatest team in the world and I'm giving you the best people. I don't deserve the credit. These people deserve the credit."

I thought I was being magnanimous, but I was being dismissive and flippant. And it cost me not only a nice piece of business, but a dream client.

Schulman: Your attitude was fully charged with promoting and supporting your team and reassuring them. The client interpreted that differently.

Turkel: I could have done a much better job of answering the question. I could have said, "I'm on top of this. My name's on the door. You and I are going to work together at the fifty-thousand-foot level. We have amazing people who are going to make our vision a reality." I could have handled it totally differently.

Schulman: I'm sure you've thought about it a lot.

Turkel: You have no idea.

Schulman: Did you ever see a need to change your attitude?

Turkel: My wife, Gloria, was an emergency room and cardiac care nurse for years. When the kids were little, she worked for an insurance company, and she would look at doctors' records for malpractice insurance. Because she could read the charts, she could read the EKG, she could tell what happened.

And she came up with a theory. Good doctors get sued all the time, but nice doctors never get sued. Some physicians were clinical geniuses, but they didn't have great bedside manner because they were scientists. And they would deal with the most difficult patients with the most difficult problems. Often, they would have a high mortality rate, not because they weren't good at what they did, but because they were dealing with people who were in such bad shape.

Then, there was the doctor who looked like 1960s TV character Dr. Kildare, who came in and kissed everybody and knew everybody's name. When the patient didn't do well or took a turn for the worse and perhaps died, he cried with the family.

She said, "I read one doctor's records, and I realized this doctor was terrible, clinically terrible. He wasn't necessarily killing people, but he certainly wasn't saving them. However, his attitude and the way he dealt with people meant he was bullet-proof because they loved him."

It dawned on me that when I'm in situations where I'm trying to show clients ideas that might scare them, I have to go out of my way to be less scary. I learned I had to come out of my shell.

FOOD FOR THOUGHT

1. What is your attitude at work? How is it affecting your status? What attitude shift could make you more valuable?

2. What is your attitude at home? How is it affecting your home life? What attitude could might make your home life better?

SECTION 3

● ● ●

ATHLETES AND COACHES

CHAPTER 16

REPETITION

*Featuring **Jim Abbott**, former Major League
Baseball pitcher and accessibility advocate*

JIM ABBOTT WAS a professional baseball player who was born without a right hand. He excelled as an All-American pitcher at the University of Michigan followed by ten MLB seasons on four teams. He was the first baseball player to win the James E. Sullivan Award for outstanding amateur athlete, and he pitched for the Gold Medal Olympic Team in 1988. He also threw a no-hitter while pitching for the New York Yankees. Abbott has worked with the US Department of Labor's Office of Disability Employment Policy (ODEP) on several initiatives encouraging businesses to hire people with disabilities.

WHAT TO ◉◉ FOR

- ➤ Believe in your dream. Try new paths and different ways to achieve it. Work hard and trust in yourself and the effort you exert to succeed.
- ➤ Don't be afraid when something you do doesn't work. Start over and keep at it.
- ➤ Reset your mind and body after a failure, so that you can look at the problem or challenge with a fresh mind.

> Practice the WINS Formula. The more wins you have, the more confident you become. Regardless of day-to-day failure, remind yourself of your hard-earned wins and gain confidence in your ability to be successful.

Mark Schulman: You must have put some time and energy into shifting your attitude to be able to create the greatness you had as a professional athlete.

Jim Abbott: A lot of people read my story at a surface level and think of it as a rallying cry for positive thinking. What played out in my attitude was more subtle. It was under the surface. I grew up differently. I knew what it was like to be on the outside. I knew what it was like to want to fit in and be on a team. Those ambitions drove my attitude, and they drove my motivation.

My attitude was informed by trying new things and doing them in different ways because for a lot of the things I wanted to do, there was no paradigm. There was no role model at the time. This was before social media, and there just weren't many stories about people who played baseball or basketball or football with one hand. So, my attitude was one of optimism and belief that, with enough hard work and repetition, I could find a way to do things just as well as anybody else.

That was my attitude growing up—the willingness to do things differently, to try new things and not be afraid when they didn't work—to start over, to keep honing, refining, and looking for ways that might ultimately breakthrough.

Schulman: Was there a signature moment when you made an attitude shift?

Abbott: I don't know what it is like to be a drummer. As a kid, I don't know if you imagine being in a world-famous band or backing up a world-famous artist or playing in front of huge crowds. Making the major leagues felt like a distant dream to me growing up. It was so far off. It seemed so magical. My goals, honestly, were just making the next team.

My success was based on moving past little downs and keeping the momentum going because it was a fight for me all the way. It was a fight for me to make the ninth-grade team. I was the only guy who didn't get a hit. To think that I might be in the major leagues in ten years would be absolutely the last thing anybody on that team could possibly imagine.

I was helped by so many people who believed in me when I didn't believe in myself, who helped me find different ways to evolve and field my position and hold bats—to discover faster, more efficient ways to do those things as the competition got stronger.

I went to the University of Michigan, which was a dream come true for me. I always wanted to do that growing up—to play baseball at Michigan. It really opened doors for me. It really started to make me believe that I could compete on a larger scale because we were playing really good teams.

Because I did well there, I played on the Pan American Games team (1987) and the Olympics team (1988). I was playing with the best college baseball players in the United States.

That was a breakthrough moment for me in terms of attitude. My goals became much bigger. Playing with those guys who I knew were going to be drafted in the first round, who I knew were big-time, major-league prospects, opened my eyes to the idea of being able to compete with anybody. It didn't matter—one hand, two hands. The next step became very clear, and that was professional baseball and ultimately the major leagues.

Schulman: In ninth grade, you didn't have a hit. That must have been disappointing and might have discouraged you. What happened after that?

Abbott: I hated losing. I hated being a failure. It was corrosive to me, and there were times I didn't handle it well. Failure ate away at me in ways that weren't always pretty. Those moments of struggle—and I can pin it down to particular games—were as formative to attitude as winning.

I had to reframe what was important. Small victories helped me battle back. But in a lot of ways, struggle and disappointment framed my attitude and behavior as much as great achievements. They were affirmations, and they were an incredible sense of belonging and achievement. Digging deep; setting small, attainable goals; and starting the process over—a lot of those moments were framed by disappointment.

Go back to the no-hitter I pitched for the Yankees. That was a wonderful moment, right? Pitching for the Yankees, whether you like them or you don't, is just so different—New York City, the pinstripes, Yankee Stadium—the scrutiny. I was really aware of that. That year was frustrating for me. I had been traded from the Angels, a team I loved. I was thrown into the New York cauldron, and I battled expectations.

In my start before the no-hitter, I pitched against the exact same team, Cleveland, and I was terrible. I went out, and I didn't make it through the fourth inning.

I was frustrated. I went for a long run *during* the game. I just left the stadium, trying to run out the frustration and the anger. As a starting pitcher, that's how your life is. You've got five days between games to completely reframe your attitude and your mindset and do it all again.

We flew back to New York City. There was a process to rebuilding and stepping back on the mound with an attitude of being able to compete and confidently throw the baseball. That's where the battle lies. That's where careers are made. That's how you make yourself into a successful starting pitcher.

Schulman: Tell me about the process. What happened in the five days? Because something must have shifted in you. It's not just luck to pitch a no-hitter.

Abbott: Physically, it was a routine. The day after a start, whether you did well or poorly, was a recovery day. I used it as an endurance day—a long distance run, a bike ride, a bit of weightlifting. You let the body reset, and that's a big step forward.

There was also mental cleansing. It was that physical release. It could be a celebration of a great victory, but in this case, it was more of a release of anger and frustration and pouring effort into starting over. You got back on the mound that second day and practiced off the mound. You worked on the mechanics of things that didn't work well or reinforced something that did.

Layered over the top was a lot of visualization—visualizing the next start, the next stadium, the next line up, the next opponent—putting yourself out on the field before the experience even happens and imagining things going well. That was a big part of the buildup.

With those physical and mental steps, you stepped back up on that mound five days later with a clear focus, a new task, a new day, a new challenge. Baseball is a game of confidence. Whether you're stepping in the batter's box or getting up on the pitching rubber, how confident are you when the national anthem finishes playing?

Schulman: You had talked about hating failure, that it could be corrosive to you. What would you do to shift your attitude from anger to motivation?

Abbott: A lot of it is physical. A lot of it is just getting back to work. The blessing of my career has been meeting with a lot of kids and families who are dealing with challenges like mine. To this day, I get cards, letters, and notes from families around the country asking, "What did your parents tell you? What did you learn? What was your experience?"

I tell them that I know it hurts. I remember not being picked for a team. I remember feeling unsure of myself in junior high school. I remember shooting baskets by myself or throwing a baseball against a wall, and it seemed like that pain and insecurity would go on and on for days.

But little by little, by making the right friends and choosing the right things, I pursued sports and grades and found little successes. I found that those times of loneliness happened less and less and the duration that you spend feeling like that doesn't last as long.

We get stronger. It's a muscle that, with training and with experience, aids us as we face life's challenges. I had a lot of training in that realm. So, when difficulty came, it didn't lessen it, it didn't make it less painful, but it just gave me the belief that I could come out of it—that as bad as I felt in Cleveland, Ohio, five days later, it could be different.

Schulman: That is your fundamental attitude, and that is what has brought you success. It's the WINS Formula, you're stacking up your wins, which builds confidence. Every single day, I acknowledge my wins. It gives me the power to continue to go on and let my mind remember that, yes, I will do better, and yes, these wins are mine. I've earned them. I've done the work.

FOOD FOR THOUGHT

1. Utilize the following formula daily.

   WINS FORMULA

   a. Wins: Review recent wins (ignore everything but successes).
   b. Improvements: Consider what you can improve.
   c. Next Wins: List the next wins you intend to achieve.
   d. State: What state of mind are you choosing for the day. Ex: Confident, Joy, Courage or Gratitude

CHAPTER 17

AMBITION

*Featuring **Julia Landauer**, NASCAR
driver and two-time champion*

JULIA LANDAUER IS a NASCAR driver and two-time champion from New York City. Since making history as the first and youngest female champion in the Skip Barber Racing Series at age fourteen, Landauer has amassed dozens of wins in several different racing series. After becoming the first woman in her division to win a NASCAR Track Championship at Motor Mile Speedway in 2015, Landauer graduated to the televised NASCAR K&N Pro Series West in 2016. She became the first woman to lead a lap in the Canadian NASCAR Pinty's Series, and currently races in the NASCAR Euro Series. In 2017, Landauer was selected as an honoree for the *Forbes* 30 Under 30 list in sports.

WHAT TO ◉◉ FOR

> ➤ There will be individuals who don't like you, often because of things you can't control. Recognize it and let it deflect off of you.
> ➤ Take feedback you can use and disregard the rest. People bring with them their own experiences and perspectives.

An appropriate action for one individual may not be your best option.

➢ Focus on the you that you want the world to know.

➢ Visualize success and celebration.

Mark Schulman: You're not even thirty, and you've raced for different divisions of NASCAR. You're a top keynote speaker. I would love to hear about times you made conscious attitude shifts to drive your life.

Julia Landauer: My perspective on my own attitude has shifted over the course of my lifetime. When you're young, you only have so many experiences. The trajectory of life changes how you approach your attitude. But if you have a growth mindset, you're always trying to be the best version of yourself.

I have always been a can-do, will-do person. I expected that my racing career would have reached a higher milestone by this point, and it hasn't. But I still am just as driven to make that happen. A big shift that has helped me continue is changing how I view other people's feedback or approval.

That was really hard. Because, for the most part, I have been a people pleaser. I want people to like me. But *someone's* not going to like you, and it's likely for things you can't control—you're from New York City, you went to Stanford, you have brown hair. It took a while to get authentically comfortable with that. Shifting that opened a whole world of opportunities—to just go after what I want and have that can-do attitude.

Schulman: I tend to be a people pleaser myself, and I've looked at things like age as restrictions. I'm fifty-eight years old, and I'm the drummer for P!nk. My speaking career has just started to blossom. I'm reaching my prime! But a lot of people share their limiting behaviors. I've learned to take what works and disregard the rest.

Landauer: An extension of that is not taking it personally and understanding that everyone comes from their own perspectives. This is why diverse perspectives are so important because everyone's coming from their own experience. So, their feedback might make total sense in their life—but it might be a little less relevant in mine.

It's taking a less personal and emotional approach and a more academic, intellectual analysis—and learning to do that quickly so you don't waste a lot of time. When you try to just do what other people tell you, it detracts from your personality, fire, and spark.

Schulman: I imagine you may have encountered a lot of adversity as a female NASCAR driver. Were there times when you consciously made attitude shifts that drove you to make this decision?

Landauer: I hadn't thought about it from a gender perspective because I'm the oldest of three kids and that comes with a certain level of confidence and cockiness, in a good way. We are a competitive family.

There were certain times throughout my career when I was treated differently because of stereotypes against women. This wasn't a conscious effort, but looking back, I realized there were certain gender stereotype boxes I did not want to get put in—like the sex symbol.

I've got a low tolerance for stereotypes—in movies, in comments around the garage—or people who enforce societal gender norms. I don't laugh at jokes that I don't think are funny. Being uncomfortable is the worst feeling, and I don't want to encourage people to do things that make me uncomfortable, especially if we must work together as a team.

At the end of the day, racing is a team sport. I wouldn't be able to do what I do if I didn't have incredible mechanics and engineers working on the car. So, everyone's got to mesh well together. That's always been important to me because I want to win races.

I've carved my own path, putting emphasis on who I am as a person. It's important to have gender discussions, to talk about obstacles and recognize the significance of being a minority in a male-dominated field. But at the same time, I want to be known as the driver who pays special attention to everyone on the team and helps them be their best, who can take and give feedback respectfully, who can be funny.

You find out what works for you. I love getting older because I love this sense of calm and ease with who you are as a person.

Schulman: You're sharing an attitude of power. I got that from you immediately.

Landauer: I also am not blind to the fact that so much of that is how I was brought up. That's why discussing these gender topics is important because everyone comes from a different background and a different experience.

Schulman: Share one more story related to attitude—positive or negative.

Landauer: I'm not upset by a lot of my attitudes throughout my life. I've remained professional. I will be first to criticize myself when things don't go the way I want, and then figure out what I can do differently.

But there was a season in my late teens when I was racing part time. I was in a new school. It was the first time I raced in the south. Culturally, there were big differences, and I wasn't doing particularly well. I felt hopeless. It was the first time I had broken out of the bubble of my youth.

There was this expectation that every driver in the stable would be really good, and we weren't doing well. There were a lot of factors working against me. It was a mix of homesickness and not having the support system at the track that I was used to. I got grumpy.

I don't know if we would have been successful if I had the best attitude ever, but I know that I did not help anything and I did not encourage my team to do the best they could. I did not inspire anyone around me because I was in a bad mood. Every photo taken candidly of me at the track was a mix of sad and angry. I had a totally wrong attitude.

I've decided never to do that again. Even if I'm down, even if I'm disappointed, my number one job off the racetrack is to make everyone else feel like we can do it. I decided I will always be positive and help the team be the best they can be. Feeling like you could have done something differently that might have led you to success is the most agonizing feeling. I want to avoid that.

Schulman: Was there an actual point of attitude shift, a light-bulb moment?

Landauer: That year was the exception. It shifted after the second or third race when we continued to under-perform. I didn't improve during that whole season. The next time I got in a race car was the following spring, and I did a lot better. I had a really supportive team, and we worked hard—fresh start, new team, new situation.

That school year, I went on *Survivor*, which was a time of big personal development for me. I made it halfway through. The season's winner said he was tempted to say I had a vanilla personality, but feared that would do a disservice to the flavor of vanilla because people actively seek out vanilla-flavored products and no one seeks out me. That aired on national television. It was humiliating.

I also was a case study for a class in our design school called Superfans and Their Heroes. It looked at Stephen Colbert, Michael Jordan, and Dale Earnhardt Sr. and how these individuals got such large and loyal fan followings. The feedback about me was just awful.

All these things came to a head at one time. That was the very aggressive knock on the head that I was doing something wrong, and I had to fix it.

Schulman: Is that the moment you got back in the race car?

Landauer: Definitely. There's so much hope and optimism when you join a new team. I wanted to have fun again in a race car. When you have really bad seasons, you can forget why you're doing what you're doing. At the end of the day, I love going fast. I love making all the pieces fit together.

I did visualizations. I realized that I hadn't imagined myself winning in a long time. Going to bed every night, I would literally visualize crossing the finish line first, celebrating and remembering why we do what we do. And I started winning.

FOOD FOR THOUGHT

1. How can you learn from the opinions of others while staying true to your own?
2. How can you keep your best aspects "front and center"?
3. During your daily routine, when is the best time to stop and visualize successes?
4. How can you best celebrate your successes and the successes of others?

CHAPTER 18

SOUL

*Featuring **Keith Mitchell**, former US
football player and celebrity yogi*

KEITH MITCHELL IS a former All-Pro NFL football player turned internationally renowned Celebrity Yogi. As a motivational mindfulness coach, holistic health and fitness advocate, community activist, and humanitarian, he is committed to providing purposeful holistic tools that help others achieve optimal health, peace, and aliveness. After a life-changing football injury left Mitchell partially paralyzed, he utilized yoga and meditation to fully recover.

WHAT TO 👀 FOR

➤ Behavior is learned, so it can be changed.
➤ There is no box, so stop trying to think inside it or even outside it.
➤ Human connections feed the soul.
➤ Only you can define what success is for you. Deflect the outside voices who claim to know better.

Mark Schulman: How important do you believe attitude has been in developing your career?

Keith Mitchell: My first realization comes from fighting to prove my validity playing football. I teach a class, "Accessing Your

Greatness Potential," because if we were never told we were great, then we assume that we are not. I was constantly fighting to prove my worth. It was an uphill journey in a game where time is the enemy with a first cousin called injuries.

Now in my second career, I'm focused on not being attached to perfection and being comfortable with the unknown. I can be whatever title you call me, but that doesn't define me. I am accessing possibilities while doing the work and putting my practice to the test to manifest whatever I want. This is where I wish I started.

Many times, just like emotions, behavioral patterns are learned. Positive thoughts when everyone in the world believes you can't are necessary, to be bold and not sensitive to critical opinions, distractions, or even mistakes, continuing to keep your eyes on the prize and doing the work.

Schulman: Have you found that changing your attitude was necessary or helpful in developing your career?

Mitchell: The most important thing is not being linear, realizing the box doesn't exist. It's necessary to have your intention close to your heart. The human being is at the top of the food chain. We are the medicine, and then everything else exists. We are the medicine to one another. This is why teachers speak to where they have been. If I had addictions, then I'm the addiction teacher.

Your mission must be personal. This will be a continuation of your own personal healing. Then, it will not be work, but necessary for your own wellbeing. The universal exchange—the nutrition that we are typically malnourished from—is simply human connection.

Schulman: Can you think of a time when you shifted your attitude to produce a better result?

Mitchell: This reminds me of the parent who has been preaching to the child over and over, year after year, and the information is not setting in. When does the parent reflect on their approach?

I have a saying; love isn't love unless the other person can receive it. We must contemplate how we are participating in the happenings of life because it's so easy to be the victim. I've had to reflect on this when it comes to nutrition and ideologies that people hold on to. I honestly believe I've allowed this complexity to enable me to know more as a teacher, where I pretty much study everything.

Schulman: Tell me a story where attitude was a critical factor in a failure or a success.

Mitchell: When I first started sharing the practice of mindfulness and mediation, I just knew the NFL would embrace my work, considering what and where we've been with my personal health. To this day, they have not really acknowledged it the way I would have liked.

Instead, I created a program with the military and the University of Rochester to work with US wounded warriors. I am disappointed with the NFL situation, and I view it as somewhat of a failure, but I'm convinced to continue working in other ways, knowing that what we are up to is very powerful.

My definition of success is my own, and not society's. So, whether I touch one person or only two people show up, it really is no difference to the energy I bring to sharing the practice. I'm not saying I don't like a big crowd, but this is where I am. To share and connect fuels my own healing and it empowers me to continue to do what we do. I say "we" for the people who paved the way and support and guide me.

Schulman: How does your attitude affect your behavior on a day-to-day basis?

Mitchell: Anxiety is simply not enough oxygen to the brain. Take a few seconds or minutes to breathe. Incorporate the mantra "less reactive to more contemplative."

FOOD FOR THOUGHT

1. Do you recognize that all behavior is learned and that learned behavior is subject to change?
2. Are you willing to think both inside and outside the box?
3. Are you using your connections to feed your soul and the souls of your connections?
4. Have you defined what success looks like for you?
5. Are you willing for your definition of success to be different from the way others define it?

CHAPTER 19

FOCUS

*Featuring **James Samuel Morris Jr.**, former*
professional baseball player and "The Rookie"

JIM MORRIS WANTED to play baseball in the major leagues since he was five years old. Despite hard work and determination, unfortunate events and injuries scuttled his career before he was twenty-five. Doctors told him he would never play again, and he retired to teach and coach high school baseball. In 1999, he bet his team that if they won their first district championship, he would try out for Major League Baseball. They won. And so, at age thirty-five and after a string of implausible events, Morris found himself on the mound as a relief pitcher for the Tampa Bay Devil Rays. His return to the game inspired the heartwarming Disney film *The Rookie*. Morris is the author of two books, most recently *Dream Makers*, which picks up where *The Rookie* left off. Morris is a seasoned motivational speaker, and he started a foundation helping inner city children find hope and inspiration through sports.

WHAT TO ◉◉ FOR

➤ Be open to change, both from the outside and within yourself. Your attitude toward change is within your control.

> ➢ Find positive people around you who can affirm your
>   worth and teach you how to better yourself, your team,
>   or family.
> ➢ Your team is bigger than you and even your immediate
>   work department or family. Think about the micro-team
>   you impact daily and how your choices influence their
>   attitudes and behaviors.

James Morris: I'm here because of a bet. I started off poorly because the one person I wanted to please all the time I did please, and that was me. I was selfish and self-involved. All my dreams would never work out because if the doctor said to take off six weeks, I'd take off a day. If the surgeon said, "You can't throw for a year," I'd throw in three months.

I just didn't listen to people. I was told I was stupid all my life, so I believed that. I thought, "Poor me," and by twenty-four, I'm out of baseball.

I had an abusive father, physically and verbally. I never got any reinforcement other than the back of the hand or a fist. Bruises go away; the words stick with you, and you can't take that back. He demanded discipline out of me, but he couldn't abide by discipline himself. We moved constantly, and that was because of his attitude. He wasn't willing to change. He was right no matter what.

When I was fifteen, my parents moved me to my grandparent's house. It was different. There was a lightness to it; the whole environment was lighter. It was those two people, my grandparents, who taught me how to be a good human and how to treat everybody the same. They were two of the best people I've ever known in my life. I learned marriages don't have to be arguments and fights. It's not a competition; it's teamwork.

MARK SCHULMAN AND JIM SAMUELS, PHD

I was talked to for the first time in my life like I mattered. They taught me how to balance a checkbook. They taught me how to have a savings account. They taught me how to shake hands and look people in the eyes. Grandfather had me take my grandmother on lunch dates while I was in high school so I would know how to treat women.

During my senior year, he got really sick. Eventually he was diagnosed with Lou Gehrig's Disease (ALS). To watch this six-foot-two-inch, 260-pound man who led a community do it with the grace and dignity from a wheelchair was amazing to me. I learned a lot from what he said and what he did for me. I learned more watching and just seeing what was going on. And I learned a lot about attitude from him because he could have crawled up in a hole and quit.

You are one of the biggest people in your life when you're talking about attitude and how to change it. A person can cast a shadow on a household or a ballfield or a classroom or a stadium. Once they go negative, they're not coming back on the other side. But once they go positive, it's going to be hard to bring them back down because they've got that energy.

Mark Schulman: The interesting thing about attitude is how contagious it is.

Morris: It's something we're completely aware of at fifteen. We notice the differences and the nuances between good, bad, up, down, on, off. I liked being talked to. I liked being treated like I was a human being. I liked the way that my grandparents interacted with everybody else. Nobody was blaming anybody. Everyone was greeted with hellos or hugs and handshakes. They carried themselves differently.

They worked harder than anybody I ever knew in my life. But they did everything right, too. And if there was a road to take, they always took the high road.

I never heard my grandfather raise his voice to my grandmother or say ugly things that you can never take back or treat anybody with fist and anger instead of love and compassion. I saw both sides of the coin. I saw my parents do it the wrong way, and I saw my grandparents do it the right way, and I wanted the right way.

Schulman: Was there a moment that something shifted in you?

Morris: My grandfather had a men's wear store in a town of about twenty thousand people. I was doing all the Christmas stuff. We had girls from high school wrapping, and I'm out on the floor. This lady comes into the store. She's got on overalls and her boots smell like pigs. It's 5:45 p.m. on Christmas Eve, and we all want to go have Christmas. Let's shut the store and go home.

All these other men who worked with my grandfather saw this, and they ignored her. My grandfather was counting the registers out from his office, and he got up and he treated her like she should be treated. Before she left his store, she bought fifteen suits for every male in her family and paid in cash. When he walked back by me, he said, "It doesn't matter if you dig ditches or you're the president of the United States. It doesn't matter what color you are, and it doesn't matter what language you speak."

While he didn't say a lot to me, I learned by just watching how he carried himself. That lady came to our store every year after that. If he wasn't there, she wouldn't buy anything. If he was there, she was buying from him.

I got drafted by the Yankees to play. I turned it down so I could be home for the last few months of my grandfather's life. I went to junior college and got drafted by the Brewers.

Over the next five and a half years, I had six surgeries—Tommy John surgery, shoulder surgery. Eventually, I said, "You know what? This is not working." I let my dad's voice play in my head. "You're not good enough. You're not smart enough. You can't do this."

I talked myself out of my own dream. I went back to college. I blew college up, man. College was easy. When you're paying for it yourself, you become smart, because that's expensive. I found out I wasn't stupid, and I could be anything I wanted to be.

I met my future ex-wife, and we got married and had our first son. For the last two years, at twenty-seven and twenty-eight, I played college football because I missed that competition.

I bucked the system at an early age because anybody who disagreed with me I considered them an ally of my father. I was going to do it the opposite way. That made my life hard and complicated at times. It made me extremely good at being an athlete, but it also put a drive in me that made other people not want to be around me. I wanted us to be as successful as possible by trying to make me as good as I could. In doing that, I was concentrating on me, the individual, instead of me, the team.

When you're young, these things aren't as obvious to you as they are when you look back. So, I knew that I wanted to work with kids. I went back to school; I started teaching and coaching.

Schulman: You made the conscious shift to be a team player and teach kids, to share all that wisdom.

Morris: The kids I inherited in Big Lake, Texas at Reagan County High School had won one game each year for three years before I got there. They were supposed to lose. I talked two kids into coming up with ten kids, otherwise we had eight and that's not enough for baseball. The first season there, not much of what I taught was baseball. We had to learn everything. If it's not going to be a "me thing" anymore, it's going to be "we," and "we" is everybody.

This is how I explained it to my kids. I said, "We don't just represent our baseball team. First, we represent our families. Then, we represent each other, our schools, the teachers and students who go there, the community, and the state. Our team is a whole lot bigger than this team."

We're going to carry ourselves the right way. We're going to wear uniforms correctly. We're going to turn our hats around the front. When you make 9 or 10 million bucks a year, you wear your hat any way you want to, but on this field and between the lines, this is how you wear it.

We're not going to trash talk to the other team. We need to keep our composure and start learning what that is. We're going to have a good attitude. We're not going to backtalk to the umpires. You never win that battle.

We're going to thank the teachers, the students, and the parents who come watch us play when they don't have to. This is not a sport that we have to play. We get to play it. If you are not enjoying it, please leave, because we need to have fun.

We took it into the classroom. We learned to open doors for teachers and do our homework. If you're not learning, you can't dream as big as you can possibly dream. It took me longer than it should have to realize that.

Education became a big part for me. That first season, we taught the kids how to take care of the field, grass, and dirt; plant trees; make a parking lot; and put a batting cage up. They liked it because they were making it their own. This was their ownership of what they had. It was their home. When you must do the work, you respect it a whole lot more than if somebody hands it to you.

That first season we went ten and zero at home. Those were the only ten days we won, but we were ten and zero at home. The second season, this little school in West Texas, I had sixty-three kids come out for my baseball team. It told me that we were doing this the right way.

I said, "Look, our team doesn't consist of the guys on the field. It's not even the guys in the dugout. What do we do about the people who announce the score, keep the books, cheer us on, cut and water the grass, and bring you to the game? Let's be thankful for what we have, instead of complaining about everything."

Those kids ate it up, they had an adult listening to them. That meant a lot to them. They said, "Coach, why do you keep teaching us we are good when we are so bad?" I said, "Because eventually you're going to believe it. We're trying to win. Let's have fun doing it."

Schulman: You look far beyond the team. When I'm on the road with P!nk, there are 225 people with us. My job is easy. The riggers get there at 5 a.m. to hang the PA system and lights, and if one thing is hung incorrectly, people can die. I adore my drum tech, Gary Grimm, and give him so much support and love.

Sustainable companies are run by people who understand the value of human capital and meritocracy. There is a woman who puts water on the stage after P!nk has done her aerial stunts. If that water's not there, who is the most important person on the tour to her at that moment? The woman who puts water on the stage. Everybody needs to feel that they are as valued as everybody else.

I talk with IT people who are behind the scenes and don't tend to get as much recognition as sales or research and development or the C-suite. I say, "You can imagine what it's like to be on stage in front of fifty thousand people and not one set of eyes is looking at you." Because that's my reality. I'm there to be of service. I'm there to support P!nk, the band, the audience. If everybody around me is happy, and I'm being of service to everybody else, I'm happy. I don't require much.

The reason you had sixty-three kids show up is because you did the work. You got that reputation based on what you created, your attitude toward people, and your attitude toward the greater good.

FOOD FOR THOUGHT

1. How can you validate your dreams and insights?
2. How can you maintain a positive, proactive state of mind?
3. How can you take greater responsibility for embracing change, both internal and external?
4. How can you focus more on positive people who validate your worth?
5. How can you increase your validation of the people around you at work, in your home, and in your community?
6. How can you take daily responsibility for a positive attitude in you and those around you?

CHAPTER 20

EXPERIENCE AND EMOTION

*Featuring **Martina Navratilova**, tennis player,
commentator, and Female Athlete of the Year*

MARTINA NAVRATILOVA, THE most successful female tennis player
of the Open era, amassed an unmatched number of professional
records over the course of a career that spanned four decades. She
won an unprecedented 59 Grand Slam titles (including a record
nine Wimbledon singles championships) and 167 singles and 177
doubles championships. Her decades-long rivalry with Chris Evert
is considered one of the greatest in sports history, with Navratilova
sporting a 43-37 advantage. She was distinguished as the WTA's
Tour Player of the Year seven times, named the Associated Press's
Female Athlete of the Year, and declared one of the Top 40 Athletes
of All-Time by *Sports Illustrated*.

WHAT TO ◉)◉) FOR

➢ Effort is key to successful outcomes. Give your business,
  project, work, or family your maximum effort, and prior-
  itize those things that mean most to you, so that you can
  give them your best.
➢ Train yourself in multiple ways, regardless of the discipline. Think outside your current environment and uti-

    lize best practices from other industries and sciences to grow and mature.

➤ Use your emotions to find success, even those with historically negative connotations. Anger can be used in positive ways and lead to successful outcomes if it is channeled through confidence and clarity of purpose.

Martina Navratilova: Boys are generally encouraged to do sports, but girls must sometimes fight to even be involved. So, you must really want to do it. That was not the case for me, I was always encouraged and supported.

But also, nowadays, I think many kids are coddled too much. All I ever want from anybody, including my kids, is giving their best; however, you come up on the ranking. Give your best if you're ranked five or if you're ranked fifty. That is the beauty of tennis, you know exactly where you stand. There is nothing subjective about it, either you beat the person, or you didn't. You won some matches, or you didn't. You rank twenty-five because that's where you are.

I've always believed in giving the best; it never occurred to me to give less than that. I was always surprised when people didn't, but that just came from inside me. When I first beat my father in tennis, I was close to fourteen years old, and I was thrilled because I knew it was real. He didn't let me win. I earned it; and it meant something.

Because of that, I was always ready to meet challenges, and I was ready to fight for them. Giving my best just came naturally; I never knew any other option.

Many people say, "Oh you're so competitive," as if it's a bad thing for a woman. They would never say that to a man in a semi-derogatory way. For me, what is the alternative? Who goes on the court saying, "Oh, I want to lose today"? I have fought my heart out, in a fair way. I never cheated my way forward. If anything, I was a little too hard on myself sometimes.

Mark Schulman: You also had a unique approach with your training. You employed cross-training techniques and other cutting-edge things to bring you to another level and make you more successful. That must have been a conscious attitude shift.

Navratilova: When I left the Czech Republic, I left my family. My dad was my coach, so I was coach-less for six years. I was working hard, as hard as I knew how to work. My come-to-Jesus moment came when I lost three or four tournaments in a row, and I didn't get to the finals at Wimbledon.

Nancy Lieberman, who was my then-girlfriend and an amazing basketball player, said "You know you are really wasting your talent. You could work so much harder than this."

In basketball, they physically train so much harder than tennis players. So, we started training physically, running suicide drills on the basketball court, lifting weights, doing sprints on the track and playing basketball full-court. I got into unbelievable shape. That was the start of it, Summer of '81. It wasn't that I was lazy—I just didn't know any better.

At the same time, I got a coach. Renée Richards became my coach, and that was when I started rewriting the history books.

Schulman: It's interesting how motivating failure can be to create an attitude shift. But it was just a natural evolution for you. You were already programmed to have the attitude of wanting to do the best you can.

Navratilova: Renée didn't care how I got there. We worked hard on the tennis court, and then I did supplemental training off the court. I had already started doing that physical training regimen before we started working together.

Renée was very helpful with the attitude bit. If I was saying anything negative, thinking negatively, or getting down, she would say, "Replace that thought with a positive one because you can only have one thought at a time in your head."

You have to realize you're being negative. It's being alert and conscious of what your thoughts are, and once you realize that, you can replace it. Positive thought means solution. Negative thought means problem.

On the tennis court, it is essential. I was playing an aggressive kind of tennis. You can't be aggressive with your feet and your positional attitude on the court if you are negative in your head.

Schulman: Are you creating an attitude of abundance and focusing on successes and wins or an attitude of scarcity and focusing on the challenges? Your brain listens to you. We are the masters of our thoughts by making that conscious decision. We actually have conscious control over what we think. I was told by a leading psychiatrist that you can't have a positive and negative conscious thought at the same time.

Navratilova: I became friends with Katharine Hepburn, and there were a couple things that she said that have really resonated with me. One of them is "It's not what you do in life, it is what you finish." The other one was "You make your own luck."

Intensity always came naturally to me. I had that intensity in practice; it was always quality over quantity. You can't have exactly the same intensity as you have in a match, but you get as close to it as possible, so when you do it for real, you've been there many times.

I remember one match, I was so flat emotionally. I was trying to be controlled, I was losing, and I was flat as a pancake.

I was trying to be so perfect, and it wasn't working. So, I started swiping the racket against the court and smacking the ball against the ground, in a *positive* angry way. It was an attitude shift that resulted in me waking myself up, getting that intensity up, and playing much better. I ended up winning the match even though the crowd was mad with me.

You have to be really alert, awake, and switched on, and I just wasn't. So, I switched myself on during that match by just getting angry and channeled it the right way.

Schulman: There is something we call the MO skill—your *modus operandi*, or your method of operation. And there are two forms of anger. There is negative anger that is rebelliousness, and there is positive anger that is determined and extremely powerful. Determination brought up your game. If you had been residing in rebelliousness, it would have brought your game down. You recognized that power, and you did it.

Navratilova: Attitude is a choice. People can make you feel any which way, but how you respond to it depends on your attitude. That is up to you. Nobody can make you be negative, and they can't make you positive, only you can do that. You are in complete control. You can't control the weather, you can't control how much money you make, but you can control how you respond to things and what your attitude is overall.

FOOD FOR THOUGHT

1. What priority should you put more effort into?
2. What can you learn from other aspects of life that can help with your career?
3. What can you learn outside of your career that would be interesting and fulfilling?
4. How can you improve your industry by learning from other industries or from your city, region, or country?
5. How can an unexpected response enhance your communication?

CHAPTER 21

HARD WORK

*Featuring **Bonnie St. John**, paralympic skier*
and medal winner, author, and speaker

BONNIE ST. JOHN is the first Black American to win medals in Winter Olympic competition, taking home a silver and two bronze medals at the 1984 Winter Paralympics in Innsbruck, Austria. In recognition of this historic achievement, she was quoted on millions of Starbucks coffee cups and honored by President George W. Bush at a White House celebration of Black History Month. St. John graduated with honors from Harvard University, won a Rhodes Scholarship, earned numerous sales awards at IBM, and was appointed by President Bill Clinton as a director of the White House National Economic Council. President Barack Obama named her to represent the US in delegations to both the Winter Paralympic Games in Vancouver and the Summer Paralympics in Rio De Janeiro. She holds several honorary doctorate degrees, and was recently lauded with her portrait in the main hall of Trinity College, Oxford, as a distinguished alumna.

WHAT TO ◉◉ FOR

> ➤ Positive attitude is critical and "radical attitude changes your life."

➢ Put in the work instead of taking the easy way. Your effort will drive the success you are seeking.

➢ Try a lot of different methods and paths, and put effort into them. Have multiple dreams. They won't all work out, and that's OK. Lean into the ones that do.

➢ When you apply for a job, you aren't just auditioning for a role—so are they. Determine if the company is a right fit for you and what you want to accomplish, professionally and personally.

Bonnie St. John: My mother had a hard childhood. She grew up during segregation in Florida. She had to walk a mile past the beautiful school for white kids to go to the rundown school for Black kids with no textbooks. But she went on, got her PhD, became an educator, and was incredibly successful. She bought a cassette tape of Patricia Fripp giving a motivational speech, and we listened to it over and over again. My mother struggled with a lot of difficulties and self-esteem challenges, but she tried to use positive thinking and attitude to pull herself up. Part of the reason I became a motivational speaker was mother's milk. It was pounded into me when I was growing up that attitude is critical and radical attitude changes your life.

Mark Schulman: The big misconception is that it begins with behavior. It begins with attitude. Your attitude drives your behavior and behavior determines consequences. You have the power to change, shift, or choose your attitude about what happens to you. That is a moment-to-moment decision, to create an attitude that serves you or not. And when you make a decision to shift your attitude to serve you, you realize that that can alter the outcomes of your life. That's powerful.

St. John: My mother took us to Transcendental Meditation lessons. She used to go to an all-night diner and write affirmation for hours. And she gave it to us, as part of our inheritance.

When I was fifteen years old, I sent away to Burke Mountain Academy and asked them to send me information in the mail. It was a big envelope with brochures in it about this private boarding school for ski racers in Vermont, and I am one of three children with a single mom who's a school teacher, so that's not possible, right?

I get the brochures and the information, and I'm sitting on my bed with my brother looking at these pictures of kids living in farmhouses and a log cabin on the side of a mountain. Half the school has classes in the morning and trains in the afternoon, and the other half does it the other way around. On weekends, they get in buses and go off to races.

There are no Black people in the pictures. There are no one-legged people in the pictures. But I say to my brother, "If I want to be a ski champion, this is where I need to go."

I had been skiing in Southern California, but it was difficult. I had to go up to the mountains every weekend. I had a job after school to scramble together money. I didn't have a coach. I was trying to be a ski racer, but I realized if I could go to this high school where the great champions go, I could be a champion.

I went to the library, and I looked up organizations that might be able to give me money to do it. I wrote letters to Muhammad Ali and Jesse Jackson. I got some sponsorships. I got United Airlines to give me an airfare to get out there. I got a ski company to give me the ski clothes I would need. I got boots and skis. I got a lot of in-kind support, but I couldn't get any money to go.

I put in an application, and I told the headmaster that I was writing letters to raise money. But when the school year came around, I hadn't raised enough. I called and said, "I failed. I didn't raise the money I needed to go to your school." And he said, "Come anyway."

I showed him all the work I had done and how hard I had tried. I wasn't just calling him up and saying, "Give me a full scholarship." He said, "I believe in your dream. You'll be the first one-legged Black person here at our school. Let's give this a shot."

On the first day of school, they have physical tests, push-ups, sit-ups—you're supposed to train over the summer and come in strong. After it was over, I was playing on a ski simulator, and I fell off and broke my leg. But I stayed. I could still lift weights and do some of the training. Because I couldn't participate in soccer and other activities, I went to the development office and started fundraising. I was going to need money to be able to get to my races. The National Brotherhood of Skiers sponsored me, which helped me for years after to compete.

I broke my leg on the first day of school, and that became an advantage and ultimately made a big difference.

I graduated and got accepted to Harvard. But I realized I wasn't going to be able to ski very well there, partly because it was so hard (there was a lot of work) and partly because it wasn't close to a good ski area. After one semester, I took a year off. I qualified for the Paralympic team, which culminated in the January Olympics, then went back to school and finished in three years.

Schulman: That is an extraordinary attitude of focus, understanding where you want to be and finding the path.

St. John: I didn't see failure as an obstacle. I had four other ideas if Burke didn't work. I wrote in my book, *Live Your Joy,* about the idea of a portfolio of goals. You have different investments. You're not going to put all your money into one of them. I am always looking at several possibilities, and if something is working, I'll put a little more into it. If it's not working, I'll back off and do something else.

Schulman: One of my favorite attitudes is freedom. The more free you are to fail, the better your chances are of success.

St. John: You're able to take risks if you're not afraid of failure. I had fallback plans. Studying hard and getting into a good college was critical for my survival. I wanted to have a good life. I wanted to have a good job. Skiing would work or it wouldn't, but that was not going to define whether I could eat. I dreamed of going to business school. I wanted a suit. I took business courses in high school. I've always loved business.

But some of my drive to go into business was out of insecurity and fear. When I was five years old, my mother was trying to commit suicide. She was not a wholly stable person. She did her best, she raised three kids, she worked, she survived, but there was always the fear that you couldn't fall back on that because she wasn't entirely stable. She *was* giving me some of the tools she used to successfully wrestle with those demons.

Thinking about attitude, getting my first agent is an interesting story. I got one of those books on how to get an agent, and I followed all the instructions. I wrote my cover letters and my book proposals. I did my research. I sent out the letters, tracking all the responses. I barely got a reply, never mind follow-up.

I decided I was going to go to a Tony Robbins book signing. They miscommunicated the location or the time, so not a lot of people showed up. I could just go and talk to Tony. I said, "I want to write a book like you did, will you refer me to your agent or your publisher?"

He said, "Send me a video." His handler was standing in the back. So, I went up and asked, "What does he mean?" And his handler said, "Lots of people ask him for things. He says send me a video about your project, because nine out of ten people won't send the video. It's a screening device."

So, I sent him a video, and he followed up. My first book was published using Tony Robbins's agent. I got a deal with Simon & Schuster.

In a way, the second book was harder because I had one book, and it was OK. It didn't do that great. For the second book, I tried to get an agent, and I had some ups and downs. I changed my attitude from "Can I get an agent?" to "I'm going to interview ten agents and find the best one for me." Instead of "Will an agent accept me?" it was "Will I accept an agent?"

I interviewed a whole bunch of agents and found one who was a good match and really believed in me. That agent got me a five-book deal.

Schulman: That's exactly what I did when it came to auditioning. I'm probably the only person that auditioned for Cher three times. I was hired the first time for about an hour, then her former drummer showed up, and they gave him the job back. The second time, they narrowed it down to four out of twenty-five, and she chose the guy with the most appropriate astrological sign because they couldn't pick. Then, she fired him and brought the old drummer back again!

By the third time, it was almost a joke to me. I thought, you know what? I'm changing my goal. I'm changing my attitude.

Rather than looking at it as a job I needed, I shifted my attitude to one in which I was interviewing them. I was auditioning them.

St. John: I've always been interested in this idea of shifting the process, so that you are looking for partners in your success.

Here's another story. I'd been in business for a while speaking, and I was working with a whole bunch of different speakers' bureaus. I had my own office, too, so I did some direct bookings. A bureau called me and said, "You got this job, but you should have paid me a commission. You went around me."

I have integrity. I don't do that. So, I talked to her, and the truth was she never pitched me. She pitched a bunch of speakers to this client, but she never pitched me. She was trying to get a commission when she had never pitched me. I tried to act with integrity in the middle of this situation. I tried to find out what had really happened.

I put so much energy into this negative situation, and when I think about it, am I investing this much energy in the people who support, promote, and love me—the people who have integrity? It was a wakeup call. I need to not let all my energy get sucked into problems. I need to have my energy go into good people.

FOOD FOR THOUGHT

1. What goals and dreams can you add to your "portfolio"?
2. What goal do you currently see as outside your comfort zone that you can pursue anyway?
3. What state of mind will you create when you achieve that goal?
4. What legacies would make you feel truly accomplished?

CHAPTER 22

MAGIC

*Featuring **Shelli Varela**, fire captain,
speaker, author, host, and story alchemist*

SHELLI VARELA USES her unique perspective as the first female fire-fighter for Mississauga (Ontario) Fire and Emergency Services to shine the light of possibility as a leader and speaker in the personal development industry. Her mission is to help people discover their passions and ignite their purposes with both internal self-evaluations as well as actionable tactical tools that result in successful goal architecting. She's been featured in *The Globe and Mail*, *The Toronto Star*, *The Sun*, and *The Women's Post* as well as numerous television and radio broadcasts.

WHAT TO ◑◑ FOR

- ➤ Look for your unconscious limiting beliefs—those based on stories and not on fact. Have a "radical and savage disregard" for thoughts that hold you back or impede your goals.
- ➤ Find the root of your limitations.
- ➤ Don't lose the feeling in that "magical, micro-moment" of possibility you experience before the fear, doubt, and obstacles of a journey or quest set in.

➤ Turn intangible fears like that of public speaking into tangible ones like inexperience or insecurity that you can actionably change, in this case with practice and study or therapy.

➤ Take responsibility for stepping into your own greatness, and realize you are here for something that is of service to others.

➤ Passion comes from curiosity. Be curious and try new things.

Shelli Varela: We get programmed from a young age to think certain things, and we establish a norm of what's appropriate or what isn't appropriate. These norms get ingrained as unconscious limiting beliefs. So, when we actually try to make a decision about what we want to do, these stories play in the back of our heads, and we don't even realize they're stories. We mindlessly accept them as truth.

So, my approach is radical and savage disregard for limiting beliefs. But you must know that they're limiting.

The stories we tell ourselves have the ability to drive our behavior. We can accomplish incredible things, but more often than not, they keep us stuck. The truth is, you have to find the root of the problem. If you can find the root of your limitations, it is as simple as a quarter turn, and then every domino after that changes.

It's attitude plus awareness, and not buying into society's idea of what is acceptable and what isn't acceptable. That comes with labeling yourself or putting yourself in a lane, and as soon as you do that, you stop looking at the big picture.

I used to think I was Shelli the Artist, so I sought artistry jobs. Once I realized I wasn't Shelli the Artist, I was Shelli Who Likes Art, that freed me up to become Shelli the Firefighter.

Mark Schulman: That's an attitude shift, and that shift changed your behavior and is driving new consequences.

Varela: For me, it came in the form of three words: "Why not me?" When I started my journey, I didn't have any skills, knowledge, or experience, but I said yes at that zero point.

People think with their heads and they lead with logic. They ask, "What are the challenges or obstacles between me and my quest?" They stop focusing on the quest. They start focusing on the obstacles, and then they're finished.

Schulman: You literally become fixated on the barriers and lose sight of the goal.

Varela: But there is a magical, micro-moment when you allow yourself to be excited. Usually, it's a second or two. I call that moment "The Yes Effect." It's that zero point when your body tells you the truth. And if you can shift it in that one second, at that zero point, that yes effect, it's a game changer.

Schulman: Can you give me any specific examples when you consciously shifted your attitude to produce a specific result?

Varela: I was hired as my city's first female firefighter, and for two decades, I kept getting asked about that story. I'm shy, and I found that annoying for the longest time, until somebody said, "Thank you so much for sharing because I see myself in your story. I thought there were things I couldn't do, and now I'm going to go do them."

At that moment, I realized my story had nothing to do with me. It was a vehicle for hope and possibility. I thought, "I'd like to do a TED Talk." At the time I was terrified of public speaking, but I knew the message was more important than my fear. So, I had to consciously reverse engineer what I was afraid of.

Schulman: Your first impression was that you had to do it.

Varela: I had been through this enough times to understand the process. So, I hacked possibility. Being afraid of public speaking is intangible. You can't touch it or fix it, and that's convenient because you can just be afraid of it and you don't have to grow or change or fix it.

Schulman: It's a very common fear, and because of that, a lot of people just accept that the fear is just the norm.

Varela: I broke it down into the tender underbelly of what I was actually afraid of. You're not usually afraid of what you think you're afraid of. What you're afraid of is way too raw to see. I break fear into two camps: roots and wings. The roots' side is practical, tactical, logical, and task-y and the wings' side is emotional, creative, and abstract.

In my two camps, the practical tactical side was I'd never given a talk, certainly never a TED Talk. I didn't know anything about physicality or voice. So, I hired coaches. I started studying. I talked to you.

On the wings' side, I felt like I wasn't enough, like I wasn't worth it. I felt like I didn't deserve to be there. I turned that "I am afraid of public speaking," intangible into tangibles. And they were actionable.

They weren't easy. I spoke to a counselor and asked, "Why do I feel like I'm not good enough for this? I keep getting asked about this story. Clearly, it has value."

I broke it down from the intangible to the tangible, from the unfamiliar to the familiar. I demystified it. I broke it down into pillars. Then look at each pillar individually, so you don't get overwhelmed. Break it down to a small task or a habit.

Schulman: You said that from the abstract standpoint, you felt like you didn't earn it, you weren't good enough, and you shouldn't be there. Was there a point, through the therapy or coaching, that you realized that was a limiting belief?

Varela: What I realized after talking to several people: It wasn't about me. I was just the deliverer of the message. That allowed me to take the weight off my shoulders and just be the conduit. It freed me. And I love speaking now, but had I not done that one quarter turn, I would still be stuck in the pattern of fear.

If you take the intangible and make it tangible and actionable, then there is almost nothing you can't break down, as long as you're chasing the right thing.

Your vision isn't always for other people to see. If it's in alignment with what's true for you, even if everybody else thinks you're crazy—often, they will think you're crazy—you're following your thing. Those mental shifts become easier if you can tune in to your own inner voice.

Schulman: It's your truth, your authenticity.

Varela: People don't listen to their inner voices because everybody's trying to fit in. It is a worthiness problem; from the time we're little, we want to fit in. We don't want to stand out, we don't want to be different and stepping outside the norm. Risking judgment keeps us smaller than we need to be. Taking responsibility for stepping into your own greatness and realizing you are here for something that is of service to other people can make all the difference.

Schulman: You stepped outside of what would have been that normalcy just by becoming a female firefighter. Then, you expanded above and beyond to become an author and speaker and to host one of the most successful webcasts. That is all way beyond what would be considered normal or regular.

Varela: Here's the beauty of it, though. When you exercise that muscle, and you have a few wins, you figure out actual patterns.

Schulman: Building up on the wins helps you to effectively build more wins. We grow up wanting to be the same as everybody else; every kid wants to be accepted. But extraordinary people are not the same. They take on things you wouldn't think would be possible.

Everyone has a story to tell, and everyone can learn from everybody else's story. Who's gonna be bold enough to tell it?

Varela: Once you realize that it's of service to other people, it becomes rocket fuel. It takes on a life of its own.

Schulman: Get reacquainted with your *why*, if you need some inspiration.

Varela: Author and columnist Elizabeth Gilbert did a talk called *Flight of the Hummingbird—The Curiosity-Driven Life* about getting in touch with your why. A lot of people are conflicted about the word passion. They say, "I don't know what my passion is like you do."

In front of passion comes curiosity. Give yourself a break. Take the pressure off. Ask "What am I curious about?" And give yourself permission to explore that without outcome. If you love painting, take a painting class. Because you also can't see the forest for the trees. The next big thing you discover takes you to the thing that is your passion.

Schulman: Passion is the motivator. It is the fuel that drives us to do anything. But there's an evolution of passion, and it is purpose. Purpose is the why. Purpose builds more passion, and passion builds more purpose. That's what really keeps the machine going.

Varela: The thing people don't consider in that moment when they don't make an attitude shift: There is a ripple effect of things that *don't get to happen.* In that zero point, micro-moment when your body tells you the truth, it will never lie to you. If you tune into it, then you get to do the thing you love and you get to be of service to other people. And what comes of that you never even know. It could be exponential.

Schulman: That's the butterfly effect. One attitude is going to generate a variety of behaviors, which are going to generate a variety of consequences. It's for us to put out there and let it ripple.

The artist's only responsibility is to put it out there. Simply do it, and let others connect and expand and have behavioral shifts and consequences that are going to drive things for themselves, for their families, and for everyone else they influence.

FOOD FOR THOUGHT

1. What thought or belief is holding you back? What is the root cause?
    a. How can you preserve and protect belief in self?
    b. How can you overcome fear about what is possible?
    c. How can you own more of your power and be of service to others?
    d. How can you feed your curiosity to explore new things?

CHAPTER 23

FOCUS

*Featuring **Dr. Jen Welter**, first female NFL
coach and women's football pioneer*

DR. JEN WELTER is the first female to coach in the NFL serving as a linebackers coach for the Arizona Cardinals. She was also the first woman to play running back in a men's professional football league with the Texas Revolution. Following her time with the Cardinals, Welter became the head coach of the first Australian women's national team in 2017. Welter had a decorated fourteen-year career in women's professional football that included four World Championships, two gold medals as a member of Team USA in the 2010 and 2013, International Federation of American Football's (IFAF) Women's World Championship, and eight all-star selections. She was inducted into the first class of the Women's Football Hall of Fame in 2018.

WHAT TO 👀 FOR

- ➤ Focus on the areas you control, and don't waste energy on elements you have no power over.
- ➤ Define your overarching purpose and life goals, and then build small goals that get you there.

➤ Step up to challenges each day, even if there isn't an end-game in mind. It will manifest itself in time.

➤ If you are blazing a trail, there may not be rules or a path to follow. You're also not bound by what has always been.

➤ Mental state is not constant, and it is OK to have days when you feel down and unmotivated. Even superheroes have alter egos.

Dr. Jen Welter: You can't control everything. That's a premise in sports psychology. You must focus on the elements that are in your control. It's being able to get back to the moment and recover from distractions. I can't control the weather. It's wasted energy. I can't control what the other team does. If I'm just putting my energy towards them, then I'm not focused on what I must do at this moment to be the best. So, you're going to get beat on plays, especially on defense.

Same thing with a bad call from a referee. You can't control the calls that the ref makes. But a lot of athletes will lose the next three plays because they're still focused on that instead of the new play and what they must do right now to be successful.

As somebody with a master's degree in psychology and sports psychology, I was trained to talk about goal setting and breaking it down. Small goals build momentum toward ultimate goals. You may refine yourself. You may refocus. But there's a certain path.

For me, there wasn't because most of the things I've done had never been done, like playing on the US National Team. When I started playing, there was no US National Team. It wasn't even a dream we were permitted to have. If you can't have that dream, how do you make it happen? How do you work towards it when it's not this big, ultimate goal?

Success is stepping up to challenges each day and continuing to move forward to be the best, even if there's not an endgame in mind. It's about the process.

When I went to publish my book, the publishers said, "'Women in football' doesn't sell." It got turned down. I said, "What do you mean it doesn't sell? Pretty sure I was the first, so how many times have you tried?"

If you're trying to recreate a formula, you must follow somebody else's. If you're doing something from scratch and it hasn't been done, there's very little mentorship, but there are also very few rules. So, you're constantly thrust into a situation where you must be fast on your feet. It's unexpected, so people aren't used to you or how to handle you. You must diffuse that. That's when I use humor—but you also must be a creative problem solver because no one has written the rules for you. You must be willing to take the losses.

The goal every day is to keep getting better and more creative and finding a way through, so that you're clearing a path for other people to follow. I solve human puzzles. How can we connect the dots or reconfigure the dots so that there is a new perspective? We're not bound by what has always been.

Mark Schulman: Life is a series of nows. Most people talk about reinvention, but you were inventing as you went along. The importance of staying present and focused enabled you to break and form a new mold.

Dr. Welter: One of the defining moments for me was going against what I thought of myself and my role. When I played women's football, I believed that if I could be the best tackling machine, someday, people would say, "She could ball." And, by extension, they would see women playing football—if I could get one more sack or one more tackle, finally it would change things.

In 2013, my whole world flipped. I got my PhD. So, I was a football-playing doctor. I thought that having a PhD would allow me to take the practical experience I was getting as one of the best in the world and merge it with theoretical knowledge and become a unique value proposition to the sport. I could always add value because I walked in both worlds. I could be a translator and somebody who wasn't just one way or the other.

Then, I made the US National Team for the second time, and we won our second gold medal with Team USA. I remember thinking, it's been three years since our first gold medal when nobody knew we existed. But 2013 must be different; people have to care.

I shifted my mentality. Before that, I didn't want people to know what we were going through as women in the sport. I thought they would look at us differently. I didn't want people to judge us as being less valuable because we made less money. I kept that as a closely guarded secret because I was afraid that people would think our rings and the things we were doing were less valuable because we weren't making millions.

In 2013, I was just not okay with it, which was different for me. I was frustrated. How can this be, that we're defending gold medalists, and we must do car washes, sell T-shirts and fundraise to get people to believe that we have the right to play football?

We got an invitation to go to the White House after we won our second gold medal. It got changed to the White House Council on Women and Girls. We didn't get to meet the president because the government shut down. We all paid to go to Washington, D.C., for this experience. I wrote an epic three-part story about these women. We couldn't even get it published on ESPNW.

My team, the Dallas Diamonds, folded. We were in the championship. They could no longer afford to be on the field.

I got a call from the Texas Revolution, a men's indoor football league team. I had no idea why they wanted to meet with me. I ended up not only playing through training camp but being on the roster and becoming the first female to play an entire season in men's pro football as a non-kicker. It was stepping up to this challenge that I never intended to do that earned me respect.

Knowing your destiny and ability, you can't half step it. You can't second guess it or even think it out. There's really only one true choice. If I hadn't done it, I would not have had the same opportunities. Someone else would have had them.

Schulman: This is sheer unyielding, unrelenting desire to be who you are. You're a possibility creator.

Dr. Welter: The real power of being a first is that there can be a second. People see and think about it differently now that it's possible. It was physiologically impossible to run a mile under four minutes, until somebody did it. And then, what? It happened again and again and again.

But mental state is not constant. That's something we must realize. People ask, "How do you stay motivated?" There are reasons why superheroes have alter egos. There are days when Superman doesn't feel super. There are days when Wonder Woman trips herself up in the lasso of truth. Motivation isn't constant. The trick is that we take the times when we can really excel.

Some days you will jump tall buildings in a single bound. Some days you will run a marathon. Other days, the best you've got is shuffling in slippers. That day of shuffling in slippers is not a bad day. It's not a wasted day. It's a recovery day. Shuffling in slippers and allowing yourself to refocus or slow down or rethink is as much a part of excellence as going fast.

You can't go fast all the time, or you'll burn out. We must have a healthy understanding of what excellence is. Excellence is not quitting. Everything that I've done that really shook things up required me to fundamentally do what no one else was doing.

FOOD FOR THOUGHT

1. Study one trendsetter from history.
2. What attitude would you need to create a novel opportunity? Adopt this attitude, and give yourself the luxury of inventing a unique proposition.
3. Note one opportunity you can invent per day for a week. Pick one or two and take action.

CHAPTER 24

RESILIENCE

*Featuring **"Bronco" Billy Wright**,*
heavyweight boxer and author

"BRONCO" BILLY WRIGHT (BORN DECEMBER 10, 1964) is an American former professional boxer who fought in the Heavyweight division. Throughout his pro career he scored twenty-nine first-round knockouts. He was a sparring partner for George Forman in his championship fight with then undefeated heavyweight world champion Michael Moorer.

WHAT TO 👀 FOR

➤ Life isn't fair. Focus on your goals, keep showing up, work hard, and have a good attitude.
➤ You're not going to be perfect—but you can be your best. Every day.

Mark Schulman: I'm looking at your professional stats: forty-seven bouts, forty-three wins, thirty-seven Kos, and only four losses. You're one of the top performers in the world. How important has attitude been in the development of your career?

Billy Wright: With a good attitude and work ethic, you can get to anything. You can work your way out of any problem. You can accomplish anything you want to accomplish.

Schulman: Have you found that changing your attitude was necessary or helpful in the development of your career at any point?

Wright: I fought for thirty years. I had my first professional fight in 1986 and my last in 2016. Boxing is a slippery rock. If you don't sign with the right people, you'll never get a break. It doesn't matter who you knock out. It doesn't matter how many times you beat their stable of fighters. If you don't sign with them, they won't open the right door for you.

You think, "It doesn't matter what I do. It doesn't matter how hard I work or how in shape I am." You start beating yourself up. You start crashing.

I was on that rollercoaster when I was younger. I didn't fight for a couple of years because I was going to "show them." I'll take my toys and go home. But that didn't do anything. Boxing still happens. The sun still comes up. I'm the one sitting at home doing nothing. The world's progressing past me because I chose to be a baby and have a bad attitude. It took a lot of stumbles and falls throughout my career to realize, listen, keep showing up, have a good attitude, and work hard.

I won four World Boxing Council championships. I won every title they have except the world title because I couldn't get a shot. Who would want to fight a dangerous fifty-two-year-old fighter? If you lose to a fifty-two-year-old, your career is over. I'm just dangerous enough that nobody wanted to fight me. I put my hands on you, you're getting knocked out.

It's easy to get discouraged. My last comeback [was] from 2011 to 2016, and I worked so hard. But at the end of the day, I've been able to travel the world. I've been a champion everywhere, and it's all because of having a good attitude. So, I don't get a world title. That doesn't matter. I had a successful career—a career most people never get the opportunity to have. I changed my attitude, changed my focus, and enjoyed the success that I was having.

Schulman: Compared to other fighters in their primes in their twenties and thirties, you had the attitude of confidence in your fifties. What manifests that in you? What enabled you to feel like you could keep going and be a champion? Because that right there is a serious attitude shift.

Wright: As we get older, it is more difficult to do things than when we were younger. It means recovery time takes a little longer. You can still do whatever you want to do. It might take me four days to recover instead of one day, but my willingness and attitude keep me going. My last twenty-two wins were WBC title defenses with twenty-two consecutive knockouts.

Schulman: What do you do to keep yourself up? What are your specific methodologies or attitude shifts? Is there a ritual you do daily?

Wright: I'm disciplined. I don't drink. I don't smoke. I don't do drugs. That keeps me strong. I made the sacrifices necessary. If you're looking for pretty, I'm not the one. If you're looking for somebody to knock somebody out, I'm the one. I'm comfortable in my skin. Bodybuilders are too bulky and slow, so I had to keep my boxing steps: pop, pop, pop, pop. Making the moves.

I love who I am and who I've become in life. I came up rough, grew up in orphanages and foster homes. I had a bumpy life. Bad things came my way, and I haven't always handled them well. Learning from the mistakes of my youth, I've now embraced life. I'm not going to be perfect; I am going to do my best. I'm going to give you 100 percent every day.

Whatever happens, that's just how it is. You're going to get hit. You can't control that. So, just do your best in the moment. Prepare yourself. Know in your heart, mind and soul, you've made every sacrifice, and you've done everything you're supposed to do. I don't short anybody. I teach them. I'm not going to change who I am.

Schulman: That is the power of attitude. You can't control outcomes, but you can control your attitude. It's where you're looking from that determines what you see and what you perceive.

Wright: If you're up there drumming and your stick breaks, you can't control your stick breaking. Just grab another stick. That's how I live my life. People say, "I'm just going to hide here, be safe, and do just enough to live." I'd rather fail. I'd rather fall flat on my face running as fast as I can and doing my best than be safe.

Schulman: You talked about dropping a stick—that happens, and what's critical is to stay present. If you drop a stick or make a mistake, your mind might focus on that. Then, you're not performing the best you can because you're so busy worrying about the mistake. So, I stay present and stay of service—to P!nk, the musicians, the dancers, and the audience.

Food For Thought

1. What new discipline can you commit to daily?
2. Think of three recent negative outcomes an attitude shift could have changed.
3. What can you do today to love who you are with greater intensity?
4. What negative prejudice about yourself are you willing to let go?

SECTION 4

● ● ●

DRUMMERS

CHAPTER 25

KNOWLEDGE

*Featuring **Kenny Aronoff**, award-winning
drummer and bestselling author*

KENNY ARONOFF WATCHED The Beatles perform on *The Ed Sullivan Show* and asked his mom to call the band because he wanted to play with them. Fifty years later, he performed onstage with Sir Paul McCartney, Ringo Starr, and countless other professional musicians during the CBS Special *The Night That Changed America*. Before that lifetime achievement, Aronoff began his rock career touring and performing with John Mellencamp. After seventeen years, he embarked on his own and fulfilled a lifelong goal—becoming a sought-after session and touring drummer. He has played with The Rolling Stones, Lady Gaga, Bruno Mars, Sting, Bob Dylan, Bruce Springsteen, Bob Seger, Dave Grohl, Elton John, Johnny Cash, Willie Nelson, Jon Bon Jovi, Steven Tyler, The Smashing Pumpkins, Meatloaf, B.B. King, Rod Stewart, John Fogerty, and many other talented musicians and bands.

WHAT TO 👀 FOR

> ➤ If you don't have the skills you need now, learn them. Watch, follow, and listen to people who do. Sit this one out, and watch how it's done.

> ➤ Your value isn't necessarily in your individual work, but how that work plays into the work of others. Your value as a puzzle piece may be greater than your value without the rest of the puzzle.

Kenny Aronoff: I was drawn to drums because I'm a hyper-energetic guy. When you play the drums, it's a physical activity, and it releases endorphins, serotonin and dopamine, and that feels good. So, why not do it again and again and again? The same way I was drawn to sports, I was drawn to drums because of the energy, the passion, and the excitement. When I started playing, not only did it make me feel good, but I realized I was making other people feel good, too, which made me feel even better.

Mark Schulman: What is it about drummers that sets us apart? There's no closer group of musicians. We are a true community. We do clinics and trade licks. Why do you think that is?

Aronoff: Typically, there's only one drummer in a band, and we're in the back. We know what it's like to sit in that chair and drive a band and drive an audience. I want to be scoring touchdowns. I want to be scoring goals. I like to be the person who facilitates that kind of a result.

Why didn't we play bass? Because we have that energy, that excitement, that thrill-seeking feeling, and the drums are the instrument that suits us most.

I grew up in a little town of three thousand people in Western Massachusetts, and we had a Memorial Day parade every year. A marching band would come in on a big bus. My brother and I had these big fat tire bikes with baseball cards and clothespins, so you'd get a motor sound. When the drum line started their cadence, I went berserk. I was only in second grade. My brother and I just followed the marching, zigzagging around, probably getting too close.

Then, I'd go home, and I'd try to imitate the sound on anything, the floor, my knees. It was the energy and excitement of the instrument, the volume and the rhythm. Rhythm is also something that drew me to drumming. There're pictures and movies of me when I was in diapers, dancing to rhythmical music, with drums. You either love it or you don't, but I love it. I love rhythm and beats, time, and groove.

Schulman: You have a twin brother. Was he drawn to it?

Aronoff: Interesting. Because we're twins, we're identical. He's older by eight minutes, and he acts like it. When our mom taught us piano, I was the more rebellious one. I said, "Forget about the piano, I'm doing drums." My mom said, "No, you have to play piano." I took the piano music, threw it, and went running around the table. "Drums, drums, drums, drums, drums, drums." So, it was drums.

My brother stayed with the piano. He was good at it, too. He wasn't drawn to the drums.

Schulman: That confirms the drums chose us. I'll never forget a story that Mark Brown told me. He was cutting tracks with you and Melissa Etheridge in the studio. He said, "In between takes, Kenny was not hanging out with us. He was in the lounge making calls and booking his next gigs."

There are a couple of interesting things about you. One is your attitude—this incredible tenacity to work and keep yourself networked. And you communicate. You have no snobbery or judgment about people. Before I even knew you, I called you and ten minutes later, you called me back. Nobody calls or texts back in ten minutes! You have real love and concern for people. Is that a conscious attitude choice? I want to know what you've created consciously and what is just a part of your makeup.

Aronoff: That's my makeup. It's connecting and communicating so that we can collaborate. Literally, this was a four-week calendar I had. Monday, I was with B.B. King and Bonnie Raitt for *Air America*, Tuesday and Wednesday was a box set for Elton John, and Thursday through Sunday was a Bob Seger album. Then, I flew from Los Angeles to Athens, Georgia, for the Indigo Girls. I flew back, and I went right into a session with Willie Nelson. Then, I had four more days with Seger, and two weeks with Bon Jovi on *Blaze of Glory*.

Now, that is an example of a situation where you better have your communication skills together because each one of those bands is a corporation with a different producer, a different engineer, and a different record label. How can you play music if you can't communicate with somebody? But it wasn't an effort for me. It was natural. So, I'm fortunate.

Schulman: How do you shift your attitude when working with different artists? Do you pay attention and are you conscious of others and their sensitivities?

Aronoff: I'm getting better at that. I am a force of nature. I'm sure I freak some people out. I can tell that everyone's looking at me like Santa Claus just showed up. But at the same time, I pick up body language quickly. If I sense it's not working, I adjust to whomever I'm talking to.

I have three traits. I'm a hyper-achiever. I'm never satisfied. I need to keep achieving to feel good. I'm a stickler, which is a person who really looks at detail. And I'm a pleaser. These work well together for being in a band or being session drummer. I come in wanting to do great and wanting everybody to do great. I'm a stickler with detail, so I don't make as many mistakes. And I get along with all these different people. I've learned over the years how to adapt and adjust to different groups of people. You just have to be aware.

You can achieve the same goal with grace and positive energy as you can with negative energy and judgment. But you do better work when you do it from a positive place in your heart. That's what I've learned.

Schulman: Have you ever made an attitude shift and it turned a negative situation into a positive one?

Aronoff: My dream was to be in The Beatles, but there was no rule or method book or mentor to tell me how to do that. So, I studied classical music, and eventually got into the Jerusalem Symphony Orchestra. But I turned it down. My brain was saying, "You should do this," but my heart was saying, "I want to be in The Beatles."

I turned down certainty for complete uncertainty. And I spent four years trying to make it. I eventually moved back to Bloomington, Indiana, and formed my own band. I tried to get a record deal, make records and tour. It didn't happen.

So, I auditioned for Johnny Cougar, and I got in the band. Five weeks later, we were in LA working at Cherokee Studios. But my spidey sense was saying, "Something's not right." There was a lot of tension between me and John. At that point in his career, he could lose his record deal if he doesn't have a good hit. He wants ideas. He plays a song, it's up to me to come up with parts.

I didn't have that skill set yet. Who cares if I'd played with Leonard Bernstein or won a violin concerto? What does that have to do with getting songs on the radio to be number one?

John says to me, "You're not playing on the record." I was devastated, shamed, overwhelmed, afraid. My whole world was falling apart, and there's no way I had any skill set to deal with all the triggers that came from when I was younger. (By the way, it wasn't John's idea. I didn't know that until four years ago. It was the producer who wanted to replace me because he saw the tension. He wanted to get the record done in eight weeks.)

There were no pro-tools back then. You needed a drummer who could play a song from beginning to end, perfect time, feel, sound, parts—everything—and know how to be a great session player to adapt and adjust. I didn't have any of that experience. When John told me, "You're going home," I was stunned. He said, "I'll pay you for the rest of the week."

I said, "No way am I going home." That was me backed up against the wall.

The whole band was paralyzed, stunned. I said, "Listen, am I your drummer or what?" The band is grinning like, "Is it going to be a fist fight?" John said, "Well, yes, but you're not playing on the record."

Then, I'm scrambling. "Well, OK. I'm going to stay here, and I'm going to go watch these other session guys play my parts, and I'm going to learn from them." I'm off the cuff. "I'll benefit, and I'll get better. You'll benefit because I'm your drummer, right?" Silence. "I'll do it for free. I'll work for free. I'll sleep on the couch." He said, "Good."

I felt so embarrassed. I went every day, though, and I did learn. I took notes. The drummers were Rick Shlosser and Ed Greene. I watched, learned, and asked questions. I made adjustments with my drum set. I realized at that point, I had to look through a microscope, which was a different direction, but just as legitimate, and learn how to serve this guy's music. He's getting songs on the radio to be number one hits. I revamped my whole business model.

I went home, and said, "OK, what do I need to do to serve this guy's music?" Once again, no mentor, no rule book, no teacher. I started getting records—ACDC, The Stones, Creedence—bands I thought were comparable to John's style, and I vowed to be on the next record. That next record won two Grammys, with "Jack & Diane," John's biggest number one hit (and the hardest track I've ever made).

Schulman: I was one of your biggest fans. You created interesting and unique drum parts that were simple and complimented his music. You had this hot drum sound, too. So, you accomplished exactly what you wanted to accomplish, and your tenacity is admirable. Obviously, you made the right decision. But you were really sincere. "I am your drummer, so I'm going to learn. I'm going to stick around." That attitude is really gutsy, but that's part of who you are. It's part of your three personality analysis types.

Aronoff: It wasn't calculated. You're right. As soon as "Jack & Diane" became number one, he'd look to me every time—"What have you got?" That's why I kept coming up with beats.

Schulman: I remember a story you told about "Hurts So Good," where you played left-handed?

Aronoff: When he'd play a song, I'd think, "What am I going to come up with?" So, I'd been practicing left-handed to simplify my plan. I was a beginner, left-handed. Johnny goes, "Aronoff, what's that beat? Why haven't you played that beat before?" I'm thinking, "Well, I have for two years, but right-handed."

Compliments to him. He noticed it. So, I recorded left-handed at Cherokee Studios, where I'd gotten fired. They played it back, and I got it. My contribution was to be the piece that fits into the puzzle. It wasn't about me. I suddenly saw the value in what I was doing as a piece of the puzzle.

FOOD FOR THOUGHT

1. How can you become a better learner?
2. What extraordinary lessons are you missing by not leaning into new opportunities?
3. What brave steps can you take to learn from someone else?
4. What puzzles do you complete?

CHAPTER 26

JOY

*Featuring **Gregg Bissonette**, drummer,*
music legend, and educator

GREGG BISSONETTE IS a music legend, who has played drums for celebrated musicians, directors, and producers, including Duran Duran, Andrea Bocelli, Ray Charles, ELO, Don Henley, Santana, Robert Downey Jr., and many others. After a childhood of playing drums and trumpet, Bissonette became the drummer for the famed North Texas State Bissonette recorded *Eat 'Em and Smile* and *Skyscraper* with David Lee Roth and *Luke* and *Live in Osaka* with Steve Lukather. In 2001, he played with English rock band Spinal Tap. Bissonette also toured with Ringo Starr to promote *Ringo Rama*. Most recently, Bissonette has established his own school through Drum Channel, titled the Gregg Bissonette Drum School, for which he has been filming and preparing for the last decade.

WHAT TO 👀 FOR

> ➤ People want to work with positive people. Joy is infectious. Share it with others.
> ➤ Strive to make other people happy, and you will be happy too.
> ➤ Be the drummer of your organization; be its heartbeat.

Gregg Bissonette: Growing up in Detroit, my dad, Ringo Starr, and Buddy Rich were my drumming heroes, in that order. My dad played Italian weddings; Chaldean weddings; Jewish bar mitzvahs, bat mitzvahs, and weddings; Italian tarantellas. I watched my dad, and he was making people happy. He was bringing joy to people.

I like making people happy. Drums bring a lot of joy. I like being the guy that counts off the tunes and controls the dynamics. When you're bashing, they must turn it up a bit. When you're playing cross sticks off, they have to play soft, or they won't hear the time. You telegraph the sections. You're the musical director. People dance to the drums and that brings joy. I'm all about trying to bring joy into the world.

Mark Schulman: Talk about an attitude! You'll do anything to make people happy. If there's tension in a session, you're the guy who cracks a joke.

Bissonette: Our gift from God is drums and music, and the joy we bring—but it's also the humor. I have always been an optimist. When I was a kid, I got a scholarship to go to one of the greatest music camps in the world, Interlochen Arts Camp. It's an intense, two-week, summer music camp. I auditioned, and I got the scholarship from the Detroit Optimists. It's this club of people who are optimists.

If you're playing drums and you're making people happy, you're making yourself happy, because that's what I love. It's God, kids, family, friends, playing the drums with Ringo (my hero), and Dodgers baseball. If I'm not playing the drums, I'm watching the Dodgers.

Find the things that bring you joy.

Schulman: That is what we do. What do you believe sets drummers apart? What's the attitude of the drummer?

Bissonette: I keep going back to my hometown, Detroit. We made cars back then. People moved from all over the world to the motor city, Motown. We were the engine. Drummers are in the engine rooms, and they're putting it together. They're on the assembly line. We're shoveling the coal in there. We might not be upfront doing the guitar solo. We might not be on the mic. But man, we are the heartbeat. We pick the tempo.

Schulman: We're the shepherds of the band. We're the foundation. I'm a low maintenance guy. If everybody else is taken care of, I'm taken care of. If everybody around me is happy, I'm happy.

Bissonette: When I was a kid, I used to go with my dad on his bread route. He'd get up at 4:30 a.m., and he would sell bread to grocery stores, schools, mom-and-pop delis, and nursing homes. I would go with my dad into nursing homes.

He would bring light with his attitude and the nurses would say, "Hey, Bud, come talk to this patient. Is that your son, Bud? He looks like a little Bud." I'd be Little Bud. My dad's attitude was so positive. When he'd go to these grocery stores and delis, they'd say, "My son's having a bar mitzvah. I want your band to play." They didn't even need to hear his band. They trusted my dad because he had an amazing attitude and he loved them. People are people, all over the world, it doesn't matter who you are.

Look at Ringo's "Peace and Love." That is not an act. Ringo is at peace. It's not what happened yesterday or what's going to happen tomorrow. He's in the moment. There's faith, hope, and love, and the greatest of these is love.

Schulman: You must tell me about the chronology of getting to play with Ringo. How did that happen?

Bissonette: I picked up my landline. It was midnight. Mark Hudson, a dear friend, called. "Gregg, I'm doing a Steven Tyler album, and we need you on a song." I love Steven Tyler. I said, "I'll be there at ten in the morning." He said, "No, bro. We need you now." I said, "Now? It's midnight." He goes, "Yeah. We need you now. There's a drum machine on this song. Steven hates it. I just finished producing Ringo's new album. His drums are still set up. You can use them if you come down."

"I'll be right there."

Mark Hudson walked in the room. He said, "Man, I know you've been asking me to come hear your Beatles tribute band for the last couple of years. I'm sorry I haven't made it. I know you're a Ringo fanatic. I'm going to be on a Ringo and The Roundheads tour next month. If Ringo's staff is out with The Who, then you got the gig."

I said, "Like that? That easily?" He said, "Yeah. He'll trust me. I'll tell him that you go around the world doing seminars about how he's the greatest and how he inspired you to start a band."

The phone rang three days later. "You got the gig."

FOOD FOR THOUGHT

1. How can you ensure you are a positive person?
2. How can making others happier make you happier too?
3. How can you focus more on your organization's heartbeat?

CHAPTER 27

SERVICE

*Featuring **Dom Famularo**, drummer,*
educator, author, and consultant

DOM FAMULARO HAS traveled the globe preaching the gospel of drumming for more than forty years. An intense performer, Famularo is one of the most respected solo drum artists in the world, with a career built on his unique skills as a drummer, educator, author, and motivational speaker. He has directed and emceed major drumming expos around the world, and has been one of drumming's most sought-after private instructors. Students regularly fly from around the globe for intensive study with Famularo, who is currently teaching more than one thousand students from twenty-plus countries at his WizDOM Drumshed studio in New York. A major player in the percussion industry, Famularo acts as an education consultant for Sabian Cymbals, Vater Drum Sticks, Mapex Drums, Remo Drumheads, SE Microphones, and Wizdom Media, where he oversees programs worldwide.

In the wake of developing this book, Dom contracted pancreatic cancer which has virtually a 0 percent survival rate. Dom survived the unsurvivable. He just gave a speech at a music conference in LA. Study this man's attitude. He is truly remarkable.

WHAT TO 👀 FOR

- ➤ Live in service of others and reap great benefits.
- ➤ Your attitude ultimately impacts your words, actions, habits, character and, eventually, your destiny. Success starts with attitude.
- ➤ Stay present, you cannot change the past—but living in the moment can positively impact the future.
- ➤ Attitude is a tool you can use to increase positive outcomes, but a positive attitude requires discipline.
- ➤ Show others that you value them, and they will demonstrate the same. Share positive affirmations that help them feel empowered, heard, and relevant.

Dom Famularo: If you're constantly learning, then there's development and change. And development and change lead to a much healthier life.

Mark Schulman: You're expanding. There's a philosophy that you're either growing or dying. I always want to grow. Regardless of what I'm doing now, in a year, it's going to be better—who I am, who I can be for other people—because I want to be of value.

Famularo: It's not about me. It's about me improving myself so I can better serve. My parents were community-minded people who served. That was the example we grew up with. My brothers and sister are the same way. They're all positive, healthy, happy, and help others. I don't know what tomorrow brings, so I must be the best person I can.

Schulman: How important do you believe that attitude has been in developing your career?

Famularo: It has been the fundamental key to my success. As long as my attitude is positive, open, and healthy, it gives me the results I need—to help more people in the journey of life, for however long I have breath of air in me. Attitude is the power of choice, to discipline my thoughts and achieve results.

Watch your thoughts, for they become words. Watch your words, for they become actions. Watch your actions, for over time they become habits. Your habits become your character. Watch your character, for it becomes your destiny. Destiny is the result. So, if I want to have a better destiny, I must go back to the beginning, which is thought. How do I think of myself, and how do I want to act in the future?

Schulman: It's the foundation of being conscious and present. You are paying attention.

Famularo: It's important to pay attention and to live in the moment. I learned not to worry because I have no control over anything outside of my life. I have met people who were regretful. They were living in the past. I have met people who were anxious and worried about what was going to happen. They were living in the future. The process to find peace within myself was to be in the now. What is in the past and future, I have no control over, so I enjoy this moment.

Schulman: That's all we have. This moment. And the next moment and the next moment. It's a sequence; I call life a series of "nows."

Famularo: If we learn to tie those "nows" together, that becomes life—a healthy, positive life. My next book is called *Owning Now*, and it's about being able to live in that moment, find peace within, and understand the potential of this attitude. I see attitude as a tool I use in life that assists me.

I like doing work around my house, so I have three types of hammers: a little tack hammer, a framing hammer, and a sledgehammer. The reality of understanding how to use this tool of attitude is knowing where it will work. Would you use a tack hammer to break cement? It's going to take you much longer. It's not as effective, and you might even damage the tool. Would you use the sledgehammer to fix a picture frame? If it is the only device you have, you could use it, but you're really gonna struggle to get results, and you might not get the results you want. Attitude is a tool to use in the right place to achieve the best results, whatever results you're trying to achieve.

Attitude is a choice. A person who has a negative attitude all the time is a person making a bad choice. It's possible to have a positive attitude if you find the discipline. Discipline means self-control.

Schulman: That is an attitude choice—choosing to be disciplined. We make these moment-by-moment choices every day. What do I choose to do right now? Am I going to choose something that is of service to me and to others, or am I gonna choose to do something that's going to affect me and other people negatively? These really are choices and attitude shifts that you consciously make.

Famularo: There is a four-way learning process. There's unconscious incompetence—you get on the drums and you just play. You're not aware that you're not good. You're just having fun with it, so you really don't care. Then, you hear somebody better, and you become aware. You have conscious incompetence.

Schulman: And that hurts.

Famularo: Exactly. You're aware that it's not working. This happens with attitude too. Then, you move to the next level— conscious competence. You're aware of what you must work on, and that becomes the journey. You try to reach unconscious competence, where the skill base is a part of you. You're not even thinking about what you're doing. That applies to attitude at the highest level.

Schulman: My co-author, Dr. Jim Samuels, calls unconscious competence "super-conscious competence," because it's mastery. You have mastered that with your attitude. It's just your go-to.

Famularo: People are not aware that they are negative.

Schulman: That's dangerous.

Famularo: They're not even aware of it; it's just how they are. You hear it in the way they speak.

My wife says, "You teach people how to treat you." If someone is yelling at me and I respond to them, I'm letting them know that their yelling worked. If someone is yelling at me, I never respond until they bring their voice down. If their voice goes back up, I don't respond. I teach them how to speak to me in a healthy way.

Schulman: Have you found that changing your attitude was necessary or helpful in your development? Was there a point where you slipped or realized something wasn't working and you needed to try something different?

Famularo: When I was in high school, I started to become more acknowledged as a drummer and played with different bands. I was looking for the results of healthy relationships. When I had an open mind and I had a positive personality, I would listen to people and not just hear them. I started to understand compassion for others.

I started to go back and forth to see what worked. I would test it, and I started to see very clear results. Because I was around friends and people all day, I could see how they responded when I was complimentary, when I criticized, or when I was negative, and I would immediately see the results. I became conscious of trying different processes to see what was going to get me a better result.

After time, I leaned toward the success that I got when I had positive, listening, compassionate, open-minded conversations because it made people feel they had value.

Once I gave someone value—showed their life was valuable to me—they became closer to me. That's the opposite of what happens with a negative mentality. It devalues the other person. The more you devalue someone, the further they step away. It's the person who calls. You pick up the phone, you listen to their negativity, and after two minutes, you can't even interrupt them. You feel yourself getting upset. I began to really become conscious of people like that.

Being a stammerer when I was younger, I wanted to speak less and listen more. When I did speak, I spoke in short, concise words that could be arrows of positive direction. I could get a fast result by speaking less and stuttering less. So, that became a tool to use. Someone would say something, and I would say, "Fantastic."

Schulman: Which you still do. Classic Dom. "Fantastic."

Famularo: Or I'll say, "excellent" or "beautiful" or "amazing." I would say these gifts of positivity so someone could feel it, and it wouldn't interrupt them. It would complement them with a positive push to allow them to continue seeing more value in themselves. From that, I developed deeper relationships, and with deeper relationships came a higher quality of life.

Sometimes our greatest challenge can be our greatest asset. I had to turn this around because I couldn't survive. People made fun of me. They played a game, Two Syllables, guessing what I was saying. It frustrated me, which made me stammer more. So, I had to pull back and find out what skills I could learn. How can I survive and still try to make myself feel good?

You must learn to trust your instincts. Because if you trust your instincts, you're good. This is why I don't plan my lectures or speeches. Before each lecture and speech, whether it's a drumming or a motivational event, I walk out and I meet people. I shake their hands, I ask questions, and I get a feel for who's in the audience. I'm doing research that first hour, inside the audience, before I go out there and deliver my message. I see how they laugh, how they listen, how they feel, who they are. I have a better chance of reaching them faster on stage than if I'm using that time to find out who they are.

Schulman: That's an attitude you've adopted of compassion and empathy. But can you tell me a story where attitude was a critical factor in a failure for you?

Famularo: There was a time in my research of who I really wanted to be that I started to see myself as a victim. When you see yourself as a victim, then everyone's against you. And you feel sorry for yourself. It failed. Every time people came to me with, "I'm so sorry. I feel for you. I know that was tough." That wasn't a fun reaction from people.

I wanted to meet other musicians and play with them, but I was not connecting with them because they are extremely sensitive people. They felt that victim mentality and didn't want to be around it. There were top musicians who I wanted to play with, but because of my attitude, they didn't allow me to meet them. I witnessed this failed process—thoughts turned into words, words into action, action into habits, habits into character, and my destiny was failing me.

I finally sat down and went through a re-evaluation stage. I changed, a "180 and let me see." If it doesn't work and I'm getting the same results, then I'm just gonna book it and do what

I'm doing. So, I began to change, and I saw immediate, obvious results. Suddenly, people started moving toward me. They liked what they were hearing from me. I met more people. I developed more opportunities.

I started playing in more bands. I started meeting more musicians. I started connecting with more teachers that had more they could offer me. This circle that I created began to grow. That began the journey, and that's why every day I start with me. How is this day gonna go? Am I in control of this day?

FOOD FOR THOUGHT

1. How can you better serve others?
2. Consider your attitude right now. Name it.
3. How can you improve your attitude to get more out of what you are doing?
4. Discipline is an action. How can you better discipline your attitude to your advantage?
5. How can you raise the tone and tempo of those around you?

CHAPTER 28

INTENTION

*Featuring **Hannah Ford-Welton**, musician, vocalist, drummer, and Christian minister*

HANNAH FORD-WELTON BROUGHT a dynamic, multi-faceted history as a world class drummer to her role as the rhythmic backbone of Prince's 3RDEYEGIRL, the artist's explosive four-piece rock band. Formerly the drummer and vocalist of Chicago-based rock trio The Hannah Ford Band, Milwaukee-based crossover Christian band Bellevue Suite and her one-woman *Peace Love & Drums* multi-media show, Ford-Welton's versatile performance history covers all styles of music, from pop and rock to jazz. Launching her professional career at age twelve by joining a blues band with her trumpet-playing father in the Windy City, she is the only female to win the Louis Bellson Heritage Days Drums Competition (2006) among other prestigious accolades, awards, and best-of lists.

WHAT TO ◉◉ FOR

➢ Positive intentions and attitudes together lead to positive outcomes.
➢ Find a greater purpose for your work—whether that is through a higher power or a philosophy of service to others.

> Lean into your skills and talents and practice them. Don't skate on what you have, grow into something even better by continuing your development.

Hannah Ford-Welton: We have so much power in what we choose to believe. As a female in a predominantly male industry—and even in just understanding my studies, faith, conviction, and mentality—belief is huge. And our behaviors follow our beliefs. Attitude is foundational to how we communicate with and see others, how we talk, how we interact, and even in our personal decisions.

We may have good intentions, but if we have negative belief systems or attitudes, we can unintentionally end up in the wrong place and lead our families to the wrong place. Good intentions but bad belief systems can also lead us somewhere we don't want to go.

Mark Schulman: When you decide, you cut off all other possibilities, which gives you enormous power. Making that decision is an attitude shift based on the choice you made. I want to get the chronology right. What was the first band you were in?

Ford-Welton: Technically, the first band I was in would have been when I was seven and first started drumming. But more so than a band, it was a percussion ensemble. Currently, it's known as the Louisville (Kentucky) Leopard Percussionists. When I was in the group, it was confined to the kids who went to my elementary school, and it was known as the Fabulous Leopard Percussionists.

[Diane] Downs founded the group in the early '90s when she happened to find some percussion instruments in her school classroom. She decided to dive in and learn these instruments with her students. Years forward, she's built a massive percussion ensemble. If you were in her class, you automatically learned how to play.

You finished your reading lesson or assignments, and you would go learn drums. So, the first instrument I learned was marimba.

If you wanted to audition to join the group officially, you could—and I did. That's where it started for me. We would travel all around Kentucky. I got my first taste of being a working musician, so to speak, as a seven-year-old girl with a group of kids who learned how to play by ear with our instructor. We put on records, songs like "Don't You Worry 'Bout a Thing" by Stevie Wonder, and she would assign parts.

I didn't realize at the time that I was getting intense ear training, and I didn't learn how to read music until much later. It was in high school when I started getting serious about it. But I'm so grateful for how it started. It was just so much fun.

Schulman: Discipline is a very definitive attitude, especially if you want to reach the level of success that you've reached. Was there a point when you realized that you needed to have an attitude of discipline?

Ford-Welton: At the age of twelve, I moved to Chicago with my dad and my little brother. We started gigging with a blues band around the city of Chicago, little me on drums, my dad playing trumpet, and these other dads. I had no business being in bars, but it was such a cool experience.

I never left my dad's side, and I was always protected, but also exposed to things early on. My dad would teach me what to do in different scenarios. You're in control over the decisions you make. "See the decision someone's making here. What is the snowball effect of every consequence after that? Do you want that for your life or don't you? If you don't, then don't make the decision."

Schulman: Attitude, behavior, consequence.

Ford-Welton: In high school, I began to think, "Do I go to college? Do I audition? Do I just go out to Los Angeles, try to get sessions, and grind, work hard, and network? What do I want to do with my life?" I was at that crossroads. My dad would tell me, "You're not going to be the cute, little twelve-year-old behind a drum set your whole life. That's not always going to work for you. At some point, you're going to have to really be able to deliver."

He wasn't saying that to scare me. He's always been honest and encouraged me to practice. Because, like any other high schooler, I wanted to go to the movies with girlfriends and have boyfriends.

I had to sacrifice those fun decisions to go to band rehearsal, gig, and practice my drum set. Sometimes, I would get really upset, but this is what I knew I was called to do. Most high school kids don't know what they were put on Earth to do yet. I had that advantage at an early age, so I had to isolate my thinking—to not just live life, have fun, and be carefree. I had to make the decision to be disciplined.

Schulman: Share about your work with Prince, one of the most influential artists in history. I would love to learn about your attitude, his attitude, how it worked, and when it didn't. What can you relate to the concept of attitudes?

Ford-Welton: I had my own band for a while and met my husband. We got married in 2011. We had some friends in Atlanta, Georgia, who kept saying, "Come stay with us. Don't worry about rent—you are newlyweds. Focus on your careers. We want to support you." So, we moved to Atlanta to do just that. We also got plugged into a church there, where we served the teen ministry, playing music for praise, worship, and drama.

Then, I got a really cryptic email that read, "Hey, I work for a well-known musician who came across some of your YouTube videos, and he wants you to audition for a project. But first, I need to know if you can keep a secret."

What kind of message is that? Honestly, I would brush off these types of messages because they include zero information. It's creepy, with social media and all. I wrote back, "Hey, I'm glad you're into my stuff. I'm super honored. But before I commit to anything, I need to know a little bit more about who this person is and what they're looking for."

They wrote back the next day—we were at church—and it was Prince. He said that before he ever saw me play, he wanted to meet and get to know me based on a video of me speaking.

I never asked him about it, but I believe it was the time that I was on the Drum Channel with Terry Bozzio. Prince was huge on female empowerment. I think he probably heard the snippet about me talking about the grind that I went through in high school being on the drum line as one of the only females—and the only female on the snare line.

When it came to working with Prince, attitude was everything. It was about more than the music; my husband and I specifically wanted to make sure that Prince knew he had people in his life who genuinely loved him, not because he was Prince the artist, icon, or greatest musician ever. It was a blessing—a legendary gig that I did not take lightly—but it was about more than that for us.

What a lot of people see on TV and in performances is just a small part of what really goes into that time in your life. It wasn't easy. It wasn't always rainbows and roses. We played the Hollywood Emporium, and that was the longest show Prince ever played from start to finish. I was on drums. It was a big band—the NPG and 3RDEYEGIRL, the horns and background singers—there was a drum solo when everyone else would leave the stage, and I stayed and delivered.

Before the encore—I didn't even know how much longer there was—my hands were so blistered my tech just kept taping tape and I just kept playing through it. You have those moments where it's so fun but so intense and emotional from learning so many parts to the pressure of that seat for that gig.

Your attitude is so important when you're carrying that mantle. It was a high-pressure job, but God kept us going. He preserved my heart, mentality, and attitude, and I kept on. This was not just about music. It wasn't about me at all. This was about relationships and personal impact. We got extremely close with Prince, and it was about more than the music for him as well.

Schulman: It's an attitude of service. When I'm on stage with P!nk, I'm there to be of service to P!nk, the band, the dancers, the singers, the road crew, the audience—everybody.

Ford-Welton: The drums are not about you. The drummer literally holds the foundation and makes it comfortable for the other musicians, singers, and performers. You hold that back beat, you sit in that pocket, you keep that rhythm. It's service. My entire life, no matter what season I'm in or what my focus is on, has revolved around servitude—whether it was drums, motherhood, a wife, a minister, or a pastor.

Schulman: Was there ever a point when you had an attitude of failure, one that didn't serve you and didn't serve others?

Ford-Welton: I had to buckle down in high school and have that attitude adjustment. Playing drums has always come naturally to me. For a while, I took advantage of that and didn't practice. I've always been a performer. I've always been a people-person. I like to entertain. I did not enjoy practicing because I was by myself doing something that I had to break apart and take my time on.

It wasn't the same exhilarating feeling as being on stage. So, for a while, it was easy for me to ride the natural gift and not have that discipline—until a time came when it wasn't easy. There were moments where I could feel myself physically needing to enhance my technique and get better.

Then, there was another attitude adjustment about life. "Why am I here? I don't need to go to school to learn how to perform. I already know how to do that." It was just such an immature, arrogant way of thinking that I didn't realize at the time. I was a young kid with eyes on the prize, wanting to just play and perform, and slacking in school.

My dad was straightforward and helped me realize that I didn't want my love and passion for music and performance to be the reason that I failed at something else. I never wanted it to be a crutch that caused me to not succeed in another area of my life. Don't let it be an excuse. Make it a reason and motivation.

Schulman: Regardless of career path or occupation, what advice do you give to individuals as they seek to create better consequences for themselves and those around them?

Ford-Welton: Whatever you want to do with your life, it's got to be bigger than you. What do you want to leave behind? What are you leaving behind for the future leaders of the world? At this moment in history, there's something in you that other people need. And when they get that, it's going to birth something in them that shows them that there's something in them that other people need. And it's a perpetual cycle of giving rather than taking.

If your foundation is firm and rooted in something that's bigger than you, it's going to keep you anchored and knowing and focused on the goal.

FOOD FOR THOUGHT

1. Give an example of how your beliefs shaped your attitude to serve you.
2. Give an example of how your beliefs shaped your attitude and did not serve you.
3. How can your spiritual beliefs shape your attitudes?
4. How can your current attitudes define and improve your legacy?
5. Can you take your natural gifts and use them as anchors to improve your attitude in other areas of your life?

CHAPTER 29

LOGIC

*Featuring **Thomas Lang**, super drummer,*
clinician, composer, writer, and producer

THOMAS LANG IS a native of Vienna, Austria, and took up drumming at the age of five. In addition to lessons at local music schools and years of private tuition, he attended the Vienna Conservatory of Music. He has worked with dozens of artists including Robbie Williams, Kelly Clarkson, Sugababes, several Spice Girls, Nina Hagen, Steve Jones, Mick Jones (The Clash), George Michael, and many more. His 1995 solo release, *Mediator*, topped the charts in Europe and garnered rave reviews for its innovative Jazz/Dance/ Prog Rock sound. Lang has been voted "The World's Greatest Drummer" by *Rhythm Magazine* and "Best 25 Drummers of All Time," winning awards and accolades from critics and peers for more than three decades.

WHAT TO 👀 FOR

➢ Teach others what you know for an even greater understanding of that knowledge, skill set, or ability.
➢ Create a scale for career-related decisions. Decide what the non-negotiables are for you and use them as a lens for saying yes or declining opportunities, when necessary.

Thomas Lang: When I was four years old, I saw a drummer on television. I was intrigued by the fact that he was the only one sitting down in the band. It seemed like he was privileged to be allowed to sit while everybody else had to stand. Then, he counted off the tune, started with a big drum fill and the band arrived. He was commanding and conducting.

And even as a four year old, that intrigued me. The drummer was a leader. He was the engine, the motor, and the conductor. A week later, my parents took me to a local fairground, and there was a band playing. I walked onto the band stand (while the band was playing) toward the drum kit. I held onto the kick drum from the front while the guy was playing. That moment infected me with the drum bug. I remember feeling the power, the air movement, and the thud on my chest—looking up at the symbols moving and the shiny chrome, his leg was moving and arms flailing.

It isn't just banging and bashing on drums and cymbals. There is coordination, dance, and choreography. There are cerebral and physical elements, the brains and the brawn. I play other instruments as well, but I never got such a kick out of playing any other instrument. Drums combine all my favorite elements and components and an intellectual and physical challenge. It's primal, yet sophisticated.

Mark Schulman: It seems like the older you get, the more you do, the more you expand, and the more excited you become. I can't tell you how much gratitude I have for what you do for the drumming community because we need people to propel us forward. Every time you post drumming videos, it gobsmacks me because you've taken it to another level. That attitude is so motivating for the rest of us. Where does it come from? What drives you?

Lang: I differentiate among playing, working, and teaching. For me, teaching equals learning, and that's why I like it. I like to share because every time I explain something to somebody else, I gain a deeper understanding of what I'm doing. And by repeatedly explaining myself—how I got to a certain point or what my goals are or how I want to achieve them—I get a clearer vision of how to do that and how to tweak my own learning to teach someone else.

If I can tweak enough people's learning and support it, then it becomes easier for me to learn. And I discover easier ways by explaining what I did to other people. Sometimes when you're teaching, you underplay certain things and exaggerate others to make it appeal more to the student and to get a point across. By analyzing why I do that in my lessons, I learn a lot about myself, my own habits, and the dark areas in my skill and in my methods of learning. So, teaching equals learning as well. That's why I like it. And at the same time, you get feedback from people that I find extremely motivating.

I enjoy being in a room full of people who genuinely love the same thing I do, who are completely like-minded and just as motivated as I am. Maybe they aren't at the same level of playing, but it's not about that. It's about the group dynamic and the energy. I find that inspiring. I walk away from every camp or teaching situation feeling inspired to learn more and to tweak my own playing and approach to teaching. Every time I teach a camp or a class, I feel like I just took a lesson myself.

Schulman: Did you make a conscious shift with your work at any time? You're an extreme drummer, you have bootcamps, you're a soloist and a champion for the drumming cause, you still do a lot of sessions—but you were also a successful touring musician.

Lang: When we had our children, I scaled down the amount of touring deliberately because I didn't want to be away from home for that long and I used to be on tour for eighteen months at a time. I focused more on things that I had control over. I didn't want to depend on other people's calendars and diaries anymore. I started organizing a lot of educational events, my own online schools, instructional products, and method books. That allowed me to be a lot more flexible in regard to my schedule and only do tours that I really wanted to do with people that I really enjoyed hanging out with.

There are three factors in my decision-making for touring: How much money is it? Do I love the people? And what kind of music is it? Two out of three is good no matter what. There was a shift from being a busy touring and recording drummer to being independent and able to schedule my own life in a more efficient and comfortable way. I spend more time with my family and am also more selective about the type of work I do.

Schulman: It all begins with your attitude about who you are and what you want to create. That generates behavior and consequences. Tell me about your greatest playing experience. What sticks out to you from a drumming perspective?

Lang: I remember being a young teenager and practicing in my parents' basement for hours and hours. I remember sitting down when it was light outside after school and just going nuts because I knew my parents weren't home and I had the house to myself. I remember snapping out of it at ten at night. I was completely soaked. I had blisters on my hands. My ears were ringing. It was this transcendent experience. I remember lying in bed that night like I had just traveled the universe. I felt physically exhausted yet satisfied. I felt mentally inspired, like I'd achieved something special and been to a special place. And it just felt amazing. From that moment on, I have tried to recreate that trance every time I sit down to play or practice. It became really addictive to me to experience that state of mind.

I have had many extremely memorable drumming experiences with artists on tours in huge stadiums where everybody's dancing and singing and I was the only one playing. "Break down. Drums only." Everybody sings the chorus and it's just you and a stadium of seventy thousand people. I've had many wonderful drumming experiences being a quiet leader in the band, being the driving force behind the machine in a humble and serving way, being reliable and able to turn on the energy for a whole stadium when necessary.

And then I have other fond drumming memories that are all about achievements—working on something daily for nine months, something difficult to play with physical or intellectual challenges and complex layers of rhythms and polymetric structures. Reaching that goal and transitioning to a higher level of playing is a real achievement.

FOOD FOR THOUGHT

1. How can teaching a skill improve that skill for you?
2. How can teaching specific knowledge sharpen that knowledge for you?
3. Define, in writing, your personal desires and requirements for engagement.
4. Which of your opportunities are in accord with those requirements?
5. Fully commit to those opportunities.

CHAPTER 30

IMPROVISATION

*Featuring **Stanton Moore**, Grammy Award-winning drummer, author, musician, and instructor*

STANTON MOORE IS a drummer, performer, and educator especially connected to the city of New Orleans and its culture and collaborative spirit. In the early '90s, Moore helped found funk band Galactic, which continues to amass a worldwide audience. Moore launched his solo career in 1998. He has nine records under his own name, the most current being *With You In Mind: The Songs of Allen Toussaint*. Throughout his twenty-five year career, Moore has played and recorded with a diverse group of artists including Maceo Parker, Joss Stone, Irma Thomas, Leo Nocentelli and George Porter (The Meters), Tom Morello (Rage Against the Machine), Corrosion of Conformity, Donald Harrison Jr., Nicholas Payton, Trombone Shorty, Skerik, Charlie Hunter, Robert Walter, Will Bernard, Ivan Neville, Anders Osborne, and the Preservation Hall Jazz Band. He has also appeared numerous times on late night television shows, including Jimmy Kimmel, Conan O'Brien, and Seth Meyers.

WHAT TO 👀 FOR

➤ Regardless of what you do, your role or job, be a joy provider.

➤ Improvise with the tools and equipment you have on hand so that you are ready when the time is right to move to the next level.

➤ Realize the consequences of how you react in situations when you have been let down or hurt, and think about how you can amend your reactions to lead to less negative results. Consider other perspectives and other causes of the behavior of others.

Mark Schulman: You have a unique attitude when you're playing that is unrivaled. The way you navigate rhythms is really special. Nobody else does what you do. I'm trying to figure out the unique attitude of drummers. What makes us different or unique?

Stanton Moore: I started being affected by drums at the age of three or four, when my mom and dad brought me to Mardi Gras parades, and I witnessed the power of the drums in the marching bands. I started going home and hitting on stuff. I kept asking about it, kept hitting on pots and pans. Eventually they said, "If you still want this next year, you can join the elementary school marching band."

It started with piano lessons in second grade. In fifth grade, I could start playing a snare drum. They made me work, or at least *want*, for it.

I knew from a young age that I wanted to play drums. It impacted me, and I aim to impact others that same way. I want to make other people feel what I felt when I was a kid—a sense of joy.

So, sometimes when I'm talking to people who don't know who I am or what I do, I say, "I'm a joy provider." I play drums, but I try to provide and propel joy to people.

Schulman: You are truly unique when it comes to playing drums. We all have our own styles and expressions, but you really have configured this drum set that's totally unique. You come up with wild sounds and bits of percussion to put on your kit. How did you formulate that attitude? Where did that come from?

Moore: That came from wanting to be unique. I did seek to have my own voice. Jazz drummer Johnny Vidacovich would show me a simple sticking. At the time, I couldn't afford cow bells or Mini Timbales (those didn't exist at the time) or pandeiros. So, I would set up frying pans, mixing bowls, and Pyrex dishes and put them on TV trays. Once I could afford or acquire different percussion instruments, I already had stickings and patterns worked out. And I felt comfortable. I would just improvise with simple ideas, and then try them out on different elements.

I had this can-do attitude. If I don't have the instruments right now, but I can figure things out on pots, Pyrex dishes, and frying pans, then when I get to real instruments, it's going to sound pretty cool.

I wanted to sound like a drum-set player, mixed with Mardi Gras Indians with a tinge of second line and marching bands. I could hear all that, but it didn't sound like what I wanted it to sound like yet. I knew once I could start switching things out, I could get to that. I could get to the sounds I was hearing in my head.

Schulman: You're like a little kid sitting with pots and pans, but you're a professional. Now you can communicate and teach. And you won't stop coming up with creative ideas. What is your greatest experience playing drums?

Moore: The first time I ever heard drummer Russell Batiste is the closest thing I've had to a religious experience. I was seventeen years old, and I went to see him outdoors on the quad at Tulane University, playing with George Porter Jr. I've got my shirt off, I've got long hair, I think I'm cool. I started getting closer and closer and more and more excited.

He was six-pack ripped, wearing no shirt and purple MC Hammer pants. As I got up closer, I literally started jumping up and down. I couldn't control it. It was like seeing the drummer Zigaboo mixed with Dennis Chambers mixed with punk rock energy. It was the most raw, funky, energetic thing. Russell has a way of demanding sound out of the drums. I had no idea how he was getting that sound.

I'm a pretty shy guy. I like to be introduced. I don't just go up to people and start talking, but I lost control of myself. I went up to him and said, "That was the greatest thing I've ever seen. I want to study with you. I want to follow you around."

He said, "Man, I don't know anything about lessons, but we can hang out." And we did. I started carrying his drums around for him, driving him around town, showing up and sound checking for him. Eventually, I started showing up and sitting in on rehearsals and some of his other gigs. I filled in for him for three gigs with George Porter Jr., and I realized I wasn't ready yet.

It was an unbelievable experience for me. I still think he's one of the greatest drummers of all time. That was just one of those moments when I was overcome with joy, happiness, and excitement about drumming.

Schulman: In your life, have you ever had any situations where you had a negative attitude that you consciously needed to readjust, or as a result of that negative attitude, something negative happened and it was a learning moment for you?

Moore: There have been times when somebody who's supposed to be there on the side of the stage is not there or is looking at their phone. And I get upset, because I'm giving 1,000 percent and I need help. All I'm asking is that you give 100 percent. There have been times when I got upset. And I realized that's not helping anybody. I can't let that happen. I've had to get better at that and adjust my behavior and my attitude when things happen that are not within my control.

I wind up bumming out the band and the person I'm upset with, and that is something I've had to work at getting better at. That's something personal to me.

Schulman: Have you ever had a shift in the middle of it, like you were getting mad and you made a conscious effort to shift your attitude to chill out?

Moore: Yes. I try to take it in stride and laugh it off. But what can we do? There are times when there are people on your team who you might feel are not giving as much as you are at that moment, but you don't always know what they're dealing with. You don't know why they're not giving their all.

You can control your behavior. So, don't respond. Don't react in a negative way. Figure out what's going on and try to handle it. React in a more constructive, less destructive way. Understand the full scope of what's actually happened from all the angles and perspectives, not just your own.

FOOD FOR THOUGHT

1. What opportunity to provide joy are you missing or ignoring?
2. What joy can you generate and include for no reason at all?
3. How can a positive attitude accelerate your learning?
4. How can you turn a destructive impulse into a constructive action?
5. What help can you offer a teammate who is underperforming?

CHAPTER 31

ADVENTURE

*Featuring **Nate Morton**, drummer for*
The Voice *and studio and touring musician*

NATE MORTON HAS self-taught drumming from age five, but his formal drum set training began during high school. He continued his education in Boston, Massachusetts, as a performance major at the renowned Berklee College of Music. He moved to Los Angeles in 1999, where he has amassed live performance and recording credits that include Paul Anka, Michael Bolton, Natalie Cole, Miley Cyrus, Madonna, Richard Marx, Pete Murray, P!nk, Paulina Rubio, Paul Stanley, and Thalía among others. Morton was also the hard-hitting force, driving the house band on several Mark Burnett shows including *Rock Star: INXS* and *Rock Star: Supernova*. He cites Animal from *The Muppet Show* as his first and biggest influence. Now, he grooves during prime time on the NBC hit show *The Voice*.

WHAT TO 👀 FOR

> ➤ Break stuff (in a positive way). Put that amount of energy into the universe.
> ➤ Whether you are the first one in or the last to leave, enjoy the role you play in any successful adventure.

> ➤ Use people who say "don't" or "you can't" as motivation to prove that you will and you can.
> ➤ Change your mindset from "have to" to "get to." Reflect on how fortunate you are in any given situation.

Nate Morton: When I was four years old, like many four year olds, the most fun thing in the world was to pull out all the pots and pans and bang on them with salad spoons. And that never became unfun. So, I'm still just a four year old banging on pots and pans with salad spoons.

Drums spoke to me. My father would take me to hear bands periodically, primarily jazz fusion or pop jazz like Spyro Gyra or George Howard. A thread in that medium grabbed my ear. It was different. I also felt like drums were kinetic. I like to move. I like to put out a lot of energy. Drums were an avenue at a very early age for me to get that out.

My friend Irv Madden, who's a bass player, used to call me to play gigs when I was in high school. He was a grown man, and he always said to me, "Every drummer is the same person. They're that person who would be breaking something if they weren't playing drums."

So, that's it. I get to break stuff. I get to put energy into playing drums.

Mark Schulman: What makes drummers unique? What makes our attitudes different from other musicians?

Morton: How many drummer jokes are there? There's a certain shared experience, and it's not a competitive one. We had to get to the gig two hours before everybody else because we had to set up all our stuff. We were at the gig an hour and a half after everybody else because we were still breaking down our stuff.

We thrive on sharing. I've known guitar players who will cover their rigs with a towel so no one can see their settings or take acetone and rub the numbers off their pedals. Drummers by nature are the opposite. "Hey, Mark, what's that cymbal on your right-hand side?" "Oh, man. That's my eighteen-inch cymbal. Sounds like this. Check it out. Oh, I've got this lick, it goes like this off the cymbal." Cut to an hour later, you're having an impromptu drum clinic.

Schulman: We play the most fun instrument.

Morton: We play the most eye-catching instrument, the most aesthetically noticeable instrument.

Schulman: You're a very successful, highly acclaimed player, and you literally have the coolest gig in the entire world. You're the drummer of *The Voice*. Have you made conscious efforts to shift your attitude at any point to achieve a more positive result?

Morton: A lot of my positivity and forward motion and drive have been inspired by all the times I was told I would fail. Not a lot of people say, "Yeah, that's a super practical thing you're going for, being a professional musician. You got that one in the bag." No. It's usually, "Oh, you're going to be a drummer? How are you going to make money?"

That inspired me. I don't know if that made for a positive attitude, but it could've gone either way. For example, I had an instructor once tell me, "I'm going to give you the advice that I give all of my students thinking of being a professional musician. Don't." It was their tough love. However, if "don't" motivates me to prove them wrong, then it works out for me in the end. It's like the coach who says, "You'll never be good enough to play in this league." What do you do? You either say, "Yeah, you're right" and quit or you work your butt off to prove them wrong.

I've always been able to step back and think about how fortunate I am. There were definitely hard times, but there's also a certain liberation in feeling like you don't have a choice. I never felt like being a drummer was something I chose to do. It wasn't up to me. That can be very liberating.

My college friend Tom Witt said to me, "You know, Nate, if you ever start to second guess your choices, just take comfort in knowing that there's no turning back at this point."

Schulman: Making a choice is a very powerful attitude shift. Because when you make a choice, you cut off other possibilities. It gives you an enormous amount of power because you are focused and committed. My first book was about the three Cs—clarity, capability, and confidence. You have clarity about what you want to do, so the choice is clear. But if you don't develop capability, then false confidence can put you in a very negative position. So, you worked hard.

Morton: The "I get to" point of reference is extremely important. I get to do this. That's what drives my positivity. I constantly remind myself how fortunate I am to get to do what I do.

Schulman: That awareness is such an extraordinary motivator. *The Voice* has a grueling schedule. You might record thirty-two songs in a day. If you approach it like you get to, that keeps you remembering what an extraordinary accomplishment it is. Because there are only a handful of people on the planet who could do it.

Morton: It's a muscle that you build.

Schulman: Was there ever a negative attitude that you needed to shift because you were creating negative results and you consciously made a change?

Morton: When I was in college, I was a pretty good player. I wasn't great; I was pretty good. But I had this attitude like I was awesome. My friend Jeff Gallegos, who was like a big brother to me, pulled me aside one day and he said, "Hey, look, man, you're a really good player. You have some skills, but there are people who won't call you because you're too cocky."

If an authority figure tells you that, like a parent, teacher, or administrator, you might say, "Nah, you don't know what you're talking about." If your peer tells you that, you listen. That was a turning point because it was something I didn't realize. As I progress in life, it is my great hope to continually become more and more self-aware and understanding. Understanding why I see and do things certain ways, why I project certain things. Nineteen may not be the peak of one's self-awareness. That was the point when I actively changed my attitude.

FOOD FOR THOUGHT

1. How can you improve your performance by "breaking stuff"?
2. How can you improve your life by driving more joy into it?
3. What "can't" in your life needs to be proven as a "can"?
4. Think of something you have to do. How can you generate a "get to" attitude?
5. How can you better appreciate how fortunate you are?

CHAPTER 32

ENTHUSIASM

*Featuring **Rich Redmond**, versatile drummer,*
author, producer, and songwriter

RICH REDMOND HAS been the touring/recording drummer with multi-platinum country rocker Jason Aldean for nearly two decades. He has recorded twenty-six No. 1 radio hits and plays to millions of fans per year in iconic venues across the globe. Redmond has also worked with artists such as Kelly Clarkson, Ludacris, Bryan Adams, Bob Seger, Chris Cornell, Miranda Lambert, Eric Church, Keith Urban, Luke Bryan, and many more. He is a busy keynote speaker, producer, songwriter, label owner, educator, and actor. He is also the author of the book *CRASH! Course for Success: 5 Ways to Supercharge Your Personal and Professional Life.*

WHAT TO ◉)◉) FOR

➢ Keep it simple. Not everything needs to be complex. Focus on getting the job done and the message across, and play it up when that makes sense.

➢ Enthusiasm is contagious. Use it to create a positive environment in which everyone is motivated to create successful outcomes.

> ➤ When someone gifts you an opportunity, thank them by overperforming and excelling.
> ➤ Analyze your failures. What went wrong and why? Can the why be mitigated or avoided, and will the outcome be different next time?
> ➤ Start your day by thinking about all of the things you are grateful for to set a tone of positivity and joy.
> ➤ Take care of yourself, or you won't be able to help others.

Rich Redmond: The drums found me. I was a high-energy New England kid. I was hitting everything in sight. My accountant dad and nurse mom said, "You want to play the drums, son? We're going to take you to get drum lessons." I think my dad secretly wanted to play the drums and live his fantasy through me. So, we got a Gladstone pad, a blue sparkle snare drum, my first set of sticks, and some Joel Rothman books.

I got a little kick drum and cymbal, playing along to KISS and Queen records. We moved to Texas, which has an amazing music education culture.

Then, The Police came out with *Synchronicity* and Van Halen with *1984*. And I was air drumming like, "This is what I'm going to do with my life." I haven't stopped. I love the drums. They are a manifestation of passion, soul, and God-given energy. We play our personality on the drums. So, I'm fortunate that in 1976, when dinosaurs roamed the earth, I found my passion.

Mark Schulman: What is the attitude of a drummer? What drives who we are?

Redmond: We play them as a form of communication. And, as a speaker, I use the drums as a vehicle for my message. It's such a great way to get people's attention because it's so primal and loud. A set of drums is like a jetliner taking off. To my ears, it's beautiful music. And it's a physical manifestation of our personalities, our personas.

In bands, drummers are usually the most high-energy performers. If you get a bunch of drummers together at a nightclub, we're going to walk in at 9 p.m. and they are going to be kicking us out at closing because there's this amazing fraternity. You don't see bass players going to conventions or guitar players exchanging numbers, wanting to get together and talk shop.

Schulman: We are a community that is unique. That's why we're known for having huge drum clinics. Both our speaking careers evolved out of doing drum clinics, speaking to hundreds of drummers. We realized we could take that message to other people.

Redmond: You must give it away to keep it, right? If I share information with others, and they use it as conduits of inspiration, it's going to manifest itself and sound completely different. Two different drummers can get on the same set of drums on the same day, play the same licks, and sound completely different. That is a beautiful, beautiful thing.

Schulman: We are all unique, but so connected and supportive. How important do you believe attitude has been in developing your career and manifesting all these amazing things that you have done as a drummer and beyond?

Redmond: Boom, whack, boom-boom, whack. It became a focus of my career to take simplicity and elevate it to high art. Studying band leaders, songwriters, and artists over the years, they don't want to have to fight through the clutter of drum-isms. They've been trying to tell a story. They have finally got it right with three chords and the truth, and it's our job to bring it to life. So, there's not always a lot of room for sha-ga-ta-boom, sha-ga-ta-boom—just boom, whack, boom-boom, whack—but elevating that to the highest art, where every eighth note in that measure is equally important.

Drummer Steve Jordan says, "Simplicity is not stupidity." When I was in college playing big band, it was great to push the needle in that direction. But as the time went on, my drums got bigger, I played less, and I worked more. Having this kind of self-awareness is important in life. Just as important as attitude.

Attitude is 99 percent of life—playing our instrument well, showing up on time, having a smile on our faces. But you can wield positivity like a sword. And it is going to move you far ahead. It's going to separate you from the pack. Attitude is important.

I can pull up in an imported car with Italian shoes, custom clothing, a Swiss watch, and expensive shades. People will think, "Great dresser—maybe this guy makes a lot of money." It's a good icebreaker, but people aren't going to remember that. They're going to remember how they felt in my presence and the experience we had together. People will always remember your attitude. I haven't written a scientific study or looked through beakers and used footnotes, but enthusiasm is contagious, and you can change it. You can use it to shift the molecular structure of a room.

Being professional, over-prepared, exceeding expectations—all that is an expectation. But with attitude, you can surprise people. You can use it to open doors. If somebody gives me an opportunity, if they're nice enough to crack the door for me, I'll kick it open. And then, I will do a great job. That's my way of saying thank you.

Schulman: I have not stopped smiling this entire interview.

Redmond: I didn't get to play Madison Square Garden or the Hollywood Bowl until I was forty-one. That's twenty years of hearing the word "no," of roadblocks, setbacks, and slammed doors. But if you stop the pursuit of your dream, you're at the back of the line. So, for twenty years, I believed in myself and I kept working hard. I did it, not because I'm more talented than anyone else but because I didn't stop. I had a dream, I was positive, and I showed up enthusiastically every day.

When I moved to Nashville, I surrounded myself with like-minded individuals. I found a rhythm section that I've been playing in now for twenty-three years. We met a young singer-songwriter, Jason Aldean. We championed each other. We did forty showcases for labels that turned into a record deal. We traveled around in a fifteen-passenger van and later a tour bus with a velvet painting of dogs playing poker. The bus would catch fire and break down.

We played for five people at the bar, and then fifty, and then five hundred, and then five thousand. It didn't happen overnight. It took twenty years.

Schulman: You got knocked down. You had some failures. The most successful people I've studied say that if you're going to fail, fail big. Go for it. Do you have any stories about failure in which you made a conscious attitude shift to pull yourself up or continue?

Redmond: When I was in Dallas, Texas, I wanted to make the leap to New York or Los Angeles. Nashville wasn't even really on the radar. But I got an audition with Trisha Yearwood, and I flew myself to Nashville. I overprepared. I was only supposed to learn five of her songs for the audition, and I learned her entire catalog. I bought a live VHS recording of one of her concerts. I made charts of everything because I wanted to exceed expectations. What if we do the five songs, and she loves me and asks if I know the B-side on her second record? What if I'm the only drummer who knew that?

I had a great audition, but I didn't get the job because I didn't live in Nashville. The people I met during that audition turned me onto an audition with Deana Carter, though. So, I flew myself to Nashville. I nailed the audition...but I didn't get the gig because of location. They turned me on to an audition with Barbara Mandrell. I went; I nailed the audition. "Where do you live?" "Dallas, Texas."

I didn't get negative about myself. I played my best, and I didn't get the job. But you know what? There was a big group of people I met in Nashville who championed me, who fell in love with my drumming. So, I went back to Dallas, I gave my band two weeks' notice and I packed up my pickup with my set of drums and my black cat, Chacha. We went boldly into the night.

I kicked the door open to my first Nashville experience, and I kept building on that. If I let myself get down in a dark place, I would have never taken that leap to the next level. I'm so glad I used it as inspiration to push me forward.

Schulman: That's what we can accomplish when we control our attitudes and utilize them to obtain what we want. How do you keep that attitude daily?

Redmond: Play from the heart. It will set you apart. When you add your patch, your zest, your essence, and your personality, you bring the heart. It makes people want to work with you. If you add your heart to everything you do in life, it's going to make you a more high-performing, happy, positive person.

Every day, I do my gratitude list. Gratitude and humility are so powerful because they set your path. They set the wheels in motion for a quality day. Life is a collection of experiences. So, I thank God (my higher power) for health, family, friends, love, a roof over my head, colorful food in my stomach, and this gift that I recognized, cultivated, and nurtured.

I've been able to fulfill my purpose in life, which hopefully everyone will find. When you find it, write it down. Laminate it.

My purpose in life is to affect people in a positive way and change lives. I can do that through music, entertainment, and education.

I try to take care of myself too. On an airplane, they tell you to put your mask on first before you try to help others because if you're not around, you can't help others. So, to positively impact the world daily, I have to take care of myself, which usually includes some sort of exercise. Some of the happiest, most positive moments in my life are when I put myself first—exercising, doing my gratitude list, drinking tons of water, taking my vitamins, eating colorful food, and practicing my craft.

Schulman: That's a magic formula. Not literally.

FOOD FOR THOUGHT

1. Describe your life in one sentence. Add a sentence about why that is exciting.
2. How can you encourage others to be excited about their lives?
3. How can you over-deliver on what is expected of you?
4. What failure have you experienced that you can learn a positive lesson from?
5. How can you continuously express more gratitude?

CHAPTER 33

DIFFERENTIATION

*Featuring **Antonio Sánchez**, Jazz drummer,
and five time Grammy Award winner*

ANTONIO SÁNCHEZ BEGAN playing the drums at age five in his native Mexico City and performed professionally in his early teens in Mexico's rock, jazz, and Latin scenes. He pursued a degree in classical piano at the National Conservatory in Mexico, and in 1993, enrolled in Berklee College of Music and New England Conservatory, where he graduated *magna cum laude* in Jazz Studies. Since moving to New York City in 1999, Sánchez has become one of the most sought-after drummers in the international jazz scene. In 2014, Sánchez's popularity soared when he scored Alejandro González Iñárritu's *Birdman or (The Unexpected Virtue of Ignorance)*, which earned four Academy Awards (including best picture) and for which Sánchez won a Grammy Award. Additional film and television projects include EPIX network's *Get Shorty* and *Hippopotamus*, among others.

WHAT TO 👀 FOR

> ➤ Look for ways you can differentiate your brand, product, service, or art from that of others.

- There is always more to learn, no matter how great or skilled you are in your craft or career.
- Say yes to opportunities, even when they are scary or outside of your comfort zone. Rely on your skills as a professional to excel in these moments.

Antonio Sánchez: Drums chose me for a strange reason. I've always loved airplanes; I'm fascinated with cockpits. So, maybe it had something to do with feeling completely surrounded and having my own control board. You're the band's pilot in many ways. I realized later the meditative aspect with your four limbs, that you have to be incredibly concentrated and at the same time not think about anything else.

So, it's a combination of the left and right side of the brain. You're suspended between two worlds. When you find the harmony among the four limbs, you can do this pattern for a long time, while the synapses start absorbing the finesse of the movement. It's just fascinating.

Mark Schulman: You are an extraordinarily unique player in the way you fuse different styles. Was that a conscious decision or was it something that you evolved into?

Sánchez: It was a combination of conscious decisions and what happens when you travel the unknown path. I copied a lot of people in the beginning. I was trying to sound like everybody. But I realized that it was not a currency, to sound like anyone else. You're just going to be a bad-copy cliché.

That was a conscious decision. At the same time, I was going through a fruitful part of my learning life. I was absorbing Latin music. I was hanging out with a lot of Latin cats, jazz cats. But I always loved rock 'n' roll, and I had my fusion background too.

So, everything started coming together, partly because the gigs demanded it from me. They were very complex rhythmically. By osmosis, stuff started slipping in. I love polyrhythms, and I always tried to incorporate them in an approachable way. I wanted to do stuff that would sound good, instead of in theory. And all these great musicians shared the storytelling, the musicality, the dynamics. I was incredibly fortunate to be hanging out with people who were musically profound. It was the best schooling I could have gotten. I became a hybrid of all these things.

Schulman: Did you find that you had a lot of ego that you needed to work beyond or manage?

Sánchez: Ego was a big problem for me, especially coming from México. I started developing and impressing people quickly. It got to my head. And I was incredibly harmed by the things I didn't know. I compared myself to my little friends, and among them, I had been playing for longer. I had no idea how much I didn't know.

I was into Rush and The Police. I thought that was it. What else is there? Those were the gods for me. Somebody at school gave me a tape of the Chick Corea Elektric Band, and I discovered this other world. I thought, "I need to start practicing again." I was obsessive. I loved doing it so much.

When I got to Berklee College of Music, I had a healthy ego because of what had been happening in México. And I realized the teachers were teaching a vocabulary that I didn't understand. I'm talking about jazz, and what you need to know in order to interact with other musicians tastefully and in the right way.

I was like a machine gun. I kept doing it without thinking about it. I had the tools, and I wanted to use them all the time. I had to re-learn a third of what I could do, so that it would satisfy the music.

I had a few very poignant ego bursts that completely destroyed me in front of other people. That started me down a different path, learning things the right way.

Schulman: An ego burst can also be an attitude shift, if that's what happens. You come in and you learn. You were obviously open to the experience and open to evolution, which a lot of people aren't. Now, you are one of the humblest people I know.

Sánchez: This was the time to learn and be humble, to accept all the things that I didn't know and make the most out of it. It was a good decision, obviously.

I was fresh out of México when I came to Berklee. I thought I was going to kick butt. I had been studying classical music and piano for four and a half years—that was my major in México. I knew a lot of classical theory, harmony, and counterpoint. But I did not understand how to interpret drum charts or a lead sheet—things that pertain to jazz. I knew how to read notes on the drums, but if you put slashes and a few hits, I had no idea how to interpret that.

So, my first semester, I'm walking down the hallway, and Ron Savage, the great drum teacher, asked, "Hey man, you play drums, right?" I said, "Yeah, what can I do for you?" He said, "I'm leading an advanced bebop ensemble, and the drummer didn't show up. Would you like to play? Do you have time?" I said, "Yeah, of course."

So, I got my drum set from this humongous locker. I had a big Yamaha Power V Special. I had a bunch of cymbals, two hi-hats and a couple of splashes. I came into the room excited to do this. The kids are from eight semesters. It was the big leagues. I started setting up my drums, and I realized that they're looking at me like,

"What is this guy doing?" But I wanted to set up my whole kit, so that I could show my stuff.

It took me a while. By the time I was ready, Ron put a lead sheet in front of me. It says, "Penthouse." I could read the melody, but I didn't know how to interpret anything. Conceptually, I was not there. I had not played bebop at all. So, they counted off. To begin with, in México, this was one and three for me...

Schulman: Oh, no.

Sánchez: The whole system is different. I couldn't figure out what was happening. I stumbled a little. And then, when I started feeling confident, I stopped looking at the chart and paying attention. I stopped listening and I started trying to show off. First little flurries, and then more and more. I had my double pedal—and this is a bebop ensemble. Ron is just looking at me from a corner of the room.

I looked at him out of the corner of my eye, and I thought, "I'm really impressing him." So, I kept doing it, doing more. I was crossing my arms. I mean, I had no idea at all.

He started tearing my drum set, as I was playing. He took one tom, a cymbal, another tom. He left me with just a high hat, bass drum, snare drum, and a ride cymbal.

He said, "OK, now solo. You've been wanting to solo the whole ensemble, so do it." I had just woken up from a coma. I had nothing. It was humiliating. And it was great. He made me understand in real time, what I was not doing—and what I was doing.

Then, the ensemble was over. He could see I was down. I was depressed. He said, "I can see you put a lot of work into the instrument. And that's great. I respect that. Now, we just need to transform that into music. So, I'm going to give you a discography. Check it out. Study with me." That's what I started doing.

I started going deep into the rabbit hole, checking out all the drummers and really building from the ground up, taking lessons. I took the necessary steps to get out of the trip I was on because, thankfully, I had a lot of technique and I had the foresight. It was a great four and a half years at Berklee, learning and transforming and really improving.

Schulman: Tell me about your experience scoring *Birdman*.

Sánchez: Iñárritu saw me play with Pat Metheny in 2005, and we met afterwards. He was a really cool guy. I told him I was a huge fan. It's funny because I talked to him for ten minutes before I realized who he was. I asked him, "So, what are you doing?" And he said, "I direct films and commercials." But we're in Los Angeles, there are a lot of people who direct films and commercials.

I asked if he had done anything I'd seen, and he said, "*Amores Perros*" and "*21 Grams*." We had a laugh, and we stayed in touch. In 2013, I got a random call from him. We never talked; we would always email.

I was driving a rental car in Miami with my wife, Thana, and her grandmother. We were coming out of the symphony. I said, "I better answer this."

He said, "I'm thinking about my next movie, a dark comedy, and I'm thinking it'd be really cool to have a score that would be just drums. Are you in? Do you want to do it?" I said, "Of course." He said, "Alright, I'll send you the script. And we'll talk."

I had never done music for movies or for visual media. I didn't have any points of reference for how to do it. I sent him some demos. He asked me for something fast, something comedic, something pensive. He wrote back, "That was all beautiful, thank you, but completely the opposite of what I'm looking for." I said, "I really don't know what you need from me." And he said, "You're a jazz musician. I want jazz. I want you to improvise. I want it to be organic."

I thought, "OK, maybe I just need to do what I do and react to the storyline and the visuals, the same way I would react to a band." And that's what I did. And it worked, thankfully.

Schulman: Did you get to see the whole film first, or was it scene by scene?

Sánchez: We did it with the script because they hadn't started shooting. He would explain the scenes and what he saw in his head. He said, "Sit in front of me, and we can imagine the scene together."

I just started improvising. I would see his hand go up, and I would change the vibe. We did the whole movie like that. He's a genius and a visionary. He's a jazz filmmaker because he's improvising and going with the flow at all times—being in the moment, which was beautiful.

He grabbed those demos, and then when they started shooting the film. They superimposed those demos on the rough cut of the film. I went to L.A., and they showed me the movie with those demos. It was a very rough cut. It didn't grab me because I watched it on a little TV with bad sound and no editing.

We went to another studio in L.A. and re-did everything but based now on visuals. He told me what he really liked about the demos. I had to go back and relearn some of the things I had improvised, and then try to do them in a way that felt improvised again but based on the previous demos. He wanted me to change the drum sound because the first demos were very neat. My drum sounded beautiful.

He said, "This movie happens in an old Broadway theater. So, make it sound like they've been in storage for fifty years." Actually, the first thing you hear in the movie is some clanking of me tuning and detuning the drums and my voice in Spanish.

When I went to see the movie for the first time, and I heard my voice, I thought, "What is going on?" And then all of a sudden, the letters started peeling with drum hits. And I'd never heard my drums in a movie theater. To hear them in quadraphonic sound—I was floored. I cannot describe the feeling.

FOOD FOR THOUGHT

1. What trait best expresses your individuality?
2. What is a great learning goal for you at this point in your life?
3. How can failing be the early stage of learning?
4. How can being free to fail open new doors for your career?
5. What new experience could be rejuvenating for you?

CHAPTER 34

INSPIRATION

*Featuring **Matt Sorum**, Rock and Roll Hall of*
Fame drummer, businessperson, and entrepreneur

MATT SORUM'S SKILLS at the drum kit have earned him induction into the Rock & Roll Hall of Fame and helped to define the soundtrack to *City of Angels*—from the propulsive wail of The Cult, to the wild excess of Guns N' Roses, and the bellicose grit of Velvet Revolver. It's his reputation as a musician's musician that has placed him squarely at the center of Hollywood's A-list community of artists. From Camp Freddy to Kings of Chaos, his side-projects have drawn a staggering number of fellow Rock & Roll Hall of Famers—from Alice Cooper and Steven Tyler and Joe Perry (Aerosmith) to Billy F Gibbons (ZZ Top), Joe Elliott (Def Leppard), Robin Zander (Cheap Trick), and Brian May (Queen).

Sorum is also the founder of six startup companies, and sits on the Global Blockchain Business Council at UCLA. He gathers each year with top global leaders in business, government, and academia at the World Economic Forum in Davos, Switzerland. He is also the brainchild behind a vinyl club curated by top musicians called experiencevinyl.com.

WHAT TO 👀 FOR

> ➤ Learn from those with experience until you have experience yourself.
> ➤ Pick your battles. Try not to be the cause of drama.
> ➤ Don't think outside the box. Think like there's no box.

Matt Sorum: I asked my mom for a drum set. I got this little Sears kit. My two older brothers hated it and busted it up. So, I was banging on everything all the time, pots, pans, and cardboard boxes. They finally gave in. "I guess this guy's a drummer."

In high school, you were able to take three electives. I chose three band classes: wind ensemble, jazz, and marching band. My teacher really influenced me to become a professional. He pulled me aside one day during my junior year and said, "Matt, I think you got what it takes for you to go all the way."

My mom was a music teacher, and she was nervous about me getting into that game. In my mind, I was already manifesting the big stage. I'd go to the Forum, see bands, look at my buddy, and say, "I'm going to be up there someday."

Mark Schulman: You just knew it. I was myopic, man. I didn't see anything else. My parents are both college professors. The last thing they wanted was a drummer. I was just so clear-focused on it.

Sorum: You had to be. Even when we were coming up, you and me, it was do or die. We're work-ethic drummers. The musicianship was of a high standard. And then, attitude. You had to be a cool person, you had to be on time, you had to get along with people. A drummer is there to lift the environment and make everyone feel good. You're the foundational person laying it down and giving everyone the energy they need.

MARK SCHULMAN AND JIM SAMUELS, PHD

Schulman: Did you have any situations in the past when you really messed up because you had a bad attitude and then you made a conscious shift and you really learned from that?

Sorum: When I first came up, I was just happy to be there. The Cult was my first big band. I just remember it feeling like I'd arrived—and I'm not going to ruffle any feathers. I was on a tour bus, and I had my own bunk. This was everything I'd dreamed of. It was Billy Duffy and Ian Astbury's band, and I was just there. When I started to say a couple of things, it didn't serve me well. I understood my place.

When I joined Guns N' Roses, it was the same thing. But we had a real musical collaboration, especially with me, Slash, and Duff McKagan.

But when it came to business, I didn't have anything to say about any of it. They were the main guys who made the decisions. Fast forward to Velvet Revolver. I was a founding member and had to make more decisions. Scott Weiland and I were the leaders of that band and the visionary approach. It was the first time they looked to me for that sort of guidance.

Then, I started to find my voice through that part of the business. When I came out of that group, I was a changed man. I morphed into more of an entrepreneur because of my business dealings and learning about how to connect with people on business ideas. I made mistakes along the way. There's the old expression, "Pick your battles." Don't be the person who is always drama.

Schulman: Being an entrepreneur is a very different attitude. You created a clothing line and store. Now you're part of a science-based nonprofit. Your attitude really shifted. Is that because you allowed it or was that because you learned? Did you notice a shift in yourself?

Sorum: I don't know if people understand how much work goes into building a band like Velvet Revolver. It was eighteen months just building the machine. It wasn't us lollygagging. It was all day every day. And after that, I was exhausted, and I wanted to try something different.

So, I formed my own band, Kings of Chaos. I decided I'm going to be the only guy. And I'm just going to hire people, go out, and do gigs. I got the coolest crew, the stage was killer, all they had to do was show up.

Now, I've been brought in as a consultant to pitch ideas. I've gone to Davos, where I've spoken about some of the startup companies I'm involved in. Learning to negotiate from music and rock and roll, I've cut myself a pretty good deal. I've got about six startup companies I'm involved in now.

When I was in GNR, I had tunnel vision, it was all about that band. And then, after Velvet Revolver, my eyes opened up. I don't want to be that guy sitting on the curb asking what happened. I must reinvent. I must move.

Schulman: I'm blown away by how outside the box and outside your comfort zone you think. There's no box.

Sorum: I wake up in the morning, and think, "What's going to happen today?" I get excited. The startup world is not much different than music. It's like navigating life. But all that navigation I learned from being in volatile bands. If I can live through that, I can live through anything.

Schulman: It's all about navigating relationships. Every relationship is nuanced, and you need to pay attention if you want to be successful and you want to thrive—the band is going to stay together. It's one of the hardest things on the planet, to keep a band together, especially a band that's as big as GNR, because there's so much at stake and there's a lot of pressure.

Like you, I wake up every day asking what can I do next? How can I make this life exciting and meaningful? What can I leverage? You're leveraging your celebrity for really good things. Recognizing those opportunities is an attitude that few people possess.

FOOD FOR THOUGHT

1. Who can you learn from?
2. What is the best, most productive battle to engage in?
3. What "box" is limiting your thoughts and beliefs? How would you see the world if that box did not exist?

SECTION 5

CREATIVES

CHAPTER 35

FREEDOM

*Featuring **Judd Apatow**, film director,*
producer, screenwriter, and comedian

JUDD APATOW WAS born in Syosset, New York, and attended the University of Southern California, where he studied screenwriting. Early in his career, he worked as a stand-up comedian, before writing for programs like *The Ben Stiller Show* and *The Larry Sanders Show*. He created well-known series *Freaks and Geeks* before getting into film, where he has excelled as the director of such classics as *The 40-Year-Old Virgin* and *Knocked Up*. He produced *Anchor Man*, *Superbad*, *Step Brothers*, and *Bridesmaids*, among other films. Apatow has cemented a reputation for creating popular work around men coming to terms with growing up.

WHAT TO 👀 FOR

> ➤ Be prepared to fail again and again and again. Learn from your failures until you perfect your craft.
> ➤ Appreciate work you are proud of, regardless of how successful it is in the eyes of others. Know you can always improve on what you've done in the past. You can always do better.

> Think of one thing you have done personally or professionally that you are most proud of. If that is the greatest thing you ever accomplish, would you be satisfied?

> Find your flow—the times of day you are most creative and most productive. Carve out time to reflect or meditate. Keep a notebook or device with you always to take notes on key ideas.

Judd Apatow: I always connected attitude to having certain philosophies about work that would help me be in a better mental state to attempt to break in. So, when I was young, I interviewed a lot of comedians. I wanted to meet comedians. I wanted to get advice. I started a radio show for my high school radio station where I spoke to comedians.

A lot of them said it takes seven years to find your voice on stage. For me, that was an important lesson. It taught me patience. I thought, seven years—it's like becoming a doctor. You can't rush it. I didn't think I could be great in three months. It's going to take seven years.

That changed everything. A lot of people today feel like it's supposed to happen right this second. But if you have patience, that leads to other philosophies—maybe I'm supposed to make a lot of mistakes and maybe I'll learn from my mistakes. There is an old Jerry Lewis quote: "You learn nothing about how to be funny by getting laughs, you learn by not getting laughs."

I took that to heart as a young person. I thought, "This is going to be painful. I'm going to have some rough nights on stage. I'm supposed to." And because I thought I was supposed to, it didn't depress me. I still would be scared before shows because I knew a lot of the time it wasn't going to go well, but I thought, "I'm on this path of growth." So it was: "Can I be in a great mood and have a great attitude while sucking? If I can just keep doing it, joke by joke, I will get better."

So, I chose to have a positive attitude during a rough road because standup comedy is the only art form you must learn how to do *in front of people* and you're only going to learn it by failing. So, that's how attitude affected my approach.

Mark Schulman: You're in a constant testing period.

Apatow: Yes. Every joke is an experiment. You don't ever know if a joke will work. You don't know if a movie will work, or a story will work, or a character will work. There's something terrifying about all of it. You only can trust your instincts and pray they're right this time.

I assume it's like writing songs. People write thirteen or fourteen songs for an album and might have some sense of which ones they think people will like the most, but sometimes they're wrong. The one they hated becomes the hit. That's what's so mysterious about it.

Schulman: Because you developed that attitude early on, that enabled you to have the patience to fail. Your attitude about failure is that you welcome it.

Apatow: You're always trying to get better. You're always thinking there's more to learn. I'm going to do my best and the result will be as good as I can do right now. That's all that I really can do. I have artists who I admire who suddenly put out the best movie of their career or one of the best movies very late in their careers. For some people, the best movie they made was the first one. They never match it.

You don't really know what that sine curve is going to be in terms of your successes and your failures. It's always helpful to think I can do better. I could go deeper, or I can learn more. Out of the blue, Bob Dylan will put out *Time Out of Mind* and you're like, "Wait, that might be his best album yet."

You're always hoping you'll connect with people in a big way. You also learn that sometimes a project you thought wasn't successful at the time, ten or fifteen years later, people are still talking about it. Maybe the one that didn't make any money is now on TV and streaming as people's favorite movie.

[Jake Kasdan and I] have a movie we made with John C. Riley called *Walk Hard*. It's a parody of music biopics. At the time, it made no money, but every time I turn on Netflix, what movie is trending? *Walk Hard*. People are watching *Walk Hard* by the millions eleven years later. So, that's its journey. You learn that you never know when your work will find its audience.

Schulman: Do you think that attitudes are shifting about entertainment?

Apatow: People are looking for interesting work. There is a difference between what you would leave your house and pay for and what you would watch at home. So, maybe when you see a commercial you think, I'll wait for that to be on TV. And it might become your favorite movie on TV. But you had an instinct that you didn't want to pay money and leave the house to see it.

Schulman: Could you talk about one or a few of your biggest failures, and did you consciously shift your attitude to help deal with those?

Apatow: There was a period where I was doing a lot of television. I did a show called *Freaks and Geeks* with Paul Feig, which was about potheads and nerds in 1980 in Michigan. We loved the show, but it was melancholy. It was about how hard school can be for certain people and how you lean on your friends to survive. There were a lot of episodes that ended sadly. They were not uplifting; they were tough.

There was an episode in which Jason Segel, who was a drummer, auditioned to be in a local band. You see him audition, and he's so excited and he's terrible. He realizes that he may not be good enough to have this dream, and he must decide whether he will give it up or keep practicing.

It was heartbreaking to watch, but that's part of growing up for people. "I'm good at this. I'm not good at that. I like doing this, but maybe I'm not gifted at it."

The show was canceled before the first season was over, although I was very proud of it. At the time, I thought this might be the best thing I ever do. I know that it has its own crowd—and it may not be an enormous crowd—but this will be certain peoples' favorite thing.

It was painful when it was canceled. I had back surgery. I really took it on my shoulders, and it was very sad. After that, I did another show about college called *Undeclared* and that also got canceled during the first season. These shows starred all my favorite people like Seth Rogan, Linda Cardellini, Charlie Hunnam. Kevin Hart was in *Undeclared* with Amy Poehler who guest starred.

I got depressed because I thought, "Am I conflicting with popular taste?" I like what I'm doing, but it's not really connecting. Because I wasn't getting any hits, people didn't really want to work with me much anymore. I had a few projects that didn't get picked up.

But I thought, "You know what? I'm proud of the work. At least I'm in the game, and maybe one day something will connect." I remember I was walking with Ben Stiller on the Sony lot, and he just looked at me and went, "Man, you need a hit."

It's hard to win these creative debates when you haven't had a hit because they don't trust that you know what you're doing. Because you've never proven that you can have success.

I took about eight months off while my wife was pregnant, and I just read. I thought, "I'm going to read everything I was supposed to read—F. Scott Fitzgerald and Alice Munro." My writing got deeper. When I came back, my career took off. It was important for me to not lose faith in myself.

Then, I wrote *40-Year-Old Virgin* and *Knocked Up*. All that happened right after I had this moment where I was really depressed and didn't know if I ever would connect with the larger audience.

Schulman: You did what you could control. That was your attitude shift. I've got a thirteen year old, and when she was born, I took some time off from the road, but I don't know if I used my time as wisely as you did to educate myself and continue to read because that is a choice. That is an attitude shift. You're asking, "What can I manifest and what can I control?" to get more in sync and learn what you need to learn.

Then, you wrote those incredible scripts for those amazing movies. That's certainly a way of shifting your failure into manifesting success.

Apatow: I thought, "I like what I've done, but I still think I can do better." That was the key. I also did something mentally with my attitude that helped a lot.

In my mind, to take pressure off myself, I focused on this idea that *Freaks and Geeks* was my highest creative achievement. I thought, "At least I did it once. At least something came out exactly the way I wanted it once. I couldn't love it more. If that's it for the rest of my career, it's enough."

That took some pressure off. I'll keep experimenting, and I'm going to have courage because I already did it. It was almost a mental trick. I thought, "I've won the Super Bowl. It'd be nice to win it again, but just have fun. Be creative. Be daring. You did it once."

That's helped me a lot over the years, those types of mental tricks to keep me experimenting. I'm not trying to hold on to anything that's happened.

The King of Staten Island [2020] is a daring movie. It's about grief. It's about someone trying to get over the loss of a parent. I'm trying to do it with humor, but I'm trying to be very dramatic at the same time. It's an interesting mix of drama and comedy.

It's certainly not what the audience is necessarily screaming for. "We need another movie about grief." It's not a comedic subject. But I liked the challenge because it was human, and it would touch people. It's something we all go through, and that's the space I like to be in. I always feel like there's some risk in what I'm doing because it's not generic. I'm trying to go as deep as I can.

Schulman: You embrace an attitude of freedom, being free for things to happen and free for them not to happen. You had freedom because you thought you'd created your ultimate work. At that point, you were free to succeed and you were free to fail. You don't feel like you *have to* do it. You feel like you *get* to do it.

You're also talking about real things. I lost my mom. I lost my dad. I try to have as much levity as I can with things, but dealing with grief with a sense of humor, that's quite a challenge.

Apatow: I did a movie eleven years ago with Adam Sandler called *Funny People*. It was about Adam's character, who's a famous comedian, getting leukemia. He was going to die, and then when he doesn't, you think he will have learned all these great lessons. But he doesn't. He becomes a bigger jerk. It's about how things crash

MARK SCHULMAN AND JIM SAMUELS, PHD

in for him after that. Then, he finally begins to learn to be more loving, to try to connect with people in a real way and not just be an egomaniac.

I wrote that while my mom was suffering from cancer, and she died not too long before we started shooting. I realized years later I was trying to process my emotions around that through my work.

Art forces you to think deeply about your life and your loved ones—how you move through the world, what lessons you take from it. With most of the work I do, there aren't big villains. It's always just life. Life is enough of a villain. It's hard enough as it is. A normal day is hard, I don't need an assassin. Just getting through today is tricky. And that's what I like to write about.

So much of what we do with our creative lives is about getting into a place of flow. I'm always interested in reading about flow. There are a lot of books about it, often about athletes. How do you get into the mental space to go down that hill, flip eight times, land perfectly, and *know* that you can do it? How do you have the confidence to not lock up combined with the creativity to do it?

When it comes to writing, it is about getting into a mental space—and an attitude—where you can shut off your critic and let creativity bubble up. You can't hear the muse if there's a voice in your head saying, "You're not good at this."

A lot of the work is understanding how your mind works. What time of day is best to write? What seems to slow someone down? I've read a lot about how creative you can be the moment you wake up. So now, the second I wake up, I grab a phone or my laptop and—before I talk to anyone, before I even get out of bed—I think about the project I'm working on, and I just type anything that pops into my head.

Every morning, something cool just pops into my head, like my brain has been working on the problem all night. It's the same reason why people are creative in the shower or while driving. You get into certain brainwave states where you're in flow and your creativity can come.

Schulman: When I'm playing with a band and I get in that flow state, I am outside my body. It's an interesting place to be because, on one hand, you're completely in the present, and on the other hand, you're looking ahead.

I study entrepreneurs and read a lot about successful people. A commonality I see is that people are their most creative in the morning. A lot of people get up early for that reason. I get up early to write down my wins from the previous day and project my future wins. I meditate, I work out, and I get into this flow.

I don't meditate to shut off my brain. Sometimes, it shuts off, but I get some of my greatest thoughts and ideas when I just allow my brain to quiet. I'm giving myself the luxury of calm.

Apatow: I had a therapist who said, "When you meditate, it's okay to put a notebook next to you." So, if you happen to think of something you're not terrified you'll forget it. You think there are hard, fast rules. But there aren't.

Schulman: Know yourself. Understand your flow and when you work best.

Apatow: I know if I check the news, I'm done for hours. I won't think of a joke, a story, anything. Don't get into real world problems. Stay in your fantasy imagination state as long as you can before the world intrudes.

FOOD FOR THOUGHT

1. Can you embrace failure as a learning experience and clarify the lesson(s) learned?
2. Say out loud your biggest successes. Could any of these be the highest accomplishment for your life?
3. What time of day is naturally the most creative and productive for you?
4. How can you best utilize that time and permanently record your insights?

CHAPTER 36

TRUTH

*Featuring **Michael Franti**, poet, musician,*
and social justice advocate

MICHAEL FRANTI IS an American poet and musician who is also an outspoken supporter of many different peace and social justice movements. While attending the University of San Francisco, Franti began writing poetry. Soon thereafter, he purchased a bass. In 1991, Franti helped form The Disposable Heroes of Hiphoprisy, a politically charged band that wrote lyrics about injustice. The band's lyrics touched many, and they opened for U2 during the Zoo TV Tour. Currently, Franti is a member of the Michael Franti & Spearhead band, which he started in 1994. The band released its first album, *Home*, in 2004. The album's sound draws from funk and soul music, instead of Franti's usual hip-hop industrial sound. Franti is an active advocate for peace in the Middle East. His film, *I Know I'm Not Alone*, was a three-week journey to view the cost of war in the Middle East. In 2001, Global Exchange awarded him with the Domestic Human Rights Award.

WHAT TO 👀 FOR

➢ Enter every situation with a positive mindset. It is something you get to do, rather than have to do.

> ➤ Practice positive thinking when things are going well, that way, when you are experiencing stress or tough situations, you are able to lean in and see opportunity. Positive thinking is a muscle that needs to be stretched and actively worked on.
> ➤ Work hard and be kind to everyone. The seeds of kindness you sow will lead to new opportunities and growth.
> ➤ Always do the dishes. When someone offers you kindness or support, offer the same in return. Or at the very least clean up.
> ➤ Speak your truth but also become a skilled listener.

Michael Franti: In 2008, I bought some land in Bali and built a small hotel—just five rooms and a yoga studio. Since that time, it's expanded to thirty-two rooms, an organic rice farm and restaurant, and four yoga studios. It's a boutique rock and roll yoga hotel in the jungle.

Mark Schulman: I got the chance to go to Bali briefly, and it is stunning. You've had a path of high integrity and consistency, and it's grown your spirit and everything you represent. I saw the U2 Zoo TV Tour and Heroes of Hiphoprisy way back in the 1990s. But you've expanded into doing so many other incredible things. You're changing your world, literally. And it all really stems from your attitude. How important do you believe your attitude has been to develop your career and who you are as a human being?

Franti: It's the centerpiece of everything I do. I believe in the power of optimism. I have never gone into anything asking, "What if this fails?"

There's always a fear somewhere in the back of my head, but it's never the driving force or the reason I do anything. I built the hotel in Bali because I love yoga. Yoga changed my life. I wanted to create an opportunity for other people to have a deep-dive experience into yoga and have it be fun.

That's what the mission of the hotel is—to create transformational experiences that are fun. So many times, we think of transformational things as painful or arduous or difficult or challenging. We attach all these negative things to them. They are challenging, for sure. There's no transition in life that doesn't challenge you. It's the difference between saying, "I have to do this" and "I get to do this."

Schulman: That is one of my main attitude shifts and mantras in my life. It's so simple and people really understand it. "I have to" feels like a chore and "I get to" feels like a choice. "Have to" is the effect and "get to" is the cause. That reframe is powerful.

Franti: I practice gratitude, being grateful for every opportunity we have. Throughout my adult life I've battled anxiety and depression. The thing I learned: If I can change my thoughts, I can change how I feel. It's something you must practice when things are relatively good. If you wait until you're in a dark place, it's going to be really hard.

It's like Steph Curry or LeBron James going to the free throw line in Game Seven of the [NBA] finals. They look over to the coach and say, "Hey, coach. I didn't practice this year." That's how it is when we get into pressure situations in life. But if we've worked on it when things are relatively good, practicing that shift of thought, it really works. It's a muscle you have to learn to flex, and you have to strengthen that muscle. When you do, it becomes easier when you're in stressful or challenging situations to be able to get to hit the switch.

Schulman: Gratitude is a like a vaccine that protects you from focusing on what you lack. It's got so much power. We have the most power when things are going well, but we get lazy. If we exercise those muscles, when we're in the challenging times, we can call on them. And that is the practice. That's the practice that LeBron James does. He's practicing when things are good. He's not practicing when things are bad. I love that you say, "Work hard and be nice."

Franti: Those are values I grew up with. My parents came from the Midwest. They grew up on farms. If you don't do the work, who's going to provide for you? They had that ethos, and they brought that into our family. My mom was also a stickler for being nice. She was a schoolteacher.

Schulman: Me too—both of my parents.

Franti: Both of my parents were teachers. So, you know. There were five kids in our family. [My parents] had three [biological] kids and they adopted me and another African-American son. My parents were Finnish-Americans and second-generation immigrants. We grew up in a mixed melting pot of a family. My mom raised five kids on a teacher's salary.

So, everything was about how we could find something creative to do in the house, rather than spend money to send five kids to the movies. We just didn't have that money but [we could] make something out of old newspapers or find something to do in the yard—plant some seeds and grow a garden, play cards or a board game.

My mom spent an incredible amount of time just refereeing us five kids, showing us that we could all get along, so it was more fun. She taught us to be nice to the other kids in our neighborhood. It didn't matter if they played on a different baseball team, if they had a different skin color, if they spoke a different language at home, if they had two moms or two dads.

We were supposed to treat every kid we met the way we expected to be treated. She was really fierce in the attitude that everyone deserves respect and kindness and that it comes back to you a million-fold. It comes back to you in ways you never expected it to.

That's something I've learned as a musician, as a touring artist for thirty-three years. I remember one of the first tours I did. I had this little punk-rock, industrial, political band called The Beatnigs. We were touring with D.O.A. (Dead On Arrival), those hardcore punk rockers from Vancouver. Lead singer Joey Keithley said something I'll never forget. After each show, he'd get on the mic and say, "Hey, does anyone have a place we can crash?"

There'd always be one punk rock house everybody would go sleep at. He said to me, "Michael, when you go to these houses, always do dishes." I thought "There's this guy whose guitar is made out of a toilet seat telling me to always do the dishes."

He said, "Always do the dishes. There's going to be a house that opens the door to you. You're going to roll your sleeping bag out on the floor. They're going to cook you a plate of spaghetti with some salad with way too much Italian vinaigrette on it. Eat the meal, and then go in the kitchen and clean up, so that your band will always be invited back, but more importantly, all the other bands that come behind you will also be invited back."

So whenever someone joins our touring party, whether it's as a musician in our band, a crew person, or even tour manager, I always share that story with them. We want to work hard and be nice to other people along the way. As a musician, there are some years you've got a hit record. Everybody wants you. There are other years when it's like, "Hey, can we get a gig at your club?"

You just don't know what it's going to be. But if you're some-body who's consistently working hard and being nice to other peo-ple, promoters and fans will stick with you. During those years when things aren't riding as high, they're going to [bring you back]. That consistency is the key to personal happiness and also long-term successes as an artist or as an entrepreneur in business.

Schulman: That's a foundational attitude—a decision you made. You learned good morals, ethics, and habits from your mom and family, but it's up to you to uphold those attitudes and keep them consistent. You are also influencing and impacting other peo-ple with that attitude. That is so critical.

You made a film about [peace in] the Middle East. You con-stantly inform. You share your attitude with your lyrics. You hav-en't strayed from who you are.

Franti: It was 2004. I was on our tour bus watching the news. There were generals and politicians talking about the economic and political cost of war. They weren't talking about the human costs war. What was it like for people on the ground in Baghdad? What was it like for US soldiers over there?

My friend said, "We should go."

I hopped on a plane and flew from New York to Amman, Jordan. Then, I hopped on a sixteen-passenger plane from Amman to Baghdad. I brought my guitar, a few friends and video cam-eras—home video cameras, no major film crew. I just walked on the streets of Baghdad and played music for people. At night, I'd play for US soldiers. I went into the house of a family, and they took me into the basement and showed me where they hid their kids during bombings. They put blankets over the children when the bombs fall because glass in the building shatters.

It blew my mind. I sang this song to them called, "Bomb the World." "We can bomb the world to pieces but we can't bomb it into peace."

I thought this was going to be this really profound moment. The father of the family, he looked at me, and I could see there was anger and tears welling up in his eyes. He said, "How dare you?"

He was translated to me; he was speaking Arabic. He said, "How dare you come to my house and sing that song while your country is bombing us?"

I was taken aback. It wasn't my intention. He said, "What we want is for you to sing us songs that make us laugh, dance, cry, sing, clap our hands. Anything to just get away from this. We're living in this world all the time. We don't need to hear about the righteousness of peace from you."

It made me think about things differently, about the way music works. Music helps people to shift their attitudes, helps people find light in darkness. When we approach a situation, it's important as musicians that we express the full rainbow of human emotion— from deep sadness to incredible and intense elation and joy— because we're helping people. When you share a song that's from your heart, it's an invitation for someone else to say, "I get that. I feel that too. I understand that feeling."

I played in Folsom Prison. This guy said, "Michael, twenty-two years I've been in this prison. We haven't had live music one time. When you played, it's like the walls went away. Prison is like a pressure cooker. If you are a dark person inside, it will cook you into the meanest, darkest, most violent, intense person ever, but if you can find light here, in your heart, it will cook you into this beautiful person who is radiant and full of joy and optimism. What a gift that is, to share your light in the place that has the most darkness."

He said [at first he was] mean and angry. Then, an elder taught him that lesson. From that point, he learned how to read. He graduated college. He started working in the library, teaching other people there how to read, teaching them this light of shifting their focus. If people can do this in war, if people can do this prison, I should be able to do this when I have all this freedom available to me.

Yet, on some days, I don't. Some days, to be authentic means I cry and let it out. Some days, to be authentic means to get naked and throw ice at a concert. There's the full rainbow of human emotion. Within that, there's always a decision we can each make. Are we going for the light or are we going for the darkness?

Schulman: It is a daily decision. It's a moment-to-moment decision. Can you think of times when your attitude was critical to failure or success, when you actually made conscious shifts?

Franti: One of the great things about being married is that it's a constant challenge. There's not a day that goes by in my marriage when I don't [mess] up, when I don't say something that hurts my partner's feelings, or do or say something I later regret. When we get into an argument, [we say,] "Do you want to be right or do you want to be close?"

Schulman: Do you want to be right or do you want to be happy?

Franti: That's it. We make decisions in life about what we say and what we do, and we do it in connection with people around us. I want to feel like I'm someone who's bringing good energy into the world, but if I'm not a skilled listener to other people's needs and feelings, I'm not doing it. So, I try to be a skilled listener, both in my personal relationship and also listening to the world. Right now, we see this broad range of political tribalism, racial difference, the environmental war that's raging between human beings and the planet.

The way we cure it, is not to get higher up on our soapbox and louder and stronger with our message. The way we cure it is to speak our truth when called upon, listen as skillfully as we speak and take in other people's experiences, so that we can find ways to move the ship in the right direction.

Everybody wants not only prosperity for people, but everybody also wants the planet to be healthy. Everybody wants everyone to have jobs. Everybody wants people to be educated and practice religious freedom, but sometimes we get stuck in our own isms and schisms, and we don't create opportunities for other people to live the way they want to live. The cure to a lot of it is, rather than speaking louder, to listen more carefully.

FOOD FOR THOUGHT

1. How can you set a positive attitude *before* you enter each situation?
2. How can you practice setting a positive attitude even when you don't need to?
3. How can you increase the kindness you extend to others?
4. How can you "always do the dishes" more in your daily life?
5. How can you become a more skilled listener?

CHAPTER 37

EMPATHY

*Featuring **Andrew Macpherson**,*
author, artist, and photographer

ANDREW MACPHERSON WAS born in London and currently resides in Los Angeles, California. His career as an award-winning photographer and artist has spanned more than thirty years. Traveling the globe, Andrew has photographed many of the world's most celebrated and iconic musicians, models, actors, and designers. He also created multiple bodies of personal work that range from *American Landscape* to *Flowers, Spirit, The Goddess,* and a study of objects to create a visual poem of *Land, Sea and Air.* By his mid-twenties, Macpherson was a regular contributor to magazines such as *Rolling Stone, The Face, Elle, Bazaar,* and *Vogue.* Currently he is collaborating on several personal projects, including an exploration into romanticism and pictorialism called *Pagan Spirit* and a photographic representation of our planet, called *The Crucible of Life.*

WHAT TO 👀 FOR

➤ Study your attitude and your reactions to circumstances. Learn humility in everything you do.

➤ When you encounter a difficult moment or person, realize that it's not about you. You don't know where they are at that moment in their life.

> One person's bad attitude can poison an entire work environment. Be open to coaching and advice from others, and to offering the same to those around you.

> You never know who you are talking to and how they may be able to help you or you help them. Be kind, gracious, interested, and authentic in every interaction. You never know where it could lead.

Andrew Macpherson: When I was a kid, I was lucky enough to be an apprentice, or assistant in photography, to a great teacher. He worked with actors, musicians, playwrights, and dancers in London. He became famous because he married the Queen's sister. His name was [Antony Charles Robert Armstrong-Jones, 1st Earl] of Snowdon, and he taught me that the greatest asset and the greatest identifier of true talent is humility.

I spent two years exploring and observing humility at work with him, and it was really true. The greatest actors (Sir John Gielgud, [Sir] Ralph Richardson), the most incredible composers, dancers, and musicians who we photographed were also the most humble, most open, and least difficult people to deal with.

That was the beginning of my education in attitude and behavior. When I fell into my first long-term relationship (relationships are the greatest mirror of life), I started realizing the behavioral patterns that were driving my life and their destructiveness, their lack of ability to serve my greater good.

I was in my mid-twenties. I started going to different forms of therapy to try and learn how to unravel the behavioral patterns that I'd been born and gifted with by my youth. That was how my search began, and the search has never finished. It's a quest, still now all these years later, not to be the victim of your reactions and to look at everything with openness, humility, and the lack of ego.

Mark Schulman: So, humility drives your behavior and its consequences, vastly differently than an attitude of inflated ego. As a photographer, you capture the greatest moments and essence of people on camera. If they start from a place of humility, it's going to create a different behavior, and you're going to get better photos.

Macpherson: [I'm] a searcher of the truth. Through my journey, I've realized that humility is absolute because the truth is always changing. In writing my book, *Question of Spirit*, I interviewed Nobel Prize–winning scientists, and they said science is dogma. [There are questions you can't ask] because the answers can only be conjectured. The Latin word *scientia* means knowledge. The mystery is always greater than the science; the unknown is always greater than the known.

The known can always be contained in a library, or if you want to pull back, on planet Earth. But the universe is so much bigger than planet Earth. The mystery is wisdom and humility. Humility is the cornerstone of how to view everything—whether it's dealing with people or looking at mystery, wisdom and traditions or trying to find our spiritual truth.

Schulman: Can you think of a time when you consciously shifted your attitude to produce a better result?

Macpherson: When you get put into positions with combative or difficult people, the most important thing is not being reactive. When a difficult person arrives in your life, what you need from them is a moment of truth. I need to create an image of an icon that people recognize. I'm fascinated by the idea of iconography. I'm trying to find the icon of who someone is, but there's not much of an icon in a grumpy, ill-tempered brat.

You always must put yourself in the position of understanding. Growing up in England, there were two people in history who were super criminals—Adolf Hitler and Napoleon [Bonaparte]. When I was fourteen on a school trip, I went to France. Napoleon was on all the bridges, street names, bank notes, coins. It's just a matter of perspective.

When I started reading Carl Jung, I really understood everyone is the hero of their own story. So, when someone arrives and they're a brat or a brute to you, it doesn't mean that you should take it personally or react personally. You must understand where they are in their story.

Did their girlfriend just break up with them this morning? Did their husband just throw a fit? It's not about you. It's about where they are in their story. That's an important perspective for diffusing difficult situations. Kindness and compassion are useful attitudes in any situation of difficulty. Reacting as if it's a personal affront is not a useful attitude.

Schulman: Where you look from determines what you see. If you work with a client who is combative, do you consciously make an attitude shift or is it natural?

Macpherson: Everybody has their own dance, and within their dance is the icon of themselves. So, if someone is combative and difficult, I try to find the warrior spirit within them. I try to find the thing that speaks of that. I want to find somebody's truth.

When I moved to New York in the '90s, I rented an apartment for two years that had a pool table in it. Growing up in England, we don't have pool, we have billiards. So, I didn't really know how pool worked. Every time someone came to the house, they would always ask, "What are the rules of the table?" I said, "No rules. What are your rules?"

I learned thirty different variations of the game of pool through having no rules. Who knew there were so many variations? That openness allows somebody the space to be who they are and be honored in who they are.

Anything we do in life revolves around having other people help us. It doesn't matter who you are or what you're doing, there is nothing that can be done entirely alone, on the crucible of your own soul or your own ego. The story I have to share is one of witnessing a young actress turn an entire film crew and studio against her through her bad behavior.

Schulman: Because it starts with attitude.

Macpherson: I got this job, and I was really excited to fly from Los Angeles to Rome to photograph an actress and the actor who was in the film with her. We were meant to have three days on the ground in Rome. The first thing we heard was how difficult this actress was being. She wouldn't cooperate with anybody or do anything to help the process. Everybody hated her, and it was really interesting to arrive at a situation where one person was drawing the wrath, the disdain, and the dislike of so many.

I arrived with an open mind, we all did, and we looked around the movie sets, which were shooting on location in the streets of Rome. We got ourselves ready to shoot. We did the pre-light. We got all the lights up, all the equipment in place. It's a big production.

An hour before the shoot, we got the message that the actress would not be photographed that day, and we would have to wait until her pleasure to photograph her. We broke everything down, sent it all back to the rental houses. There was me with this incredibly expensive, super-high megapixel Hasselblad camera system, a digitech, my assistant, and the client.

I said, "I've always wanted to go see the ruins of Rome. Let's go." So, I get to walk around Rome for three days waiting for the actress to give us permission to photograph her, taking pictures of the ruins in beautiful weather, in beautiful light, with a $70,000 camera system and my assistant and digitech.

When we eventually did get to photograph the actors, I've never seen so much eye rolling. Everybody hated her and her behavior. Nobody could be bothered dealing with her. No one wanted to make her look good. It was really hard not to get caught up in the disdain for this person who had caused so much trouble for everybody.

We got pictures in the bag. We left Rome and I thought, "This woman is never going to work again. This is the end of her career."

After the film, somebody took her aside and [spoke with her]. Because today, ten years later, she has a really successful career, and she's starring in a lot of films. In my world, you hear people talk. And I know a lot of people who have worked with her since who say she's [wonderful to work with].

That's a story of walking to the precipice of failure, but through getting the right advice and taking it, she was able to walk it back. She could have very well never been booked again, never gotten another job, but by taking advice and by learning, she turned around an imminent failure.

Schulman: She's fortunate because there are several other artists who we both know that have not been, who either have not listened to other people trying to coach them to shift their attitudes or have been so rebellious that they've hung onto negative attitudes, and they have really bad reputations.

Macpherson: The reactiveness of behavioral patterns is massive. The power of our subconscious is so much greater than the power of our consciousness and our ego. Often, people are victims of storms raging within their subconscious, and despite getting advice, they don't have the tools to reign it in.

Self-defeat is something that I have witnessed in a lot of people, and it's almost as if they are addicted to failure. It's a chemical addiction. They're not taught at school the tools to triumph over behavioral patterns. I didn't even know that there was a behavioral pattern or understand the power of the subconscious until I was twenty-five—which is ten years after I left school.

From the age of ten or eleven, [I would have liked to] start learning about how the subconscious is actually the powerhouse—not the ego, not the self. The subconscious drives our life, and it is only doing what it believes is best. If you grow up in a family of shouting, hatred, abuse, and anger, it's what your subconscious learns to deal with. It will always draw you into those situations, and you don't have the freedom of choice. Your subconscious is way more powerful at putting you where it thinks you need to be—the place that it comfortably recognizes—because it knows how to deal with it.

People talk about chemical attraction, but often that is your subconscious feeling like it has found its home. If your home is, or as a child was, not nourishing to you, it's pulling you back into a situation that isn't nourishing to you.

Schulman: Do you have any experiences where you consciously shifted your attitude to create success?

Macpherson: My first ten years in this business, I worked as a fashion photographer. I was obsessed with the details of fashion: hair, makeup, hem lengths, prints, planes, colors, color blocking, the effect of clothing on the subconscious, the effect of clothing on the conscious. Fashion is an archetypal endeavor, and I really enjoyed it. But I started craving more. Fashion's fun to break into, but after seven years of making ugly clothes look nice, I started yearning for more.

I got a job with a magazine in New York to photograph an actor. I'd already been to Hollywood and shown my portfolio to all of the big movie houses. They all said, "You take pretty pictures, but you can't shoot actors." [I thought,] "Maybe this will change everything."

I woke up that morning in a bad mood. It was pouring rain. I got in my car to drive across London to the studio. I couldn't find a gas station. My gas tank was empty. I only just got to the studio. I'd heard that this actor was difficult to work with—didn't like photographers, didn't like having his picture taken.

I put up all the stuff, and a motorcycle messenger came in. Because I loved and rode motorbikes, I started talking to him. We had the same bike. We talked for about fifteen minutes about motorcycling.

Then, [I remembered,] "I'm meant to be setting up for this job." He said, "What are you doing?" I said, "I'm setting up for an actor I've got to photograph for this magazine in New York." And he said, "Oh, that's me." He took off his helmet. It was Daniel Day Lewis.

We got on so well he asked me to photograph the poster for *In the Name of the Father*, and that blew open the door of Hollywood.

FOOD FOR THOUGHT

1. How can genuine humility serve you?
2. When dealing with a difficult person, how might compassion serve you both?
3. Have you noticed how "contagious" a negative attitude can be?
4. Are you willing to receive corrections and use them to improve?

5. How might it serve you to assume everyone has the potential for mutual benefit?
6. How can you be more kind, generous, and authentic with everyone?

CHAPTER 38

CONFIDENCE

*Featuring **Chef Andre Rush**, master sergeant,*
award-winning chef, master ice carver

CHEF ANDRE RUSH is one of the top chefs in the US military and retired as Master Sergeant. He was a member of the US Culinary Arts Team, where he competed and won 150 medals and trophies. He is regarded as the Army's strongest chef, lifting more than 700 pounds. Chef Rush was also the Senior Enlisted Aide to the Superintendent of the United States Military Academy. Chef Rush has trained more than 10,000 troops in culinary arts and was called upon Army-wide to assist in teaching other senior and junior aides. He has volunteered his entire career and rendered services for the Corps of Cadets for the last ten years. He famously did 2,222 pushups a day as part of the #22PushupChallenge, to raise awareness for the estimated twenty-two veterans who commit suicide every twenty-four hours. He is certified in household/estate management from Starkey International, has sommelier expertise, and is a Certified Ice Carver.

WHAT TO 👀 FOR

> ➢ You may not be competent or proficient today, that doesn't mean you should stop trying. Practice will build

your skills and knowledge will build your confidence in yourself.

> Asking for help does not make you weak. It actually takes great strength.

Chef Andre Rush: Attitude is everything. You are your biggest fan, you are your most invaluable words, you are a marketing tool for others and yourself. Am I going to conquer the day today? What is my goal? What am I going to achieve? What obstacles do I have? If there's going to be negativity, I must get ready to face and combat it. How do I flip this?

It's hard because you can't change everyone. When you are around like-minded, like-hearted people, you can accomplish so much. When negative people gather, it empowers them to be more negative.

Mark Schulman: People get addicted to the negative chemistry generated from being angry. If you start hanging out with negative people, then you're just fostering more anger. We see that today with hate groups—it's a chemical rush they get. And it's a decision. Have you found that changing your attitude was necessary or helpful in developing your career?

Chef Rush: I'm from a small town in Mississippi. I grew up very, very poor. My dad taught me to value work ethic at a very young age. I worked, and I worked hard. And I was a stellar athlete at a young age.

When I was twelve or thirteen, I worked with him in construction, and my dad asked me to literally pick up a car. He said, "Dre, go pick up that car." I thought he was joking. I couldn't do it. Every day, I trained to figure out how to pick up that car. Finally, one day, I got behind the car, I grabbed, I pushed, and I got it off the ground. I came back to my dad with a smile on my face and the other workers were clapping. He said, "About time." It took me long enough. I just got back to work. Now, I appreciate that.

It was a very different time and era. There was a lot of racism. Even now. The last time I was called a racist name was this morning.

That's why today I am helping kids and military families, doing TikTok videos about fitness and mental health, and raising awareness about food insecurity for kids in the D.C. area and nationally. I give back that attitude. You can change someone's entire day or week with a smile or by saying hello.

Schulman: One of my favorite attitude shifts is smiling! The muscles in your face signal your body to relax and send endorphins to your brain. It becomes real, and people can feel that. Anger and rage can never be sustainable. It can only be destructive. Have you ever had a situation where you had a critical failure as a result of your attitude, and then obviously a success by making conscious shifts in the moment?

Chef Rush: When I came back from Iraq, I was destructive. I had PTSD. It was very traumatic. We were back at West Point, New York, and everybody wanted to be in charge. All the officers wanted to tell me how to do my job, but I worked for the general. It was very contrary. The general called me into his office one day and said that I needed to go to see a therapist. He said, "You served your country diligently with your time." He knew I was losing it, a big build up since 9/11. I got really upset. I said, "Do you know who I am and what I've done?" I'm talking to a general.

So, I went to see a therapist for the first time, up on a top floor, long hallway. I talked to him, but it went in one ear and out the other. As I'm leaving, I walk past someone in special forces, a big guy. I put my head down, and he did the same. I got to the elevator and was ready to push the button, when he ran back, put his hand out, and said, "Brother, if you're here, I know I need to be here too." He looked at me as an equal.

That was the time I understood it's OK not to be OK. If you need help, you need help. That's when I shifted my attitude, the one that had me lashing out at the general. It was just fear, which was never me. I just took that, and I flipped it over. If people look at me and say, "Well, he's doing it, and I know it's OK for me to do the same thing," that's a good example.

Schulman: That's a beautiful story because you not only shifted your attitude, but you helped shift the attitudes of others. And that's really being of service. That story can help a lot of people who are afraid to ask for help or believe it's inappropriate or somehow weak. It takes strength.

Chef Rush: I know I've helped people. What people don't understand is that when they say, "Thank you, Chef, for what you're doing," they are actually part of my therapy.

FOOD FOR THOUGHT

1. What practice can improve your essential skills?
2. What help can you ask for?
3. How can that help make you more successful?

CHAPTER 39

SERVICE

*Featuring **Jade Simmons**, classic concert pianist,
art entrepreneur, presidential candidate,
and keynote speaker*

JADE SIMMONS IS a one-of-a-kind artist who has built a one-of-a-kind career garnering diverse recognition from unlikely places. She's played the White House and the US Supreme Court, and her genre-bending concert adventures span Rachmaninoff to rap. For her work on and away from the stage, *Essence* magazine featured Simmons alongside former First Lady Michelle Obama on its Style & Substance List. One of the rare classical artists invited to perform at South by Southwest, her show was branded one of the Best of SXSW 2014. Simmons has remained committed to expanding the boundaries of Classical music and its presentation. She's the acclaimed host of American Public Media's hit podcast *Decomposed*, which earned spots on the Best Podcast lists for *IndieWire*, BBC America, *Esquire*, and *Time*. Simmons is also the author of the No. 1 Amazon bestselling book *Audacious Prayers for World Changers*.

WHAT TO 👀 FOR

> ➢ Make reasoned decisions based on achievability, but "err on the side of possibility."

➤ Practice empathy to understand the paths of people around you, how they differ from your own, and what you might be able to learn from them.

➤ Lean into your meaning and purpose; recognize small changes and even accidents that could play into that purpose in greater ways.

➤ Live life and business in service to others, and find the benefits far outweigh the risks.

Mark Schulman: At a very young age, you must have developed an essential attitude or mindset. Where did it originate from, and how did that drive you?

Jade Simmons: I blame a lot of it on my parents. They raised me to believe that nothing was impossible, and that I could do anything—if you believe it, you can achieve it. It was practiced into us, and they would solidify that ·way of thinking by playing into it themselves. If I brought yet another instrument home (I played probably five or six instruments when I was little), they never said, "That's enough, stop. It's too much."

I was that typical overscheduled kid. I played every sport. We were always at some game. I was on the marching band and the youth symphony. I was the student body president.

The one qualification was if you ever drop below excellence, we need to look and see if that's maybe something we should take off the list. So, I blame my parents. They were big believers that we should go after our dreams, and that's something I have continued to do to this day.

Schulman: Did you ever change or shift your attitude consciously at certain times in your life? Was there a time where your attitude wasn't serving you or you saw potential failure imminent?

Simmons: Whatever I'm going after, I'm at a deficit where reality and reasonableness are concerned. Those words don't mean anything to me. I decrease the value of whether something's logical, realistic, reasonable, or attainable.

I have a surplus in expectancy, and I err on the side of possibility.

Most of my energy time emphasis is going to be on the part that has possibility. Anybody can start from a place of logic. Analytics, common sense, all those things we need—and most visionaries have to some degree—but we can always hire people to tell us how crazy our ideas are. So, I like to spend my time on what has not been done yet and what is it about myself that I can offer to that equation.

That mindset has served me well. When it hasn't served me is in the area of leadership. Sometimes, I get out ahead of my team. I'm assuming everybody's got their parachutes on and they are ready to jump. I probably push people sometimes a little too early—like, "I didn't finish snapping that jacket on."

It's that assumption, that everybody thinks or moves like we do. The attitude shift has been to spend time in a position of empathy, in a position of understanding without judgment. Just because you don't move like me doesn't mean you move badly. Can I learn from your oppositeness?

I'm happily married to a high school sweetheart, who is the exact opposite of myself. So, I've had to live that, and I'm more prone to looking for those opportunities to understand people better.

The world of Classical music is extremely competitive. As an African-American female Classical pianist, I was a rarity in many places. I used to [play] these grueling recitals. All the pieces were way too long, and I'd sweat through my gowns. I was trying to impress the audience and catch my breath.

In between all of this impressing, I started telling stories. I'd talk about the composers. I'd let people know that Mozart was a prankster. Liszt was a ladies' man—women would throw their gloves on the stage and pass out. I would tell these stories and, lo and behold, the audiences fell in love with the stories as much as the music.

I got bolder. Instead of just telling stories about the music and the composers I would dare to share something about myself or dare to inspire them. There was a huge shift. I thought my purpose was to play the piano, but it turns out the piano was just a vehicle. My true purpose was to activate people into becoming the next version of themselves—the biggest, boldest version—and storytelling became the vehicle to spark that in others.

It was an accident in the beginning. I was trying to catch my breath. But once you discover something, you owe yourself and the people who have been impacted by what you've discovered to intentionally do it.

So, now I intentionally look for those opportunities where I can push people into purpose, into the next version of themselves. That was the most pivotal attitude shift for me. Stage fright went away, memory slips went away, because I was no longer worrying what they were thinking every time I missed a note. I was wondering, "What are they feeling right now, and what else can I make them feel?"

Eventually, I got really bold. Attitude shifting is an addiction. When you see the benefits, you wonder what else can I shift? I started pushing myself and my audience. Can I dare to bring in new genres? Can I add jazz or blues? Can I add electronics, a little bit of hip hop? I started rapping.

You can imagine the fear. I'm going to lose my audience. They're going to think I'm not serious. I'm sure I lost people, but I didn't notice it because I gained a new, diversified audience. To-date my audiences are some of the most diverse in the world of Classical music. That shift pays off for everybody.

Schulman: That's authenticity! When you are authentically yourself, you are going to attract, and you are going to repel. And that's OK. I'd rather be loved by most and have some people just not that into me than be in the middle. That's the worst.

You are in the business of moving people and shifting their states, and if you're not doing that, you're just there to pass time. You are not the woman who is just there to pass time.

Simmons: I don't have time to pass. I am an impatient person. I want change to happen quickly. People [hire me] to make change happen. I get worried if something isn't changing, I have some kind of reinvention every eighteen months. And I encourage people to get more used to reinventing and peeling back the layers.

The big shift was daring to believe that whatever made me lovable and consequential to the people closest to me I could introduce to perfect strangers. To audiences, that's the height of authenticity because you don't have to pretend to be someone and turn part of yourself off. You get to be all of you all of the time.

Schulman: It's also the height of vulnerability. Because when you're authentic, you allow your true self to come out. It takes being extremely bold, and it takes a belief that you are doing the right thing—that you are going to impact other people's lives.

You ran for president in 2020. What inspired that attitude shift? Do you remember the moment?

Simmons: I'm learning this is how life works. If you look back for the moment you think was the first, you'll find [an even earlier] moment. As a very little girl, I remember saying I wanted to be the first female president. But probably in the same breath, I wanted to be a rock star and a fireman.

I briefly considered going to law instead of music school because I had this hunger to make an impact. Then, I saw Oprah Winfrey, and I thought, "It's better to be Oprah, to hold up a book and it becomes a number one bestseller. To say, 'I'm not going to eat meat this week,' and the stock prices drop." That is influence. I began professional speaking, and I let that idea of law or politics go by the wayside.

My father is a civil rights activist. He doesn't believe in choosing your battles. He fights all of them. It was important to him that we came to the dinner table knowing what was happening in the Middle East, what was happening in Uganda. I knew that I was going to run in some capacity in the future.

In 2016, division began to really rip up our nation. I saw that division seeping into churches, seeping into homes, seeping into families. By the time we got to 2019, the way people were treating each other, I felt whatever progress we had made on race erased.

I started listening. Could I find a candidate who I could really get behind? I listened for the right voice. If you start looking for something and you don't see the answer, you have to ask yourself if that means you need to toss your hat in.

I knew the nation was more independent than red or blue. I knew people had family members who were completely different than them, but who they loved anyway. I knew there was potential to have a different atmosphere in which to conduct politics.

We knew what the odds were, but we had a different mission. How can we have victories along the way? We had a coalition of people from a wide political range. It said something about having conviction starkly different from your neighbor's and still showing love and respect and offering solutions that serve more people than not. There's nothing to regret about what we did.

Schulman: You've had a life of service, and that is such an incredible attitude.

Simmons: That's the service shift, discovering purpose. It allows you to shed title. I no longer had to explain why one day I was in a church ministering and the next day I was on stage playing Chopin. I didn't have to explain it because as long as I was being of service in all of those positions, I could say yes to them.

Attitude shifts have been crucial for me. One big one was understanding that life was happening *for* me not *to* me. That gave me the ability to reframe everything no matter how ugly or hard. The campaign was difficult but wonderful because we had support from places we didn't expect.

Talk about being vulnerable though! I was no longer just saying inspirational things that everybody loved. I was saying things that might offend people, that might disagree with people. That was a risk for me. Even in receiving wildly negative [feedback], I was getting a window into who they were—and that shifted what I was able to see. Even in your insult and your vitriol, I'm understanding something. I'm getting information I need. I may even know how to serve you better.

If you're going to make a big, bold move, you must do it for a purpose. It cannot be for you.

FOOD FOR THOUGHT

1. How can you set meaningful goals that are realistic?
2. How can you learn from more empathy for the people around you and their goals?
3. How can more attention to your meaning and purpose make you more aware of how to increase your accomplishments?
4. How can service to others benefit you and your efforts?

CHAPTER 40

ABUNDANCE

*Featuring **Erik Wahl**, artist, author,*
keynote speaker, and owner of The Wahl Group

Erik Wahl is an internationally recognized artist, TED speaker, and No. 1 bestselling author. His breakthrough experience as an artist and entrepreneur has translated into making him into one of the most sought-after corporate speakers on the circuit today. On stage, Erik's keynote experience creates a dynamic multidimensional metaphor for how to systematically embrace innovation and risk. His message: disruption is the new normal and businesses must embrace creativity in a wholesale fashion, or risk being left behind. Erik's presentation inspires organizations to be increasingly agile and outlines how to use disruption as a competitive advantage. Some companies will be disrupted, others will choose to be the disruptor.

This interview also features Tasha Wahl, artist, philanthropist, businesswoman, and founder of Butterfly Effect. She is the wife of Erik Wahl.

WHAT TO ◉◉ FOR

➢ Think in terms of scarcity and abundance, and be grateful for what you have. Consider that time is scarce, and use time strategically to accomplish your goals. Focus on what makes you and others happy.

> ➤ Meditate or employ other methods to reflect on your attitude and make adjustments as needed. Own your emotions and know when they are impacting other people in positive and negative ways.
> ➤ Overprepare, but when an effort doesn't deliver perfect results (in your mind), know that it can still have positive impacts on others.
> ➤ Rely on trusted allies to help you, and use their strengths to enable success, while also sharing your skills and abilities to help them grow and thrive.

Erik C. Wahl: It's frightening to say that attitude is everything. The trick is to define attitude. It can be values, it can be work ethic, it can be positivity.

The attitude that I've found most helpful is scarcity and abundance. It's realizing that we live on that spectrum—in that pendulum—and we have choice. How hard I choose to work, how I interact with other people, what kind of hope I experience through business, how I deal with setbacks when things don't meet my expectations.

Gratitude is a discipline. Creativity is a discipline. Joy is a discipline. Being able to shut off negative input is a discipline...having the emotional intelligence to be aware of chinks in your own attitude [is a discipline].

Attitude isn't set; it's a choice.

Mark Schulman: Do you see value in taking an attitude of scarcity? Is that something you would naturally move away from?

Wahl: I use scarcity in time. I have a finite number of minutes to prepare for a presentation—not allowing [myself] to get stressed. I want to be opportunistic with it, planning my time so that I understand scarcity on the time pendulum. Outside of that, I want to always use abundance.

If there's an attitude of abundance with time, maybe I become less disciplined. As an artist, I [want] structure and discipline and finiteness without becoming scarce, without giving way to nerve. Respect with scarcity, but not submission to it.

Schulman: Can you think of any specific moments when you created a conscious attitude shift, when you consciously checked your attitude? Did it produce the behavior and consequences you were looking for?

Wahl: I have thousands of them, but the one that I like most specifically is before I step on stage. I want to be the best possible version of myself on stage. So, I will go into quietude or meditation or aloneness prior because I need to control my attitude. If I'm not controlling it for those thirty to sixty minutes before I go on stage, then I'm at the mercy of what's happening around me.

We take an offensive approach since we've been doing this for so long. I've got a show producer on the road with me now, who does the audiovisual and handles the clients. There is a buffer zone, and I'm just taking the stage. She handles everything behind the scenes because I'm not great with those things.

I'm flawed. I'm human. I get frustrated. I get angry. I have a set patience, but these aren't real or not real. They just are who I am. You control the enterprise—the ram. Under control.

Schulman: I'm pretty blatant. I'm not rude, but I tell people that I need space. I pace like an animal. That's my thing before I go on stage. I move as much as I can because I'm creating the optimal physical state. And when people try to talk to me, I tell them I am getting ready, and they understand. They get it.

Can you think of any specific events where you messed up because you didn't have the right attitude, and it created negative consequences as a result?

Wahl: We had a product that was selling like crazy. With my live presentation stage, we wanted to scale it. So, we decided to digitize it, and we shot a video. I wrote a film, shot a film, directed a film, and then got in front of the camera. And I stopped.

It didn't make sense to me that I would suck at it. I come alive—I step into my own when I'm on stage. But when they said, "three, two, one, action," I got nerves that a lot of people get when they go on stage. I was thinking, "Are my hands in the right place? Did I say the right thing? Did I word that properly?" I couldn't get out of myself, and I screwed the entire project. I didn't prepare for that scene. I thought that I would be okay at it, and I just wasn't.

In that case, I realized I was in over my head. I didn't do the work I was hired to; I was ill-prepared and not naturally talented enough to pull it off. So, I drove the whole thing into the ground because I was so overwhelmed with my lack of preparedness for something that I thought I would be good at.

Schulman: What did you do in response to that? Did you just bag the project? Or did you get educated, and go back?

Wahl: We had a very expensive lesson that is now out there for public consumption and record. It's not what I envisioned...

Tasha Wahl: Erik is very hard on himself. He expects the absolute highest performance at all times regardless of what it is. Ninety percent is still going to affect and change people. This was a really expensive, beautiful project that took four days. We have a set of one hundred people. We're not going to quit; we're going to move forward and see it through. I like his performance; he doesn't like his performance.

Erik C. Wahl: Tasha's an attitude buffer, so I tell her everything. We don't let everyone on set know. Nobody knows. She works me through my attitude behind the scenes and gives me perspective. That's an example of attitude and behavior shaping.

Schulman: That's actually a really interesting component that nobody's talked about—how someone else helps shape your attitude.

Wahl: I'm aware that I'm sometimes erratic, that I am an emotional artist. So, processing through her to clients, to publishers, to agents, to audiovisual teams is helpful for me. I posture, so I know she's going to have the right response to the situation.

Schulman: That's like being part of a great team or great band. On a day-to-day basis, how does attitude affect your behavior?

Wahl: It's substantial; it's part of finding space for meditation on the road…[so you] have an attitude of abundance. You have the attitude of gratitude, of gifting, of sharing.

Take that time to stop and recalibrate. Did I move too far in one direction? There's a way to bring that back. There are people who are going to be listening to me in about an hour. Is my attitude in the right place where I'm going to be able to gift unconditionally?

I'm letting go of attitudinal choices done in the quietness of life, that needs to happen before a public or brand persona or messaging can be routed.

Tasha Wahl: One of the greatest things we've learned is the ability to have grace for yourself. It's easy to have grace for others, but have grace for yourself and say, "I'm not stuff. I've had a terrible attitude. I'm being a jerk right now."

That's when you let it go and start over—right then, instead of tomorrow. "I wigged myself off the waterfall. But I can recuperate and pull myself back together for the sake of the team." You can start right away. You can change your attitude immediately. And we have to do it all the time. We have to be adaptable.

Erik C. Wahl: Change happens in a moment. It happens at the time you choose to make that decision.

FOOD FOR THOUGHT

1. What priority is too easily forgotten?
2. What can you do to remember that priority?
3. What personal emotions make you and others more effective and productive?
4. Presentation is 90 percent preparation. How might you prepare better for work?
5. How can you be a better ally?

SECTION 6

●　●　●

ACTORS AND HOSTS

CHAPTER 41

CONTROL

*Featuring **Jeffrey Hayzlett**, primetime TV and*
podcast host, keynote speaker, and bestselling author

JEFFREY HAYZLETT IS the host of primetime television shows *C-Suite with Jeffrey Hayzlett* and *Executive Perspectives* on C-Suite TV and business podcast *All Business with Jeffrey Hayzlett* on C-Suite Radio. He is a speaker, bestselling author, and chairman of C-Suite Network, home to the world's most trusted network of C-Suite leaders. Hayzlett is the author of four bestselling business books: *The Mirror Test, Running the Gauntlet, Think Big, Act Bigger: The Rewards of Being Relentless,* and *The Hero Factor: How Great Leaders Transform Organizations and Create Winning Cultures.* Hayzlett has been cited by *Forbes, SUCCESS,* Mashable, *Marketing Week,* and *Chief Executive,* among many others. He shares his executive insight and commentary on television networks like Bloomberg, MSNBC, Fox Business, and C-Suite TV. Hayzlett is a former Bloomberg contributing editor and primetime host.

WHAT TO ◉◉ FOR

➤ It can take years to change a company's culture, but individual attitudes can change in an instant.

➤ During crises or unfortunate circumstances, focus on the areas you can control and the tactics and actions you can take to improve the situation. Don't dwell on things outside your control.

➤ Your attitude—good or bad—can be contagious. It can raise others or push them down. Be aware of your impact on the people around you, and choose the attitudes that will provide the most positive benefit to everyone.

Mark Schulman: How important do you think attitude has been in the development of your career?

Jeffrey Hayzlett: Oh, it's huge. For me, attitude means mood as well. You can go to a great restaurant and the food may be impeccable, but if all of the people there have a bad attitude, you don't want to go back. You can go to another restaurant, and it has [bad] food, but everybody has a great attitude, and you want to go back again and again.

[Workplace] culture's great, but it takes a long time. Mood is everything. If you can change the mood of a company, you can do about anything in the world with that company. You can have [an inferior] product, but if you've got a great mood, you can go and change it. You could have the best product, but if you've got a bad mood, it does not work.

I don't look like I did when I was twenty. I'm almost sixty years old. I look better. I look better today than I did when I was twenty. It's all about attitude. My mood is going to affect my personality. It's going to make me live healthier. It's going to make me feel better. It's going to make me a nicer person. It's going to make me more successful.

When you have a good attitude, you can go and accomplish everything. I go to bed every single night hoping I'll hurry up and sleep so I can get up in the morning and get back to work because I love what I do. Most people want to feel that way. Most people want to have great attitudes, but they've been beaten down. They've been told they can't do it or they listened to little voices in their heads saying they can't. I stopped listening to those voices a long time ago.

Schulman: Was there a specific event, time, or shift that inspired you? Was there a moment when you had a realization that attitude was critical to your success?

Hayzlett: Every day. When people ask me, "What's the biggest mistake you've ever made?" I say, "I don't know. I haven't made it yet." I'm going to continue to make mistakes. You're going to screw things up. That's just being human.

People ask if I get nervous. I've bought and sold 250 businesses for more than $25 billion. I know what I'm doing. I'm pretty sure of myself. But there *are* certain things that scare me.

I'm scared of heights. I get a nose bleed if I wear two pairs of socks, that's how scared I am. [As a kid,] when I first did the high dive, I was scared. I didn't want to do it. I got to the end, and I was going to go back. But all these kids were coming up the ladder. So, I did it. I jumped off.

Immediately, I wanted to do it again. We must learn to overcome fears and understand no matter what it is—from beginner to maestro—you're going to play bad notes, but it's only a second or two. With speaking, I just have to get through the first two seconds.

Schulman: Can you think of any specific times in your life where you made a conscious decision to shift your attitude to produce a different result?

Hayzlett: Every day. I'm not joking. But there have been situations [when] I received very bad news. Someone stole money—

millions of dollars. I went home and got pretty upset. I was in a bad mood. Then, I just pulled my pants up and got back to work. I can either be a victim, or I can choose to take control of the things I can control and not worry about the things I can't. The faster you can do that the better.

I am not a doctor. I am not a nurse. I can't even sew a mask. But during [the pandemic], I realized very quickly, I can be a business first responder and I can help other people. The more people I help, the more I give, the more I get. And that's a clear example of saying, "I'm going to do things a lot differently."

Schulman: There are two ways to manage change. You either embrace it or you resist it. When the pandemic hit, I lost nineteen speaking gigs in two days. I was very resistant to the virtual space for about two days! I was telling myself, "I can't do virtual presentations because I'm too interactive. I play drums and I'm very interactive." Then I woke up and said to myself, "What kind of pathetic story am I telling myself?" I made the decision to embrace what I was resisting. And then magically my mind started getting creative and solutions oriented. And then I said, "I'm going to come up with the coolest, most interactive virtual presentation I can. I'm just going to blow people away." It was a clear attitude shift.

Hayzlett: [In early 2020,] I planned a big event on the *USS Wisconsin*. We were going to call it "Battleship Forum," a leadership summit. I had the first female fighter pilot to ever land a Tomcat on an aircraft carrier. I had a Navy commander. I had former Navy Seals, ordnance officers, army captains, Bronze Star Medal winners, and CEOs of all kinds coming into Virginia Beach for this program.

And now I have to cancel it? No. I'm going to put it online. I'm going to stretch out a two-day program over a full week. I'm going to drive and thrive. I'm going to put battle-tested leadership on Zoom. And guess what? We had ten times more people attend. We had 30 percent more results than we expected on the bottom line, and we had a great program.

Schulman: Do you recall a time when you had failure as a result of your attitude and what did you learn from that?

Hayzlett: It's important to have good support systems around you—and your attitude leads to this. I wanted to put on a program a certain way, and my team didn't want me to do it. I rented out a former church in San Francisco. They had turned it into a meeting space, and the place wasn't ready for prime time. It was chock full of potential problems. I got so indignant about the fact that we could pull it off, that hell or high water we were going to do it.

I was in a bad mood. I was grumpy. I was putting in eighteen-hour days. I was going to Costco with a rented van and picking up water. It was the hottest temperature in over a hundred years in San Francisco that June. There was no air conditioning. And I'm making my staff work in these conditions. I made it work despite all that. And yet, it was a failure due to the fact that I shoved it through because of my bad attitude. I had to go back to my entire team and apologize and promise I would never do that again.

They forgave me. And they also realized that my bad attitude led to their bad attitudes. There were good realizations that came out of that.

Schulman: It is contagious.

FOOD FOR THOUGHT

1. Can you think of an attitude you have had that changed in an instant?
2. Can you think of a company culture that changed over time?
3. What can you positively change about your company culture?
4. What can't you change about your company culture?
5. How can you positively impact the attitudes around you?
6. What attitude change might bring the most benefit to your company?

CHAPTER 42

FULFILLMENT

*Featuring **Howie Mandel**, comedian,*
actor, and TV show host

HOWIE MANDEL HAS remained a constant force in show business for more than thirty years, serving as executive producer for such television shows as *Take It All* and *Howie Do It* for NBC, *Deal with It* for TBS and *Mobbed* for FOX. He is a judge on the hit series *America's Got Talent*. Mandel's versatile career has encompassed all aspects of the entertainment spectrum, including television, film, and stage. From his work on the Emmy-award winning *St. Elsewhere* to the international animated children's series *Bobby's World*, Mandel has become a mainstay of the American comedy scene. In 2009, he added another title to his resume—author—when he released his frank, funny, no-holds-barred memoir *Here's the Deal: Don't Touch Me*. The *New York Times* bestselling memoir revealed his ongoing struggle with OCD and ADHD—and how they shaped his life and career.

WHAT TO 👀 FOR

- ➤ Find fulfillment within and for yourself instead of relying on others to achieve it.
- ➤ Ask yourself: If there were no ramifications, what would I do in life?

> Accept opportunities when they come your way, regardless of whether they are within your comfort zone or skill set.

> Find your passion and embrace it, even if it's not your full-time job. If you live for your passion, you've made it.

> "If you say no, nothing is going to happen. If you say yes, you'll move ahead or you'll make a mistake that will teach you a lesson."

Howie Mandel: Attitude far outweighs my talent, my passion, or anything I have achieved in life. And it's accidental. I didn't go into it knowing I had the right attitude. I didn't pursue anything cognizant of my attitude. But if I look back on everything and compare it to other people who I think have a lot more to offer than I do, the only difference between them and me is my attitude.

I was born in the '50s, when there was a stigma connected to mental health issues. Later in life, I was diagnosed with OCD. I have anxiety, depression, and severe ADHD. I've also been married for forty years. I have three kids. I have two grandchildren. I have a career.

I equate it to the best philosophy I've ever read (though I didn't know I was following it) by Nike, and that's "Just Do It."

As an element of my ADHD, I don't think of ramifications. I don't have a GED. I did not finish school. I didn't have a lot of friends because I acted without thinking of the ramifications. I can't sit. I can't listen. Everything I've ever been punished for, expelled for, or had people angry at me for is what I get paid for today.

I went to a standup comedy club in Toronto. It was amazing to see young people spewing funny little anecdotes and relatable things. And, as luck would have it, the emcee came up on stage and said, "We'll open up at midnight. If you think you have the chops to do this, we'll see amateurs."

Somebody at my table said, "You should go up." I signed up. I didn't think that there had to be any preparation, that it could be humiliating, that this was not anything I was pursuing. I was not in show business. I was not in a school play. But somebody said, "You should go up." And I said, "OK."

"Ladies and gentlemen, Howie Mandel." I stood there after he introduced me. I remember seeing the microphone. This is as vivid as it was yesterday. There were all these strangers. The spotlight was in my eyes. I couldn't think of anything, and fear just enveloped my whole body—but not fear in a bad way, fear like the adrenaline you get on a roller coaster as you climb the first hill just as you're going to go over the edge.

I started saying, "OK. OK. OK. Alright. Alright. Alright. Alright." And they're giggling at me. And I said, "What? What? What? Tell me what you would do." The contorting and the fear and the "OK, OK" and the "what, what" became a signature piece.

Because I have OCD, I wouldn't touch anything. I wasn't medicated at the time, and I carried rubber gloves with me. I had my hands in my pocket, and I pulled out my rubber glove. "OK. OK. OK." I pulled it over my head and started breathing through my nose and the fingers went up and down. Then I said, "OK, good night."

I walked up stage, and Mark Breslin from Toronto [comedy club] Yuk Yuk's said, "Come back tomorrow night." And I said, "Oh, OK"—like I always do. It's the same club where Jim Carrey, Norm Macdonald, and a plethora of other behind-the-scenes writers and directors started. It became a good place for me to hang out because there were like-minded, for all intents and purposes, weird and different people there.

It's really important to find something in life that you're excited about. Once you find that, you've made it. Fame and money come and go. You're not going to be the richest person in the graveyard. It doesn't matter. The only thing that isn't fleeting in your lifetime is passion. So, if you're excited about waking up in the morning, if you go to work all day, but you've got a stamp collection at night, then you made it.

You know what bothers me? Wednesday is known as hump day. What's the connotation? You'll get to the weekend and not even do something you're excited about.

I was in California on business, and I went to The Comedy Store. There was a producer in the audience named George Foster who was doing a comedy game show called *Make Me Laugh* with Bobby [Van]. He asked, "Do you want to do television?" I said, "Yeah." He said, "Come to my office."

I went to KTLA. It was the first time I was ever on a lot. He had me try to make his secretary laugh. And he said, "You're very good. Can you tape tomorrow?" I taped five shows, went back to Toronto, continued in retail and the show aired. I started getting calls from *The Mike Douglas Show* and *The Merv Griffin Show*.

Gene Simmons from KISS called me. He said, "You're funny. I saw you on Merv Griffin yesterday. My girlfriend is looking for an opening act." I said, "OK, I'll do it. Who's your girlfriend?" He was living with Diana Ross. I became Diana Ross's opening act at Caesars Palace. I didn't have an act. I was saying, "What?" I didn't know anything. I was not in show business. I left school, and I went into retail. I was in the carpet business. I was just a middle-class Jewish kid in the suburbs of Toronto.

How are you going to make a living, buy a house, and feed a family? By putting a rubber glove on your head? Are you kidding me? I said to my wife, "I'll give it a try. Let's go to California for a year." And she said, "That'd be fun."

I got seen. I was on stage. I kept getting television shows and gig after gig after gig, and it grew into a career. But it grew into a career because I always said, "OK." Don't think about saying no. No is the first two letters in nothing. If you say no, nothing is going to happen. If you say yes, you'll move ahead or you'll make a mistake that will teach you a lesson.

The biggest mistakes I've ever made didn't [mess] up my life. They just informed me to make really good moves in the future. The biggest mistakes I ever made didn't stop my career. Life is an accumulation of successes. As somebody who suffers with mental health, the best personal therapy I can do for myself is be in the now. Be present.

If you feel like putting your right foot ahead of your left foot, do that. If you feel like putting your left foot ahead of your right foot, do that. Keep doing those things. You can end up ahead because you kept putting a foot.

Mark Schulman: Where you're looking from determines what you see.

Mandel: The issue with our society is we are taught that our success, our wellbeing, and our happiness is dependent on others. Many people look outside to give them any success they're going to have. "You know why I'm unhappy? Because she said this. You know why I'm not doing well? Because my company won't do this."

I am responsible for my happiness. I have a beautiful family and a great, supportive wife of forty years, but it's up to me. There have been times—a year in my life—when I was miserable and I couldn't control my emotions or my productivity. If we took care of our mental health like we take care of our dental health, this world would be a better place.

Schulman: Everyone needs a therapist, an objective view, a life coach, somebody to be a mirror to allow us to express and get feedback from that expression.

Mandel: Even when your teeth aren't bothering you, you go to the dentist. They take X-rays. "Mom, no cavity." But there's nothing in place in our curriculum in life for mental health. I'm not a good spokesperson for it because I have diagnosable issues, but humanity is the issue. Everybody needs a coping skill to get along in a relationship. Everybody needs a coping skill to figure out how they can be more productive at work or more creative or manage time.

It's more important to let your teeth rot out of your head and keep your mind clean and cavity free than any other thing.

Schulman: That's the impetus for me to talk to people and write this book. It's to inspire people to create attitude shifts that drive more desirable behaviors and outcomes.

Mandel: When you talk to people who are "successful" (whatever we qualify as success), you'll see it's not a secret why they're there. It's how they react to life, how they're coping. That's all it is. Success is a coping skill.

Schulman: You're a wonderful philosopher and a great storyteller. Can you think of a time when a negative attitude hindered you?

Mandel: In 2005, I felt like my career was over. I turned down movies. I said, "I don't want to do this anymore," because I didn't want to be away for three months. The last movie I did before that, I was living in North Carolina for three months, struggling away from my babies. And I said, "This isn't really worth it. I don't want to do that anymore." I turned down movies, movies that became hits. But that's OK because I was doing what I wanted.

I still wanted to be in show business, so I dropped in on comedy clubs, but ticket sales were failing. They weren't full in the theaters I was playing. I was in the hallways of casting offices along with twenty other people who looked like me auditioning for five lines and under.

I got a call from my manager who said, "I got a call from NBC. They want you to host a game show." I said, "Are you kidding me?" In 2005, there wasn't any comedian on television doing a game show. The last time a comedian did a game show before that was Groucho Marx doing *You Bet Your Life*.

My career is over, and you're calling me with an offer to put the nail in the coffin of my career? So, I said, "No."

He called me back a half hour later and said, "You know, they really want you. They're going to devote five consecutive prime time hours a week to this game show."

I said, "So you're talking to me about five nails on the top of my career. I don't want to do it."

He called again and said, "Howie, they won't let it go. They said they can't do it without you. Will you just take a look at it?" I said, "I don't want to go to a meeting. This is me saying no"—which is very unlike me.

I had already accepted that I'd move on. I was going to be a real estate guy.

He said, "Can they just show you the game?" I said, "I'm at Jerry's Famous Deli in Woodland Hills. If he wants to come and show me what this game is, I'll look at the game, but I'm not going anywhere. I'm having soup." So, Rob Smith of [production company] Endemol Shine shows up at Jerry's Deli and lays out the rules for *Deal or No Deal*.

I went home. My wife says, "Did you take the show?" I said, "No." She said, "Idiot, take the deal. You're walking out of this career anyway. Take the check. Get out of the house. You're miserable."

I called them back on a Friday, and I said, "You know what, I'll do it. When do you tape?" They said, "Monday." I said, "This Monday?" "Yeah." "Don't you have to build a set?" "We have a set." "Don't you have to hire models?" "They're all there."

I'm thinking, how far down the list am I? How many people said no when this is built and ready to go in two days? I said, "Can I hire a writer?" And they said, "Go ahead." So, I hired a comedy writer.

I was armed with so many funny things. I thought, "If nothing else, I'm going to be on prime-time network television for five nights. Even if this is the worst game, I'm going to do some funny [stuff].

Monday came. I walked out and the announcer said, "Ladies and gentleman, Howie Mandel, *Deal or No Deal*." The crowd roared. I saw my writer off to the side giving me a thumbs up.

I said to the first contestant, "What's your name?" She said, "I'm Karen Vann." I said, "Tell me about yourself." She says, "I'm a single mother. I have these three children." The three kids were right there. "I've never owned a home. I have no health insurance. So, whatever I walk away with today is going to be life changing."

I'm looking in her eyes and I'm thinking, "This is real." Up until now, I've been in movies. I'm on stage making people laugh. This is not pretend. There's a real human being standing in front of me.

My empathy took over. My humanity took over. Without thinking, I changed my cadence. I forgot about my career. I forgot about being entertaining. I just wanted that person to live in a better place than they came in.

I took the shows and when they yelled cut at the end, I got a wash of emotions. As far as thinking, "I just gave NBC five hours of nothing. I wasn't funny. I wasn't witty. I was just trying to help people out."

My wife and I took a flight out to the Caribbean. I was in Tortola at a place where I didn't have TV. I didn't want to be able to buy a newspaper. I didn't want to read. I thought this was going to be so publicly humiliating.

On Tuesday morning, I got a call from that guy who came to Jerry's, and he said, "You're not going to believe this. Last night, fifteen million people watched the show." For a game show, that's huge. I thought, "So, now fifteen million people saw this most embarrassing thing." The next day he called me. He says, "The second night, twenty million watched." The third night took off. One hundred million people watched that week.

I got back on a plane. I landed in Miami. Within thirty seconds, the first person who laid eyes on me said, "*Deal or No Deal.*" I've never had this level of success. And through that, NBC gave me a development deal, and I was under contract at Universal for five years. I'm sitting here at my own studio. I'm producing my own things.

I almost didn't take the biggest success of my career. Why? Because I said no.

FOOD FOR THOUGHT

1. How can you seek fulfillment within yourself?
2. If there were no ramifications, what would you do in life?
3. How can your comfort zone be limiting your career or life?
4. How can saying "yes" help you grow and learn?
5. How can saying "yes" bring you unexpected opportunities?

CHAPTER 43

DIRECTION

*Featuring **Suzanne Sena**, America's Confidence Catalyst, TV host, and presenter*

SUZANNE SENA IS an Emmy-nominated host, expert interviewer and broadcast veteran, publicly recognized for her years of experience on the national Fox News Channel and E! and as the hilarious Brooke Alvarez on critically acclaimed comedy *The Onion News Network*. Also an entrepreneur, Sena has coached some of the biggest names in corporate America, and is now known as America's Confidence Catalyst. In her podcast, The Confidence Connection, Sena provides inspiration to listeners in search of their own superstar success. Her mantra: "Limits exist only in the mind."

WHAT TO 👀 FOR

➤ Surround yourself with people who support you and your vision. Recognize negative actors and seek what unconscious biases, life experiences, or perspectives may be influencing their opinions. Don't take it personally, but also don't let it impact your personal and professional decisions.

> Visualize and manifest your future. Know what you want and go for it. You won't always succeed, but any direction is good and will lead to other opportunities down the road.
> Failure is not a negative word. It is necessary for learning and growth. Embrace your failures, learn from them, and use those learnings to design your own path.

Suzanne Sena: How many times do you hear somebody say, "Oh, no. I can't do that. I'm already thirty-two"? I was thirty-two when I started my national television career on the E! channel. I was in my mid-forties when I got my first lead in a TV series. A lot of people might give up. I just do something else until the timing is right for what I want.

Mark Schulman: So many people have limiting, time-bound prejudices about what they can or cannot do. The default for our brains is safety and not excellence. Your parents told you that entertainment and acting weren't "real" careers, and mine felt the same way about music. My parents were both college professors. The last thing they wanted me to be was a professional drummer.

You talk about having blinders on, with absolute focus. I only see what is possible. I was myopic when it came to my goal of playing drums for a living, and it sounds like that is an attitude you share.

Take a vision board, where vision is literally foresight; you see it. And if you can see something, it can be possible for you. I say, "Dream your life, and live your dreams." If you can dream it, if you can see the possibility of it, if you can see yourself doing it, then it's possible. Of course, it can also take an enormous amount of work.

Sena: It always does.

Schulman: It involves moving outside your comfort zone, especially based on the conditioning that you had. We're so strongly affected by the conditioning and limiting beliefs that we inherit from our families.

Sena: One of the greatest lessons I've learned is that when somebody expresses negativity—"that's too hard" or "you can't do that"—it just means *they* can't picture doing it. It's their anxiety. And they're projecting it onto you. I would have loved my father to just celebrate everything I did, but he didn't understand it. It wasn't within his realm of reality because those people on TV, they're not real. Right?

Schulman: We do get impacted by the influencers around us. I look for continuity in messages from entrepreneurs and other successful people because there are so many different viewpoints, and one thing I hear over and over again is surrounding yourself with the right people. Because if you surround yourself with naysayers, you can easily take on that attitude since attitudes are contagious and infectious. Attitude is your point of view.

Tell me your formula. Tell me your secret for being able to overcome the negative attitudes around you. It's deeper than blinders. Tell me about how you manifest success, even though you might have negative influences around you.

Sena: It's interesting you said "manifest" because I'm a strong believer in that. What you put out into the universe, makes it more real. When you prepare yourself for something you don't have yet, it makes it more likely to happen.

Don't wait until you get the opportunity to say, "Oh, I wish I could speak Spanish because that bilingual job would be amazing." Why not learn it now so that when the opportunity arrives, you're ready? I have always planned out things I want to happen. I know myself well enough now. I know that if I have something in mind that I want to do, I can get to it, but it might not be tomorrow.

I write everything down. I came up with a whole curriculum for "Hosting Classes" five years before I ever did anything with it because it just came to me.

It does help to have successful or positive people around you. But some people are very averse to risk, and there's a direct correlation to having confidence in your decisions and your comfort with risk. So, it's come from years of developing systems and methods for minimizing risk.

I would never tell somebody, "If your dream is to be a performer, quit your job, live with eighteen people, and eat peanut butter." I didn't do that. That risk would have been too much for me, and I had a bigger priority at the time.

What's important to you today may change in six years. There was a time when somebody would have offered me a daily talk show and I would've jumped at that. Now, I really like the jobs that take one day to two weeks, pay well, and then I have my life. It depends on where you are in your life and what you have around you.

Schulman: You're picking and choosing. That's an attitude of adaptation, to mitigate risks. But rather than mitigating risk and focusing on what you aren't willing to accept, you can focus on what you are willing to accept, and construct your life consciously to create that. It's a conscious decision. I'm in my late fifties already, and my speaking career has really exploded in the last couple of years. Twenty-five years ago, if you had asked if I wanted to do keynote events for Fortune 500 companies, I would have said, "Man, my drumming career hasn't even peaked yet."

Leverage and use the success you already have. You develop a certain amount of success in one area, and then you leverage that into the next area. For me, they are all related because they have to do with communication, with entertainment, with changing people's lives through what I say and do. I already had thirty thousand hours on stage. So, it is just a matter of where I focus the stage energy.

Sena: I don't really view failure as failure. I view it as a part of the next success because I learn from it. I call it failing forward. I signed a contract when I started working at E! The contract had a start date and it was for four years. So, I thought that meant the day that the contract ends, it's over, unless you get a new contract. I didn't know how things worked.

I had a show called *Celebrity Homes*. The producer said, "Okay, Suzanne, we're booking you for this date and that date." And I said, "Oh, my contract actually ends before that. I think we're going to renegotiate." I found out later that in the business you just keep working and then, retroactively, somebody says, "Oh, we need to resign her." It got to the attention of the new person in charge that my contract was almost up, and that began some not-so-happy negotiations, which never came to terms.

I ended up leaving. I can't say that I wish it had been done differently because I would never have had the lead in a TV series, which was one of my original dreams. I never would have my life now because I took a different path. I didn't know what I didn't know.

I was back home visiting my dad, we're in the car, and Kathie Lee Gifford turned in her resignation. And I said, "Oh, I want that job." And my father said, "Well, again, Suzie, a lot of people want that job," because it was way out of the realm of his reality.

I called my agent and said, "I want to be interviewed for that job. I'm a perfect fit." He said, "They've got about five thousand people on the shortlist right now." And I said, "Okay, what can you do to get me a meeting with the producer? Tell him I'm going to be in New York next week." And he said, "You are?" And I said, "I can be."

And I did. I met with him, and I got an invite to be on the show. I was one of the finalists. *Entertainment Weekly* said I was the runner up to Kelly Ripa. That was one of the highlights of my career. I thought that was the biggest it could ever get. I would never see some kind of national thing like that. The whole world seemed to have eyes on me at that moment. It felt amazing. It wasn't ten years later, and I was back on national TV on the Fox News Channel.

One thing takes you to the next. Every experience feeds the other. But how many people would never say, "I want to do that job," and then force their way in? I know people who would say, "Gosh, no, that's like winning the lottery." But are you actually buying the tickets? Are you actually studying how it's done?

Schulman: That is an attitude of tenacity. I have the same attitude, so I understand it. I had a very simple philosophy when I was younger and it makes it sound simple and easy. "Hey, someone's got to get this gig. It might as well be me!"

Sena: We're of the same brain. "Why not me?" That's the attitude.

Schulman: Switch it from the negative! "Why not me?" to "It can be me. I'm qualified. I can do this just as well—if not better—than anybody else." There is a certain amount of timing and a certain amount of luck. There are things that are out of our control, but what we can control is exactly what you did. "I'll be in New York next week." You have the power to manifest it, create it, make it happen. Because it's literally just taking that action. I love it because that's the way that I sustain my life.

Sena: When I was at E!, my life changed dramatically from what I had been doing with so much new attention and responsibilities. The very first year there, I started feeling, "How did I get this job? Why me? Why did they pick me?" I felt guilty because my friends didn't have those levels of jobs. "Why Not Me?" became my motto for the year.

The next year, when things slowed down, it changed to "Make Things Happen." I also like "'Movement is Good." If you've ever been stuck and you don't feel like something's happening, that's ambivalence. If you're being pulled equally in two directions, and you're not advancing. Movement gets you out of ambivalence. If you go a different direction, that's okay. So I guide myself. I pick a theme for the year.

Schulman: These are all magnificent attitudes. What are your daily rituals? How does your attitude affect your behavior on a daily basis?

Sena: I dance.

Schulman: I love that.

Sena: When I coach experts who are about to go on television for the first time, I always recommend music. I say, "You play that and you dance before you get out there because you're going to feel it and you move." I ironically have a book of affirmations from my father.

He was not encouraging when I was growing up. My father always questioned what I did, didn't understand. Back when E! was on cable, I bought a dish so he could watch it. He sent it back. It crushed me. He never watched. "Oh, I couldn't find that on TV. Send me a tape."

When he passed away, my brother and I went through every-thing. I opened up this little closet, and in it I found every single article about me and every single picture of me laminated, every single tape. He taped everything. For some reason, he wasn't comfortable telling me, but he absolutely was proud.

Schulman: You're just a light beam. You're shining. Is there anything else you want to add based on the premise of Attitude × Behavior = Consequence.

Sena: We gain a lot by listening. I learned by listening to you. We learn no matter who we're talking to or what we're taking in. The evolution you mentioned is pretty interesting. If you listen to what's drawing you now, you don't need to put yourself in a box.

And you don't have to just be doing one thing.

I have an opportunity right now to host a show. We're looking at that. I'm still coaching. I run my company. But it has all come together for me, and someone who knows more than I do in this space talked to me last year about doing what you're doing—developing a brand that ties it all together. What have I learned from everybody? Where has my own confidence come from? That's my brand. And I've officially launched the platform Confidence Catalyst.

I love the phrase because a catalyst is something that ignites change, and it's exciting. We don't have to deny any part of who we are. I did that for a while. When I went to E!, they said, "Don't tell anybody you're an actress because they won't take you seriously as an entertainment reporter."

Then, I got the job at the Fox News Channel. They said, "Don't tell anybody you were an entertainment reporter because you won't be taken seriously." Then, ironically, I got a job as an actor playing an anchor.

The best thing about opening my own business ten years ago is I can tell everybody everything I've done. Now my experiences, my successes, my confidence can help everybody. You should never deny who you are. I get to meet people. I love what I do, but I don't deny any of it because there's purpose to all of it.

Schulman: I'm definitely a believer that we're either growing or we're atrophying. So for me, it's a matter of gathering information and learning whatever I can. And you've been magnificent! Suzanne, you rock.

Sena: You rock. Right back at you, rock star.

FOOD FOR THOUGHT

1. How can you better encourage other people? Yourself?
2. What is a simple way to avoid nay-saying?
3. What failure taught you a valuable lesson?
4. What success taught you a valuable lesson?
5. What vision of your future inspires you and those around you?

CHAPTER 44

DREAMS

*Featuring **Tom Todoroff**, actor, teacher,*
bestselling author, consultant, and commentator

Tom Todoroff is a stage, television and film actor and executive producer, who trained at The Juilliard School (under Alan Schneider) and with Edith Skinner, Cicely Berry, Kristin Linklater and Stella Adler, at her invitation. He has played more than fifty classic and contemporary roles at theaters around the world. He has appeared and starred in dozens of television shows and films and teaches voice, speech, and acting. He directed Jimmy Buffett's yearly worldwide concert tour for seven years. Todoroff's clients include Samuel Jackson, Stella Adler, Liam Neeson, Harrison Ford, and Jimmy Buffett.

He coaches actors and directors at his Conservatory and weekly class in New York City as well as at his studios worldwide in more than thirty cities and seven countries.

WHAT TO ◉◉ FOR

- ➢ Success can happen as a result of making a series of commitments and keep them no matter what.
- ➢ Plans are the effortful part of bringing dreams into reality. Don't underestimate the power of spending time on creating plans. If you stay with the plan, realities are inevitable.

➤ Invest in your dreams. Spend the time and make the effort.

Tom Todoroff: Gravity wants to bring everything down, including our attitude. Gravity says stay in bed. But we pull the covers back, take the word "no," we flip it on its butt, and the day is *on*. In every passing year, I'm striving to have a deeper knowledge of spiritual growth—which is personal growth and professional growth. It comes down to overcoming laziness because everything's effortful.

Every minute of every day is an opportunity. What's today going to be about? It's all about your attitude.

There are some days that don't start great, and I go back to bed for another hour of sleep. I hit reset. It's like rebooting your phone or your computer. You call AppleCare, and the first thing they say is, "Have you tried turning off your phone?"

[When] coaching actors, in the beginning, they want to be reactive. They're looking for the approval of whomever is teaching them. And I say, "No. Your point of view is everything!" So, it's cultivating that and playing the positives. Positive and possibility begin with the same syllable.

When you play the positive, it opens up everything into realms you never imagined. A negative manner clears the room. But people come in with their nervousness and anxiety, and they yell, scream, and play negative stuff. Why do people go to plays and movies and watch good television? We're not looking for ways to feel worse geopolitically about what the world is doing. So, [focus on] positive, positive, positive.

Success is to make a series of commitments and keep them no matter what.

We're all transmitting and receiving all the time. If you're in a positive space, it expands. If you're not, everything contracts and now the bandwidth is severely diminished. This I'm sure of. We've all had that experience. "I can't believe you called. I was just thinking about you."

If you're in a negative space—and we all get there because gravity brings everything down—the transmission and the reception is severely diminished.

At twenty-seven years old, I went on a meditation retreat. I had never done that. It was nine days of silence. I thought I made a big mistake. By day three, it was just excruciating. And then there was some part of my brain that just said, "Listen, you've got six more days of this, so settle in and relax." Sure enough, suddenly I'm entering into conversations with people in my silence. People who I haven't talked to in years.

What came up were unfinished conversations. There were seven of them like little champagne bubbles coming up from the bottom of the glass. I was just having these conversations in silence. When I got home, I had a piece of mail or a phone message from all seven of those people. They all said, "Listen, I know it's been a long time, but I really feel like I want to talk to you." That was a transformative moment for me that I got, wow.

Mark Schulman: That is attitude—your point of view. Where you see things from determines what you see, and what you see is what you get.

Todoroff: Plans are the effortful part of bringing things into reality. I've produced movies and I've coached a lot of people. You've got to be able to see it first—to create a plan.

For a long time, I lived in New York City, and there was always construction somewhere. Some developer looked at a plot of land and had a dream. Are you going to do the effort to create the plan? What's the zoning? Can I get a tax abatement? Can I get inside my

MARK SCHULMAN AND JIM SAMUELS, PHD

left brain? If you find that stock out, get a pool of investors and stay with that plan, the building is inevitable. The dream is the easy part.

[In acting,] the people who have gotten a lot of work are most often not the ones who were the most talented or attractive. They were the hardest workers, fighting to get craft, to get the best representation and into the best auditions. It's all a fight. That's the plan price. If you stay with the plan, reality is inevitable.

Hearkening back to laziness and how it relates to attitude, so much is giving up. I get angry at the marketing of this. One of the first things I tell actors: Release the false notion of overnight success. It just doesn't exist. You have people [who think if they] get on a reality show, they'll get seen but they forgot to learn how to act! It's like thinking, "If I go to a party, I'll meet a person and get to be the drummer for their tour." You haven't bought a snare drum. You need to practice rudiments.

Schulman: We joke that it took us ten years to become an overnight success. My coauthor's philosophy is that reality is the one possibility that destroys all others. You start fighting with reality, it's going to kick your butt.

Todoroff: Mental health is an ongoing process. It's an ongoing class. It's an ongoing process of dedication to reality at all costs. Stay dedicated to reality, stay dedicated to the calendar and the clock. You want to suffer? Start to mess with the calendar and the clock. Spiritually, we are on a timer. It's like a heartbeat. The heart is telling you get on with it, get on with it.

Schulman: I would love to hear a specific story when attitude was a critical factor in a failure for you. And then a story where a conscious shift in your attitude was a critical factor in your success.

Todoroff: When I got to Julliard, I fell in love with somebody in my class and we were going to get married. It was a really terrific relationship, but through the foibles of life, it didn't happen right away. It took a year and then I started working on stuff.

This is the first time in my life working in restaurants, which I loved. It was that struggle that burnished the metal and made it all happen and that—when I was a waiter at the Copacabana, when I tended bar at the top of the Empire State Building, and when I served breakfast at the mayor's mansion.

I was out of school. I was a waiter, not a student. My attitude shifted. When I look back, everything she fell in love with disappeared because I wasn't loving me. I was angry and frustrated.

I remember thinking, "I wonder how much of this negativity she will take before she leaves." I remember saying something like that to her one night. "What do you think it would take for us to break up?" And she shot me a glance and she said, "What a stupid thing to say." And I remember thinking, "She's right." But it didn't stop me from doing it.

She left. I hurt from that for the better part of five years. I realized that we language our world, and I put it out there into words. I put it out there—"What do you think it would take for us to break up?"—when I wanted to be with her forever.

When I look back, so much of it was [because] I didn't trust me. When you're successful personally and professionally, it's your fault. If it's not working, it's your fault too.

When people get into acting, they think it's about them. It's not. It's about the script. It's about your ability to tell the story. I tell actors, when you're really nervous, you're making it about you. When you're excited, you're making it about the work. We hire you because we feel we're in good hands. You're going to be a good steward of this journey. It's effortful, but is it really that difficult?

Schulman: Are there any stories where you made a conscious attitude shift that brought success?

Todoroff: I auditioned for Julliard twice. The first time was at the behest of a teacher I had at a liberal arts college in Wisconsin. I felt like it went pretty well. I didn't get a letter for a long time, and when I did, the letter said, "We were impressed with your audition. However, you would require voice and speech work."

Speech therapy! I would need speech therapy? My teacher said, "Well, you're from Buffalo." I said "Tam" instead of "Tom." I had a mouth full of braces.

I called them because they said, "Contact us." They found a speech coach for me in Chicago—a seven-hour round-trip drive from Beloit College. I talked to her on the phone. She's $65 an hour in 1977. The last time I checked an inflation calculator, that was [close to $300] an hour. So, I got a second job to pay her for one hour of her time and a tank of gas.

I made this round-trip drive every Thursday for a year. I changed my course schedule. In the interim, there were other people in the theater program who said, "You're spending all this money to take these classes, but you don't have anything in writing from [Julliard] that they're going to take you."

I remember feeling like that could happen. They're right. But I shifted my thinking: "That is not a possibility."

A year later, [my speech therapist] and her husband said, "Listen, don't make this February drive to Chicago. Just come the night before, take a class, and you'll be in Chicago, which is fifteen minutes away from my [second Julliard] audition in the Fine Arts Building on Michigan Avenue."

I auditioned for [prolific theater director] Alan Schneider. I had written a paper on him two years earlier and had no idea he had a connection with the school.

I always say that acting is closer to a sport than it is to an art because it's about repetition. I did my two monologues—and I don't know why I knew to do this—but it was the same two monologues I auditioned with every single day for anybody who would listen.

I remember the British lady who was in charge of voice said, "Well, you've made remarkable progress, and you're prepared for a program such as ours." Alan got up, put his arm around me and said, "Listen, don't wait for the letter. Move to New York, we'll see you in September." That changed my life.

FOOD FOR THOUGHT

1. What commitment to one obtainable success are you willing to make today?

2. What negative attitude have you expressed lately? What positive attitude could you have consciously chosen instead?

3. What effort and time are you willing to commit to your dreams?

ADDENDUM

THE ATTITUDE SCALE

HERE IS A chance for you overachievers to take a deeper dive into more specific information about the many facets of how to shift of your attitude. There is a natural sequence in the order of fundamental attitudes.

This scale illustrates the natural development of both positive attitudes and negative attitudes. Each attitude is directly related to the one directly above and below it. The scale provides a roadmap for "attitude switching."

Attitude	Behavior	Consequence
+6 Confident	Displays optimism	Inspiration
+5 Conservative	Shows interest	Stability
+4 Successful	Follows through	Completion
+3 Focused	Takes correct action	Correct results
+2 Careless	Distracts	Mistakes
+1 Determined	Struggles toward	Progress
0 Critical Choice	**Conflict**	**Complaint/Correction**
−1 Rebellious	Struggles against	Regress
−2 Undermining	Disintegrates	Mistakes
−3 Failing	Takes wrong action	Wrong results
−4 Failed	Gives up	Incompletion

| −5 Defeated | Shows no interest | Instability |
| −6 Lifeless | Displays pessimism | Expiration |

The middle of this scale presents a critical choice. Should we make significant changes to save our marriage or get a divorce? Should we form a mutually beneficial peace or go to war? Should we unify our political aspirations (increasing our chances of winning) or break our voting block (and lose)?

Above and below this critical choice are two similar behaviors—struggle toward or struggle against. It is up to you, your team, or your business to struggle against an unwanted condition or struggle toward a wanted one. Either way, there will be struggle involved, demonstrating the underlying conflict(s).

Often, individuals and business leaders don't realize they *are* conflicted, but they unknowingly exhibit behaviors that belie that fact to others including their teams. Careful and thoughtful introspection is necessary to fully examine conflict and determine appropriate steps to remedy it.

Anger drives both rebellious and determined attitudes. From there, "against condition" moves down the scale and "toward condition" moves up the scale.

This critical choice reflects the result of the battle between destruction or construction, of being rebellious or determined. If you are not hyperaware of anger, you are liable to unwittingly make the wrong attitudinal decisions in the moment.

Recognizing the enormous power of anger, and the positive and negative outcomes of decision-based outcomes, a critical assessment is necessary for smart attitude choices.

Moving up the scale from "determined" is "careless," representing a relaxation of anger and the focus it brings, followed by "focus," but without the innate conflict anger brings.

Carelessness brings with it mistakes. Do not resist this; to do so would evoke conflict. Instead, watch for it, and when it appears, focus on your goal. Your newly focused attitude allows you to notice and correct mistakes bringing you one step closer to success.

Note that carelessness comes from the relaxation of focus generated by anger. This is often why well-meaning and necessary "resolutions" are not followed up on. A great idea easily distracted is the hallmark of a "careless" attitude.

This is not failing, though, rather a mechanism built into the human mind-body connection. Awareness is your defense against this carelessness. To succeed, you must intentionally move up to the "focused" attitude where advancements constructively happen.

So, when working positively through an angry reaction, you must expect a period of carelessness. Pay attention! You may find yourself unable to focus on the elements needed to move your project forward.

Be patient. It will often take time and repeated reminders to change your attitude and that of your team to "focus." A new, common goal will move your mindset from "careless" to "focused," and you will gain the value that comes from taking the right actions.

"Focused" is a renewal of focus but without the innate conflict involved with anger. Focused is an attitude driven by a single unifying center of attention—and all successful leaders demonstrate an understanding of this characteristic.

(Be careful. The scale works regardless of the quality of goals— an entirely different discussion.)

The value of your goals or desired outcomes are a matter of opinion. War: Good or bad idea? Depends on geopolitical circumstances. New product: Good or bad idea? Depends on market need and costs.

If you are coming to realize your attitude may not be one that is leading to many positive outcomes, can you change it?

First Rule: When switching attitudes move up just one attitude at a time on the scale. Each of these attitudes closely connects to those below and above. For instance, "rebellious" is an "anger" attitude, as is "determined" just above it.

The easiest way to switch from your current attitude to a more desirable one is to remember a time when you once experienced it.

Let's say you find yourself angry with your neighbors because they are not mowing their lawn. There are two problems—an over-grown lawn and your anger.

You may be in the higher form of anger (determined), but you're angry and not getting anywhere after repeated attempts at getting them to mow their lawn. You need to free yourself from the anger because it is adding a second problem to the original one.

You decide to find a way to get that lawn mowed, no matter what (typical "determined").

Your solutions so far have all failed. You need a newer, better solution. You need to "think outside the box" and come up with a new solution.

Since your former tactics have failed, leaving you frustrated and angry, you need new, better solutions.

You opt to make your neighbors "an offer they can't refuse." But you need to be careful. If your offer involves destruction or unpleasantness, you are still "rebellious." Make certain your offer is entirely creative and constructive. Find what they need to say "yes."

Maybe you pay for their lawn care because they are financially at risk. Maybe they don't want anyone to know about a medical problem that precludes the use of their lawnmower. Find the problem and help solve it.

Determined to get to a workable solution, start identifying the real problem. "They're just asses" is not constructive.

Determined and compassionate communication is almost entirely irresistible. If that fails, talk to your attorney, homeowners association, or the city office for code compliance. Remain determined.

If you want to try something even more freeing, get bored with the problem. Be careless about it. If your mind rebels, perfect! You are demonstrating the futility of rebellion. Start the process over and move from "rebellious" to "determined" and back to "careless."

For a set amount of time, even just a few minutes, don't care about it—care...less. Consider it a short vacation from the frustration the situation has created. Take the time to see the scenario differently and find new, creative solutions.

Focus entirely on the outcome you wish to bring about. Relaxed focus on your goal can open creativity. These are the signs of a "focused" attitude, which can unlock an altogether new awareness. New ways of seeing the situation present interesting new possibilities for success, leading to the next-level attitude—"success."

ACKNOWLEDGMENTS

MARK:

The brilliant interviewees that are the foundation of the content of this book took the attitude equation and brought it to life with your stories and perspectives. You made my job as interviewer so engaging and easy. You all rock!

Our editor, Jessie States, shaped the format of this book and worked interactively with us to guide the readers through "what to look for" and "food for thought" to expand the content of each interview.

Dr. Jim, you have been a profound influence and the mentor of my life for the last thirty-five years. Your creation of the attitude equation has been the impetus of not only my sanity but a gateway to the profound influence I have been able to have through sharing this concept with thousands of people in my keynotes. You have changed the world.

Jacob Hoye, our publisher at Permuted Press, has worked tirelessly and strategically to make this body of words a published body of work!

Michael Murphy, your graphic design of the book brings the content to life! Thank you, my friend.

Shannon Marvin, my agent, brought us together with Permuted Press, so you are reading this now because of Shannon!

Heather Jo Crider runs my speaking business, is my speaking partner, has been instrumental in the marketing of this book, and has showered me with true love and brilliant insight in all areas of my life, exceeding my expectations. My love for you knows no bounds.

My attorney, Stephen Stern, and accountant, Mark Grossman, are constant sources of support, brilliance and friendship, and have been for most of my life! I love you both.

My daughter, Zade, has been my constant inspiration, companion, and overwhelming source of joy, more than I could have ever imagined! Zade, you astound me every day, and I love you so much.

My dear friends and family are always there as mirrors and pillars of support through my evolving life. You know who you are; I just want you to feel my love and know how much you mean to me.

Guy Kawasaki was so kind to write such a compelling and intriguing foreword. Thank you, buddy!

JIM:

The content of this book comes from a number of years studying with some very smart people, all of whom I deeply appreciate.

Harry Lorayne, memory expert and author, from whom I learned to use my memory in some extraordinary ways. When I was a teenager, my first memory demonstration left my family stunned and in disbelief. It gave me a very sound understanding of how my mind actually worked, which I have built on and evolved ever since.

L. Ron Hubbard, founder of Scientology. Mr. Hubbard taught me the advantage of a systematic approach to learning, communicating, and resolving inner conflict.

Jack Horner, founder of Eductivism, an applied philosophy for establishing a clear and peaceful mind.

My beloved students and friends, including Dr. Francesco Patricolo, EJ Manning, Roderick Taunton, Dr. Jay Klusky, Sarah Johnson Marshall, Heather Oliver, Kent Snyder, Mark Schulman, Shirley Izaguirre, and the thousands of students with whom I have had the pleasure of working.

And you, for taking your valuable time to consider what is offered within this book.

ABOUT THE AUTHORS

Photo by Erica White

MARK SCHULMAN has enjoyed an unprecedented career over the last thirty years as a first-call drummer for world-class rock and pop artists. He was voted Top 3 pop-rock drummers in the *Modern Drummer* Reader's Poll in 2014 and was the featured cover artist in its May 2019 issue. Schulman has played four record-breaking world tours with P!nk.

His résumé includes a "who's who" of international rock 'n' roll royalty including acts such as Cher, Billy Idol, Foreigner, Sheryl Crow, Stevie Nicks, Beyoncé, and many other world-class artists. He has drummed with Velvet Revolver at Ozzfest and for a crowd of 225,000 at Glastonbury Festival with Simple Minds. Schulman has appeared on nearly every American, European, and Australian variety show. His first book, *Conquering Life's Stage Fright*, illustrates how people can harness the doubt, fear, and anxiety that comes with performance or presentation and transform it into clarity, capability, and confidence.

Schulman is also an international keynote speaker with a client list that includes American Express, Aveda, Cisco, Dell, IBM, Kaiser, Microsoft, NCAA, SAP, and more. He helps audiences "hack attitude" and boost performance through compelling stories from top performers, demonstrative drumming performances, and high-energy interaction.

Schulman was the chairman of the board for Create Now!, a nonprofit organization founded in 1996 to change the lives of children in need through creative arts mentoring. A cancer survivor, Schulman has also volunteered with the Ronald McDonald House and the Teenage Cancer Trust.

DR. JIM SAMUELS began helping others improve their memories in 1962, and he has since developed and refined his applied philosophical approach to human development. He holds a PhD in psychology from Greenwich University. In 1975, he developed the SORTing™ methodology, a robust set of techniques individuals can use to release unresolved stress while increasing understanding and self-awareness.

Soon after, he turned his attention to the world of business, integrating memory training with a strategic approach to planning and business management. In 1997, he earned the rank grandmaster of martial arts philosophy and trained numerous regional, national, and world champions, including Andrew Gainer, a three-time world champion in full-contact freestyle competition. He then created The Principles of Engagement, a communication training system for verbal self-defense. His award-winning cable television series, *The Warrior-Philosopher*, ran for fifteen years in Portland,

Oregon, and reached tens of thousands of people seeking ways to improve their lives.

He is the inventor of Re-Minding, a personal-management skill that helps people quickly free themselves from unwanted thoughts and feelings and release their natural creativity and energy. Dr. Samuels has been a prolific innovator and educator, providing people and organizations with tools to relieve stress and fulfill potential.

For the last twenty years, he has been consulting for California-based Laguna Components, which provides electronic components for NASA Jet Propulsion Laboratory projects, including among others, the Mars orbiters *Perseverance* and *Ingenuity*.